American
Government:
Reform in the
Post-Watergate Era

American Government: Reform in the Post-Watergate Era

David C. Saffell
OHIO NORTHERN UNIVERSITY

WINTHROP PUBLISHERS, INC.

Cambridge, Massachusetts

Library of Congress Cataloging in Publication Data

American government: reform in the post-Watergate era.
American Government.

  Includes bibliographical references.
  1. United States—Politics and government—1969–1974—
Addresses, essays, lectures. 2. United States—Politics
and government—1974–   —Addresses, essays, lectures.
I. Saffell, David C., 1941–
JK271.A573   320.9'73'0925   75-34097
ISBN 0-87626-021-0

© *1976 by Winthrop Publishers, Inc.*
  17 Dunster Street, Cambridge, Massachusetts 02138

10 9 8 7 6 5 4 3 2 1

For Paul and Heather

contents

preface

In large part, the readings in this book have been selected because they support the proposition that if Watergate (that is, the break-in at the Watergate building and the ensuing scandals of the Nixon administration) is to have any positive side effects, wide-ranging reform has to take place. In addition, public officials at all levels must move to operate in an open and forthright manner. In particular, the president must make himself accessible and control the activities of his staff. Only in this way can confidence in government be restored.

In this study, Watergate serves as a point of departure to examine the need for reform as well as to describe and analyze the kinds of governmental changes (cleaning-up operations) which have occurred since 1973. With the immediate issues of Mr. Nixon's culpability and the involvement of his staff in the Watergate planning and cover-up behind us, hopefully we will be able to take advantage of the rare opportunity to devote ourselves to the peaceful and orderly development of our society.

A particularly difficult question, raised in several of the readings in this book, is whether Watergate was an "aberration" or whether it was inherent in the American political system. The implication is that if Watergate was an aberration—simply a phenomenon of the Nixon administration—then specific reform measures cannot (or need not) be taken to prevent "another Watergate." Yet even if Watergate is largely attributable to Mr. Nixon's character, then perhaps electoral reform could make it more difficult for such a person to be elected president in the future. Also, we need to remember that Watergate has caused Americans to be much more critical of the entire scope of government operations, including many far removed from the specific Watergate abuses. The skepticism caused by Watergate has led to proposals for wide-ranging reform at all levels of government. Thus Watergate is viewed as a starting point for reform rather than as an end in itself. Finally, few would suggest that Watergate was not, in part, the result of "the system" as it relates to campaign finance, congressional oversight, the development of the Executive Office of the President, government regulation of business, and the organization of political parties.

As the situation developed, Watergate itself was not a divisive issue in America. Indeed, it tended to bring us together as no other acts of the Nixon administration were capable of doing. A basic premise of this book is that it is important that we act in a united way to move ahead with governmental reform, much of which was recognized as necessary long before Watergate occurred. We should not set basic reform aside with the rationale that Watergate was an aberration in the American political system, attributable to one administration and one president.

This book focuses on broad reform—redefining national security, controlling investigative agencies, increasing congressional oversight, improving presidential accountability, and limiting the influence of private interest groups—as a response to the dangers in our political system made more evident to us through the Watergate affair. Throughout each chapter attention is particularly directed to seeking ways to create a higher level of integrity in government. Many Americans expect a reordering of national priorities led by government officials who have a genuine commitment to the basic ideals of freedom and dignity. If they are disappointed again because of the power-seeking acts of high government officials, their belief in the decency of America may be completely destroyed. Still, hope springs eternal and many of us continue to believe that reform can be significant within the basic framework of American government and that confidence in government can be restored.

This book is intended to be used as supplemental material to the basic course on American government where the articles easily can be integrated into the major topics. It also is designed for possible use in courses on the presidency, Congress, and political parties. While the emphasis is on political reform, the reader is cautioned to remember that reform proposals must be carefully evaluated. Caution is in order so that we may discriminate between those reforms which will have a positive, practical effect and those which will simply make things worse.

ACKNOWLEDGMENTS

My special thanks is extended to Professor Hugh Bone of the University of Washington. Professor Bone helped set the direction of this book by suggesting that integrity in government be stressed as a means of supplementing some of the strictly Watergate materials which appeared in a previous reader (*Watergate: Its Effects On The American Political System*). Several others read the manuscript and made valuable comments. These include Professors James Magee of Eastern Michigan University, Walter S. Jones of Northeastern University, Gilbert Scharfenberger of Salem State College, and Daniel Vaughn of the University of South Carolina.

Once again, my thanks are extended to the production staff of Winthrop Publishers, especially Eric Carle. James J. Murray deserves particular credit for his initiation of this project and for his management of it from an idea to a completed book.

My colleagues—Robert Davis, Terry Gilbreth, and Mary Katherine Hammond—have been most helpful in providing ideas and materials which supported this undertaking. Special thanks is due Professor Andrew Ludanyi of Ohio Northern University for his assistance in combing the recent literature and recommending appropriate articles. To the library staff at Ohio Northern University I extend my overdue public appreciation.

D.C.S.

Reflections on Political Reform

Wilbur J. Cohen

When Charles V, writing from Flanders prior to his arrival in Spain in the sixteenth century, suggested to Cardinal Cisneros, the Regent, that reforms in the Spanish Inquisition might be advisable, the aged Cardinal replied: "The Inquisition is so perfect that there will never be any need for reform and it would be sinful to introduce changes."[1]

Cardinal Cisneros was advancing the traditional and extremist opposition to political reform which, with various modifications, has been the "conventional wisdom" of resistance to political reform over the centuries. In its basic form, the Cisneros doctrine is both a rationalization and defense of the status quo and an encouragement to revolution. It offers no real possibility for the consideration of change or reform. Thus, it poses questions which have perennially plagued philosophers, politicians, and reformers: Is a radical overhaul of major institutions through revolution the only way to achieve basic political reform? Does partial incremental political reform only postpone or prevent more basic political reform? What are the alternatives when specific political reforms are opposed, defeated, postponed? Why do individuals reject or accept change?

Major political reforms have occurred when there are major economic and/or military revolutions: the United States in 1776; France in 1793 and 1945; China in 1949. The Articles of Confederation and the United States Constitution developed out of revolutionary conditions. The far-reaching Fourteenth Amendment to the Constitution evolved from the military victory of the North in the Civil War. But the first ten amendments to the Constitution—the great Bill of Rights—emerged from a political conflict with respect to the rights of the individual and the requirements of the state. In fact, much great political reform results from redefining the rights of the individual in relation to government.

Political reform which is short of revolution is a continuous process. It occurs, reoccurs, persists and reappears in democracies or dictatorships, in capitalist or Communist economies, in Republican or Democratic administrations, and in federal, state or local governmental processes, in voluntary associations, business, labor and nonprofit organizations. It is an omnipresent factor in human society.

Political reform is as old as society itself. Probably as soon as three or more persons associated together they found a need to modify responsibilities, from

[1] Quoted in James A. Michener, *Iberia* (New York: Random House, 1968), p. 147.

From *Current History*, August, 1974, pp. 49-51, Reprinted by permission.

Wilbur J. Cohen was Secretary of Health, Education, and Welfare in 1968-69. During the 30 years he spent in Washington, he was responsible for piloting over 100 bills through the political machinery of the executive and legislative branches in an effort to achieve political reform through the legislative process. Mr. Cohen currently is Dean of the School of Education, The University of Michigan.

time to time, in carrying out their activities. Political relationships, political organizations, and political reform are an out-growth of the variety, complexity, and changing nature of human relationships in a changing environment. As soon as institutional structures were formed to carry out economic, familial, cultural, or sexual needs, the roles of the participants required periodic redetermination. As individuals react to these changing roles, political reform is advocated, supported, and opposed to effectuate changes in roles, power, or processes.

While it is customary to think of political reform as a strictly political phenomenon, it is more likely that most current political reform grows out of economic conflicts, pressures, needs, and abuses. The establishment of the Federal Reserve System and the enactment of the federal income tax and the Sherman and Clayton anti-trust laws are illustrations of political reforms necessitated by economic forces. Economic power and political power have been intertwined in American history from its very beginning. Some individuals and groups use economic power to obtain political power. Some individuals use political power to obtain financial gain. As evidence of these uses becomes perceived as undesirable, the effort to correct the abuses becomes a movement for political reform.

Politics and political reform have produced some of the most unusual and controversial leaders in history, among them Moses, Alexander, Caesar, Joan of Arc, Napoleon, Bismarck, Abraham Lincoln, Disraeli, Lenin, Mao, Ben-Gurion, Pope John the twenty-third, Franklin D. Roosevelt, Winston Churchill, Khrushchev, Nasser, Sadat, and many others. Demands for reform were reflected in the influential writings of Plato, Aristotle, Machiavelli, Mohammed, Voltaire, Rousseau, Jefferson, De Tocqueville, Lord Bryce, Marx, Lord Acton, Charles and Mary Beard, Lincoln Steffens, and Woodrow Wilson. The very list of these diverse men and women indicates the difficulty of defining and diagnosing political power and political reform outside the totality of economic and political institutions in a particular culture and period.

But although political reform is difficult to define in universal terms, it can be explained as a political change from what exists at a given moment. It may be good or bad; significant or inconsequential. It may be short range or long range. It may be statutory, constitutional, judicial; it may involve a change of key personnel. Revisions in processes, powers, or privileges may be demanded. One man's political reform may be viewed by another as political interference or political disaster.

Some political reforms do not fulfill the expectations of the sponsors. A most notable example is the Volstead constitutional amendment (the Eighteenth Amendment) of the World War I era, which prohibited the sale of intoxicating liquor, and which was subsequently repealed in a 1933 amendment. It is also not always possible to comprehend in the short run what the longer-run results of a political reform are likely to be. The full impact of the Fourteenth Amendment is still unclear. Certainly, the sponsors of the amendment in the Civil War aftermath could not have foreseen that the Supreme Court would apply it to aid the development of the modern business corporation at the beginning of the twentieth century and to protect welfare recipients and minorities in the 1970s.

Some political reforms, although defeated by opponents, still exercise an influence on American politics. In 1937, President Franklin D. Roosevelt, in a post-election burst of overconfidence, suddenly sprung his Supreme Court "packing-plan" on a startled Congress and electorate. The opposition to the proposal was widespread, hard-hitting, and successful. Nonetheless, although almost all the President's customary supporters deserted him because of his direct attack on a fundamental institution of the Republic, the Court "received the message." It began to uphold the constitutionality of major New Deal measures such as the National Labor Relations Act and the Social Security Act. Roosevelt's battle over the Court was lost; the war was won. The economic forces growing out of the depression of 1929–1933 produced one of the most far-reaching political reforms in our history without a revolution of bloodshed, a Civil War, or a military crisis.

Politics is frequently referred to as the art of the possible. But significant political reform is often the art of the improbable. In many instances, political reform appeared doomed from the beginning because of monumental opposition. The British Reform Bill of 1867, which finally gave the vote to the working class of the towns of England, is a historic case. Lord Cranborne, one of the opponents of the 1867 law, voiced the traditional evaluation of democratic attempts to broaden voting rights.

You practically banish all honorable men from the political area and you will find in the long run that the time will come when your statesmen will become nothing but political adventurers, and politicians of opinion will be looked upon only as so many political maneuverers for the purposes of obtaining office.[2]

A notable instance in recent American history was the passage of the Medicare law in 1965 after some 55 years of agitation for health insurance and some 13 years of support for medical insurance coverage for the aged.[3] Yet once the Medicare legislation was enacted, the pressure for national health insurance was accelerated.

The Watergate episode will certainly bring a number of political reforms into being. Limitations on campaign contributions and expenditures will be the most likely federal legislative action. But such action deals with only a small aspect of the abuses uncovered by the Watergate experience. Abuses at the state and local level are probably more extensive than those at the national level.

Over the past 40 years, the presidency and the executive branch of the federal government have steadily accumulated power, and the power of Congress has not been fully or promptly utilized. At the same time, economic power in the private sector has increased, while state and local governments have failed to respond to the growing needs of an urban, industrial, mobile economy.

John Gardner, the chairman of Common Cause, a citizen's group dedicated to trying to achieve political reform in many areas of American life, has recommended that the basic political change must be to hold the powerful accountable:

[2] Quoted by Asa Briggs in "Benjamin Disraeli and the Leap in the Dark," *Victorian People* (Baltimore: Penguin Books, 1965), p. 299.

[3] See Richard Harris, *A Sacred Trust* (New York: New American Library, 1966), for a most interesting play-by-play account of how political forces were mobilized in the Medicare controversy.

We have heard demands for a seemingly simple remedy: weaken the Presidency, strengthen Congress. But ours is a huge and complex society in a swiftly changing world: we can never again have a weak Presidency or Executive Branch. And Congress, in its nature, cannot play the leadership role alone.

Our only recourse is to accept the necessity for a strong Presidency and Executive Branch and at the same time to create powerful instruments for calling them to account. Most of the needed instruments now exist but require strengthening. It is not just a matter of holding government accountable. Government must help us to hold accountable the great power centers of the private sector.[4]

The most far-reaching political reform that has been suggested is some method by which the President's term of office can be terminated by some special action of Congress other than his conviction on impeachment. The proposal is an attempt to combine the essential feature of parliamentary government with our separation-of-powers approach. This effort to curb the power of the President deals with some but not all of the major abuses that have or may occur. Financial disclosure of income and assets of political candidates and elected officials; a single term for the presidency of four, five, or six years; prohibiting a President from selecting more than four members of the Supreme Court; requiring the President to appear before a congressional committee not more than twice a year; recall of the President and Vice President by petition; national referenda on national issues; a four-year term for the director of the Federal

Bureau of Investigation; payment of damages to individuals whose rights are invaded by improper or unlawful federal action; and holding elections on Sunday so more people can vote—these are some additional political reforms worth further consideration.

It seems likely that whatever political reforms come out of the Watergate episode in American history, they will not satisfy the political philosophers or social reformers of the future. Yet in the next few years the pressure for political reforms will result in some changes that may have implications for the redistribution of political power as important as the changes that occurred in 1789, 1865, 1933, and 1968.

Trust and confidence in the political institutions of the United States rest on many factors outside constitutional guarantees and statutory limitations on undersirable political activities. Political parties are not mentioned in the Constitution nor are the Cabinet, the White House staff, or lobbying groups. Essential to clean politics are an independent and fearless judiciary, a free press (guaranteed the right not to disclose sources of information), and the due process and equal protection of the laws—all safeguarded by specific constitutional guarantees. The congressional power to declare war and the power to levy taxes and make restricted appropriations are and should be used as more effective restrictions on the power of the Executive; for example, there should be congressional limitations on expenditures for the White House staff.

Academic freedom (including tenure in the educational system) is a necessary and essential element in maintaining some semblance of clean politics and potential political reform. But no politi-

<hr />

[4] "Rebirth of a Nation," a statement issued by Common Cause, 1974.

cal system and no political reform can assure fair, just, clean politics without the courageous, outspoken citizen or leader who is willing to speak out irrespective of personal cost or consequences. John F. Kennedy's book, *Profiles in Courage,* evidences a persistent quality in American political life that should be encouraged and admired. There is no substitute for the character of an Attorney General who resigns his office when the President of the United States demands an action contrary to his conscience and commitment.

Some recent political reforms have not yet been fully effective as instruments of further political reform. The growing interest in equal rights for women, zero population growth, control over the environment, energy limitations, and national growth all indicate popular interest in a more just society, one that is more sensitive and compassionate to human needs and in which a community of interests guides public policy. As life expectancy for women increases, the amendment to the Constitution giving women the right to vote probably will become more significant.[5] With the recently adopted Twenty-Sixth Amendment permitting individuals eighteen years of age to vote,[6] and laws assuring that minorities can vote, we may be entering upon a period of more rapid or more significant political reform. The Watergate episode may be only one of many factors in the long-run process of political reform.

[5] See *Current History,* June, 1974, p. 276, for the text of this amendment.

[6] *Ibid.,* p. 277.

American Government: Reform in the Post-Watergate Era

Drawing by Hunt; © 1975 The New Yorker
Magazine, Inc.

"The people want integrity? Big deal.
We'll give them integrity."

chapter one

Integrity in Government

"We are firmly convinced . . . that with nations as with individuals, our interests soundly calculated, will ever be found inseparable from our moral duties."

—Thomas Jefferson, Second Inaugural, 1805

"I will work unceasingly to halt the erosion of moral fibre in American life, and the denial of individual accountability for individual action."

—Richard M. Nixon, Radio Address, October 15, 1972

Much of the movement for reform following the Watergate affair has centered on the means for restoring integrity to government. Campaign financing has been an obvious target. In addition, reform of institutions such as Congress, the presidency, the bureaucracy, and political parties has involved proposals aimed at raising ethical and moral standards and thus restoring confidence in government. As historian Henry Steele Commager notes, "The basic problem posed by Watergate and all its attendant horrors is neither constitutional nor political; it is moral. It is not a problem posed by an administration in Washington; it is one posed by the American people." It is, of course, much easier to identify the problem than to provide a solution. The articles in this chapter outline the complex problem of integrity and seek to offer some modest and positive approaches to altering the values of American society so that they support a higher level of moral sensibility.

Watergate revealed a breakdown of democratic government in America. Individuals carried attaché cases stuffed with $100 bills, presidential aides perjured themselves to stay on the team, secret intelligence operations were set up under the guise of protecting national security, and enemies lists were compiled—all to preserve political power. After the acting director of the FBI had destroyed possibly incriminating papers in the Watergate case (at the direction of a White House aide) and the attorney general was convicted for his role in the Watergate cover-up, the Nixon campaign slogan of law and order became a mockery.

"All the president's men" seemingly had no sense of values or conception of integrity instilled in them by their family, their church, or their school. Political scientist Aaron Wildavsky notes that at the Watergate hearings senators tried to teach them and give them little sermons: "Young man, don't you understand that what you did was terrible?" Individuals often acted without a sense of loyalty to anyone or anything except their leader.

It would, of course, be a mistake to assume that only the Nixon aides, among those in government, have been guilty of gross immorality. Politics long has been tainted by moral corruption. Major government deception and secrecy has been with us since the early 1950s under both Democratic and Republican administrations. Because of this situation and the resultant cycnicism it has bred, the reaction of many to Watergate was simply to say "All politicians do it, why bother to get upset now?"

Political analyst Louis Harris (in *The Anguish of Change*, 1973) notes that Watergate brought to new depths the already low estimate that the American people had for their government. As the Watergate scandal developed in April 1973, a majority of 52 percent agreed that "corruption in the federal government was very serious" and the federal government was seen as the "most corrupt" of any level of government. Even among children, the president not only has received less positive ratings than in the 1960s, but he has received negative ratings. As compared to 1962, children in 1973 viewed politicians as "more selfish, less intelligent, more dishonest, and less likely to keep their promise."[1]

David Wise (in *The Politics of Lying*, 1973) sees the Watergate burglary and cover-up as a result of years of government manipulation, deception, and falsehood. He notes that Watergate destroyed the belief in the essential goodness and decency of America. "Somehow," Wise states, "we elected a government of eavesdroppers, burglars, perjurers, forgers, and wiretappers." While they almost "stole America," they did not completely destroy our hope that government can operate as Thomas Jefferson suggested in 1805. Restoring confidence in government is a task in which we will all share the responsibility for helping to create a new moral order both in and out of government.

READINGS

Professor Commager suggests that while the schools alone cannot reshape the morals of American society, they can perform the vital role of acting as society's conscience in the development of ethical standards. If, however,

[1] F. Christopher Arterton, "The Impact of Watergate on Children's Attitudes Toward Political Authority," *Political Science Quarterly* (June 1974), p. 274. Also see Robert Hawkins, Susan Hawkins, and Donald F. Roberts, "Political Socialization of Children: Two Studies of Responses to Watergate" in Sidney Kraus, ed., *Watergate and Mass Communications* (Bloomington, Ind.: University of Indiana Press, 1975).

Drawing by Wright; © The Miami News

what the schools say about values continues to be antithetical to the values rewarded by our society, classroom teaching will remain hypocritical and ineffective.

The article by the late sociologist C. Wright Mills, taken from his controversial 1956 study of the organization of American society, continues to be of interest in the 1970s. Mills suggests that in the absence of a moral order, individuals are subject to manipulation and distraction by an elite leadership. The "higher immorality" is a feature of the American elite (the rich, military officials, politicians, and corporate executives) which operates in institutions. Because these institutions are without moral codes or values, Mills believes they corrupt individuals.

Watergate and the Schools

Henry Steele Commager

One of the most ominous developments of our time is the widespread loss of confidence in our system of government. That loss of confidence is not confined to the United States, nor is it inspired merely by a reaction to the sins and follies of this Administration. It is rooted in skepticism about the continuing viability of the American constitutional system.

The loss of confidence in our system of government is increased by reaction against the imperialism and militarism which the American system—for all its checks and balances—seems to permit. It is intensified by the conclusion that the United States is what the Holy Alliance was in the early years of the nineteenth century and what Britain was in the latter part of the century—a bastion of reaction throughout the globe, the friend and supporter of authoritarian regimes in Brazil, Spain, Korea, Vietnam, and Cambodia.

It is aggravated by what appears— quite logically—to be the palpable racism of so much of American foreign and military policy; it is sobered and saddened by the disappearance of— even the repudiation of—that sense of idealism and of mission which Thomas Jefferson's sympathy with "infuriated man seeking through blood and slaughter his long lost liberties" and which held out the hand of fellowship to revolutionaries throughout Europe and Latin America.

From *Today's Education*, September–October 1974. Reprinted by permission of the National Education Association and Henry Steele Commager.

Though our attention is riveted on the spectacle which unfolds itself in Washington, our interest and our objective is not primarily in that. We are not concerned, or should not be, to punish Mr. Nixon and his piratical crew. History will take care of that.

We are concerned to vindicate our political system and our constitutional principles. The great question which confronts us so implacably is whether the American Constitution, which has served us so well, and the American political principles and practices which have worked so effectively over the years can continue to function in the modern world.

The American system—if I may use that evasive word to describe what we all recognize but cannot easily define— is both difficult and complex. It was the first contrived constitutional system in history—the first to be made anew, as the nation itself was the first to be made anew. Almost everything about it was an experiment: federalism; the separation of powers; the Presidential office; the independent judiciary; the principle that all authority derived from below and not from above; the new techniques of change and amendment—revolution institutionalized.

Only a mature and sophisticated people could have made it work. That the American people first constructed it and then made it work is a tribute to that maturity and sophistication. Are the American people perhaps less mature politically today than they were in the eighteenth century—less mature and less resourceful? And is a constitutional mechanism rooted in the seventeenth century ideas of the relations of men to government and admirably adapted to the simple needs of the eighteenth and the early nineteenth centuries, inadequate to the importunate exigencies of the twentieth—and the twenty-first?

Some evidence exists to support these fears. There is, for example, the ostentatious decline in political leadership—a decline so spectacular that it is superfluous to rehearse it. Suffice it to ask how, during one generation, a nation with a population only half that of Chicago today managed to produce a George Washington (as compared to Richard Nixon), and a John Adams (as compared to Spiro Agnew)?

And how sobering to recall that every one of the great political and constitutional institutions of the American governmental system was invented before the year 1800 and that not one has been invented or emerged since that time.

We have had constitutional crises before—crises more dangerous than any which threaten us now (for the present crises are in large part contrived). In the past, we have managed to cope with these crises by familiar and legal methods. We used the device of the constitutional amendment and of judicial interpretations, which grew logically out of the original document. We displayed—in the creation and development of political parties and of judicial review—an astonishing resourcefulness in adapting and modernizing the eighteenth century document. How else explain its continuing vitality?

Clearly, the Nixon Administration is not prepared to follow these methods or precedents. It does not resort to formal amendments or rely on judicial review or seek to enlist the Congress in essential adaptations of Constitution and tradition to the needs of the present. It prefers—as by some instinct—to rely on revolutionary methods to achieve what it wishes to accomplish.

Nixon has amended the Constitution—but by personal fiat. He has challenged the principle of the separation of powers. He has propounded the principle that the Chief Executive is above the law and has arrogated to himself a body of privileges and immunities unknown to the Constitution or to law. He has merged—or tried to merge—the office and the man. He has dismissed as anachronistic the protections of the Bill of Rights. He has confessed that he has no confidence in the virtue or the intelligence of the American people, or, for that matter, of their representatives in Congress, and chooses to conceal his own activities, foreign and domestic alike, in a fog of secrecy.

I do not propose to spell out these departures from constitutional orthodoxy and political morality. Indeed, Mr. Nixon has provided us with a convenient symbol in Watergate. Among many things, Watergate symbolizes corruption of the Presidential office and the widespread usurpation of powers by the President; corruption of the democratic processes; growth of a police state which covers its activities in secrecy; and contempt for the guarantees of the Bill of Rights.

Watergate does not symbolize a breakdown of our constitutional system: It is not the Constitution that has failed us but those who persistently violate the document. It is not our political mechanisms which have failed us but those who repudiate traditional political mechanisms. After all, we should not forget that the Constitution and the democratic processes saw us through crises far graver than any which confront us now—the crisis of the survival of the nation in the early years of the Republic, the crisis of the Civil War and Reconstruction, the crisis of the Great Depression and of the greatest of wars. Certainly recent experience does not demonstrate that we should jettison our Constitution and change our political institutions to meet the current difficulties. But rather that Presidents—and the Congress too—should abide by these and execute them.

But does Watergate symbolize a breakdown in the office of the Presidency or a failure of the Presidential system? That system worked pretty well up to now; are the stresses of modern world politics too much for it?

No, we do not need to abandon Presidential government, only to confine it to its constitutional limits. This does require new legislation. All political spending should have really strict limitations, and the government should bear most of the cost of campaigns. The Presidential exercise of war-making power must have a far clearer and firmer limitation. The misuse and abuse of executive agreement should be curbed in order to return treaty-making to its original constitutional character, and Congress should participate far more vigorously in the conduct of foreign relations. How odd it is that we should have forgotten the *advice* in "advice and consent."

Secrecy in the Executives Offices should end except for genuine emergencies during time of war. Executive privilege and executive immunity —two fictions concocted in the last generation but unknown to the Constitu-tion—should also end. And while we are about it, we should, in my opinion, abolish the useless office of Vice-President—a kind of appendix to the Presidency which has no function.

The basic problem posed by Watergate and all its attendant horrors is neither constitutional nor political; it is moral. It is not a problem posed by an Administration in Washington; it is one posed by the American people.

After all, we can never get away from the most elementary fact: The American people reelected Mr. Nixon by a majority of nearly 18 million votes. Either they did not know what kind of man he was, in which case they were inexcusably negligent or inexcusably naive, or they did know what kind of man he was and did not care or perhaps liked him as he was—as some Americans still like him the way he is. The latter explanation is probably nearer to the truth.

Did he not—indeed, does he not— represent qualities in the American character that are widespread and even taken for granted? In himself and in the curious collection of associates he gathered around him, he represents the acquisitive society, the exploitative society, the aggrandizing society. He represents what is artificial, meretricious, and manipulative. He represents the American preference of the synthetic over the real, for advertising over the product, for public relations over character, for spectator sports over active games, and for spectator politics over participatory democracy.

He represents, too, the widespread American conviction that anything can be bought: culture, education, happiness, a winning football team—or the Presidency.

The present mood of disillusionment seeks a scapegoat. The most nearly universal scapegoat is, needless to say, the schools. After all, did they not "train" the generation that has come to maturity—if *maturity* is the mot juste? Clearly, if we have failed, it is because our schools have failed by not having raised up that generation of enlightened citizens that Jefferson was confident they would produce.

Instead, they raised up a generation which maintained in power administrations that pursued for 10 years a meaningless, futile, and barbarous war against a people 10,000 miles away; which accepted uncritically the notion that God or Providence had somehow delegated the United States to serve as policeman to the world; which acquiesced in the increasing arrogance of the military establishment; which looked with indifference on the erosion of constitutional government and of the guarantees of the Bill of Rights; and which looked with general incomprehension on an Administration with a record of duplicity, chicanery, mendacity, and criminal turpitude without parallel in American history.

Clearly, education has gone astray. But the basic confusion here—one which permeates the thought even of the educational establishment—is the confusion between education and schooling. Almost from the beginning, Americans lacked most of those institutions which in the Old World took on the task of teaching the young what they needed to know in adult life: the church, the guild, the farm, the forge, the class system, the extended family. Therefore, Americans have tended to put more and more responsibility onto schools.

Because they were reluctant to put down roots, to form permanent attachments, to build up networks of social control, because they were always on the move—from the Old World to the New, from the seaboard to one frontier after another, from the farm to the city, from job to job, from church to church—they failed to create institutions and influences to provide the social, cultural, and moral training for the young. These responsibilities, too, they foisted off on schools—or allowed to go by default. In short, Americans asked the schools to do what in the Old World was done by a dozen ancient and powerful institutions.

But the problem goes even deeper. Americans, particularly in the twentieth century, not only abandoned much of their responsibility for education by requiring schools to provide both formal and informal education; they also foisted on the schools responsibility for inculcating a set of values and of moral standards different from and almost antithetical to those practiced by society. The more virtuous the standards they taught, the more effectively they were thought to perform the function of a surrogate conscience which permitted society to follow its own ways while consoling itself with the illusion that the schools would train up a generation with higher standards.

Thus, society requires schools to teach that all men are equally entitled to life, liberty, and happiness but makes clear by its conduct that it does not intend to take that promise seriously or to apply it to the ordinary affairs of life. Society applauds the principle of racial equality but does not itself provide the young with persuasive examples of its practice, knowing well that the example is more powerful than the principle.

Society rewards pupils who can recite the Bill of Rights, but it shows no serious interest in the application of these rights to tiresome minority groups. Society rejoices when schools celebrate (as they are expected to do) examples by great men like a Franklin or an Adams of placing service to the commonwealth above service to the self, but it rewards private enterprise rather than public enterprise.

It expects schools to teach the primary value of the mind and the spirit, but itself prefers the rewards of more materialistic teaching. It expects schools to bring home to the young the great truth that justice is the end of government but itself practices injustice in almost every area of public life. It expects schools to teach respect for the law but elects to the highest offices a President and a Vice-President who display contempt for the law. It encourages schools to teach the beauty of peace but exalts war, wages war, maintains the largest military establishment in the world, and spends more money on the military than does any other nation.

If our educational enterprise has failed us, if it is in disarray, it is in part because we have asked it to perform a miracle: to teach the young to understand and to improve the world they live in, while we ourselves display little awareness of our fiduciary obligation to the future. Much of public education today is a massive exercise in hypocrisy, and it is folly to suppose that the young do not know this.

It is against this background that we must consider the demands for reshaping society that are now made of educators and the schools. Educators have of course long been aware of the dichotomy between what is taught in the schools and what is held up for approval and emulation by so many other and more powerful institutions of society. It was an awareness of this bifurcation of education that, a generation or so back, persuaded the Teachers College group (John Dewey as inspiration; George Counts, Kilpatrick, and Rugg as activists) to launch a crusade to reconstruct society. For all its rhetoric and its high-mindedness, that crusade was a failure. And no wonder. It is very difficult for the part to reconstruct the whole, and the experience of our schools with such direct crusading has not been encouraging.

What emerged should have been clear from the beginning. Society does not produce good citizens by teaching civics but by providing the young with the spectacle of a society devoted to the commonwealth. Society does not develop internationalists by teaching a bit of the history of other nations but by immersing the young in the great traditions of the past and of other civilizations and by conducting foreign policy with respect for other nations and peoples.

Rarely in the history of education have so many been exposed to so much with results so meager. If we are to judge by results of the past 40 years, this enterprise of relying on schools to reform society, politics, and morals by direct teaching has been a failure.

What seems reasonably clear is that schools—separated from society and asked to teach things in which society has no interest and to inculcate moral values which society repudiates—cannot reform society. (What is more, schools cannot reform education, for most education takes place outside the classroom.) Society, which created a dual system of education, seems content with the perpetuation of that system. Only if society recognizes (as it did briefly in eighteenth century America and in the America of Horace Mann and Henry Barnard) its responsibility to *paideia* will it permit its institutions to work in harmony with its schools.

Yet all is not desperate, for if society imposes its moral standards, it habits and even its will on schools, schools in turn impose their standards on society. Schools are not merely the mirror of society, nor the passive agents. They are part of the formative process, and if society requires the schools to act as its conscience, they sometimes surprise society by doing just that. Schools have in fact exercised a decisive influence on American society—in advancing national unity, for example, in functioning (far more successfully than business or social institutions) as a melting pot, and so on.

The educational establishment should involve itself in politics—that is in the clarification of those great issues which concern the life and the soul of our society and of the world. These issues concern themselves with the survival of our commonwealth and, ultimately, of the commonwealth of mankind.

More than almost any other group, teachers stand in a continuous fiduciary relationship to oncoming generations. We have both a moral obligation and a professional one to influence policies. This we have not heretofore fulfilled to the extent that we might do so.

The agenda I submit is the essence of conservatism. After all, are not teachers by their very nature conservative? What is it they are about but to conserve the learning of the past for the present and the future, to conserve civilization as we have known it, to conserve children that they may grow up into useful and self-respecting citizens?

The first item of conservatism must be to conserve nature, to conserve the natural resources of the country, to pass on to future generations their rightful natural inheritance.

A second item in any policy of conservatism is to conserve mankind. This means controlling population so that we are not threatened with famine and the internecine wars which will inevitably come if hundreds of millions of peoples are without food while more favored peoples indulge in gluttony and waste. It means providing a humane environment in which the young can grow to maturity and usefulness and happiness. It means making available an education which can go far to remedy the glaring inequalities of our own society and of societies elsewhere. In a broad way it means the creation of a just society. This is not only a moral obligation, not only a practical obligation, but it is in fact a constitutional obligation.

A third item on the agenda of conservatism is closely related to the second: the conservation of life, of our limited resources, and of civilization by the avoidance of war.

Since 1945, we have spent billions on war and "defense" and are even now considering a military budget of about $90 billion. Far more serious is an armaments race which seems to be quite out of hand. The decision of the Department of Defense, endorsed by the Congress, to develop MIRV's may set off a new, more expensive, more open-ended, and potentially more lethal phase of the Cold War, which otherwise might be on the way to a thaw.

A fourth item is the preservation of those freedoms without which a democratic society such as ours cannot survive—freedom of speech, of the press, of assembly and petition; freedom of the academy and of science to pursue unhindered their search for truth; freedom from massive invasions of privacy by the new instruments of surveillance.

A fifth item is a restoration of faith in the viability of our democratic and constitutional institutions, a revitalization of participatory democracy, a reassertion of standards of what used to be called civic virtue, and the creation of an educational (not just an academic), social and moral system which will discover and encourage the kind of leadership we must have in order to solve our problems.

Schools cannot carry through this program. Teachers cannot carry through this program. If it is to be carried through, it must be by the creation of a great network of private, voluntary organizations—such as fraternal associations, the PTA, and the NEA. These organizations must be ones whose function is not primarily self-advancement, which are not by their nature part of politics, but which are and must be very involved in the great political issues of the survival of our society and of civilization as a whole.

I close with these lines from a student of fifth-century Athens:

"In the contest which we are going to watch, fighting will bring no joy and victory no triumph. For the battle which Athens has now to face is not against the Lacedaemonians or any hosts of armored men, but against the foe in her own household, the desires and ambitions she herself has nurtured."

The Higher Immorality

C. Wright Mills

The higher immorality can neither be narrowed to the political sphere nor understood as primarily a matter of corrupt men in fundamentally sound institutions. Political corruption is one aspect of a more general immorality; the level of moral sensibility that now prevails is not merely a matter of corrupt men.[1] The higher immorality is a systematic feature of the American elite; its general acceptance is an essential feature of the mass society.

Of course, there may be corrupt men in sound institutions, but when institutions are corrupting many of the men who live and work in them are necessarily corrupted. In the corporate era, economic relations become impersonal—and the executive feels less personal responsibility. Within the corporate

[1] Cf. Mills, 'A Diagnosis of Our Moral Uneasiness,' *The New York Times Magazine,* 23 November 1952.

worlds of business, war-making and politics, the private conscience is attenuated—and the higher immorality is institutionalized. It is not merely a question of a corrupt administration in corporation, army, or state; it is a feature of the corporate rich, as a capitalist stratum, deeply intertwined with the politics of the military state.

From this point of view, the most important question, for instance, about the campaign funds of ambitious young politicans is not whether the politicians are morally insensitive, but whether or not any young man in American politics, who has come so far and so fast, could very well have done so today without possessing or acquiring a somewhat blunted moral sensibility. Many of the problems of 'white-collar crime' and of relaxed public morality, of high-priced vice and of fading personal integrity, are problems of *structural* immorality. They are not merely the problem of the small character twisted by the bad milieu. And many people are at least vaguely aware that this is so. As news of higher immoralities breaks, they often say, 'Well, another one got caught today,' thereby implying that the cases disclosed are not odd events involving occasional characters but symptoms of a widespread condition. There is good probative evidence that they are right. But what is the underlying condition of which all these instances are symptoms?

1

The moral uneasiness of our time results from the fact that older values and codes of uprightness no longer grip the men and women of the corporate era, nor have they been replaced by new values

and codes which would lend moral meaning and sanction to the corporate routines they must now follow. It is not that the mass public has explicitly rejected received codes; it is rather that to many of the members these codes have become hollow. No moral terms of acceptance are available, but neither are any moral terms of rejection. As individuals they are morally defenseless; as groups, they are politically indifferent. It is this generalized lack of commitment that is meant when it is said that 'the public' is morally confused.

But, of course, not only 'the public' is morally confused in this way. 'The tragedy of official Washington,' James Reston has commented, 'is that it is confounded at every turn by the hangover of old political habits and outworn institutions but is no longer nourished by the ancient faith on which it was founded. It clings to the bad things and casts away on the permanent. It professes belief but does not believe. It knows the old words but has forgotten the melody. It is engaged in an ideological war without being able to define its own ideology. It condemns the materialism of an atheistic enemy, but glorifies its own materialism.'[2]

In economic and political institutions the corporate rich now wield enormous power, but they have never had to win the moral consent of those over whom they hold this power. Every such naked interest, every new, unsanctioned power of corporation, farm bloc, labor union, and governmental agency that has risen in the past two generations has been clothed with morally loaded slogans. For what is *not* done in the name of the public interest? As these

[2] James Reston, *The New York Times*, 10 April 1955, p. 10E.

slogans wear out, new ones are indus-
triously made up, also to be banalized in
due course. And all the while, recurrent
economic and military crises spread
fears, hesitations, and anxieties which
give new urgency to the busy search for
moral justifications and decorous ex-
cuses.

'Crisis' is a bankrupted term, because
so many men in high places have
evoked it in order to cover up their extraordinary policies and deeds; as a matter of fact, it is precisely the absence of
crises that is a cardinal feature of the
higher immorality. For genuine crises
involve situations in which men at large
are presented with genuine alternatives,
the moral meanings of which are clearly
opened to public debate. The higher
immorality, the general weakening of
older values and the organization of
irresponsibility have not involved any
public crises; on the contrary, they have
been matters of a creeping indifference
and a silent hollowing out.

The images that generally prevail of
the higher circles are the images of the
elite seen as celebrities. In discussing
the professional celebrities, I noted that
the instituted elites of power do not
monopolize the bright focus of national
acclaim. They share it nationally with
the frivolous or the sultry creatures of
the world of celebrity, which thus
serves as a dazzling blind of their true
power. In the sense that the volume of
publicity and acclaim is mainly and
continuously upon those professional
celebrities, it is not upon the power
elite. So the social visibility of that elite
is lowered by the status distraction, or
rather public vision of them is through
the celebrity who amuses and entertains—or disgusts, as the case may
be.

The absence of any firm moral order
of belief makes men in the mass all the
more open to the manipulation and distraction of the world of the celebrities.
In due course, such a 'turnover' of appeals and codes and values as they are
subjected to leads them to distrust and
cynicism, to a sort of Machiavellianism-
for-the-little-man. Thus they vicariously
enjoy the prerogatives of the corporate
rich, the nocturnal antics of the celebrity, and the sad-happy life of the very
rich.

But with all this, there is still one old
American value that has not markedly
declined: the value of money and of the
things money can buy—these, even in
inflated times, seem as solid and enduring as stainless steel. 'I've been rich and
I've been poor,' Sophie Tucker has
said,' and believe me, rich is best.'[3] As
many other values are weakened, the
question for Americans becomes not 'Is
there anything that money, used with
intelligence, will not buy?' but, 'How
many of the things that money will *not*
buy are valued and desired more than
what money *will* buy?' Money is the one
unambiguous criterion of success, and
such success is still the sovereign
American value.

Whenever the standards of the
moneyed life prevail, the man with
money, no matter how he got it, will
eventually be respected. A million dollars, it is said, covers a multitude of sins.
It is not only that men want money; it is
that their very standards are pecuniary.
In a society in which the money-maker
has had no serious rival for repute and
honor, the word 'practical' comes to
mean useful for private gain, and 'com-

[3] Sophie Tucker, as quoted in *Time*, 16 November
1953.

mon sense,' the sense to get ahead financially. The pursuit of the moneyed life is the commanding value, in relation to which the influence of other values has declined, so men easily become morally ruthless in the pursuit of easy money and fast estate-building.

A great deal of American corruption—although not all of it—is simply a part of the old effort to get rich and then to become richer. But today the context in which the old drive must operate has changed. When both economic and political institutions were small and scattered—as in the simpler models of classical economics and Jeffersonian democracy—no man had it in his power to bestow or to receive great favors. But when political institutions and economic opportunities are at once concentrated and linked, then public office can be used for private gain.

Governmental agencies contain no more of the higher immorality than do business corporations. Political men can grant financial favors only when there are economic men ready and willing to take them. And economic men can seek political favors only when there are political agents who can bestow such favors. The publicity spotlight, of course, shines brighter upon the transactions of the men in government, for which there is good reason. Expectations being higher, publics are more easily disappointed by public officials. Businessmen are supposed to be out for themselves, and if they successfully skate on legally thin ice, Americans generally honor them for having gotten away with it. But in a civilization so thoroughly business-penetrated as America, the rules of business are carried over into government—especially when so many businessmen have gone into government. How many executives would really fight for a law requiring a careful and public accounting of all executive contracts and 'expense accounts'? High income taxes have resulted in a network of collusion between big firm and higher employee. There are many ingenious ways to cheat the spirit of the tax laws, as we have seen, and the standards of consumption of many high-priced men are determined more by complicated expense accounts than by simple take-home pay. Like prohibition, the laws of income taxes and the regulations of wartime exist without the support of firm business convention. It is merely illegal to cheat them, but it is smart to get away with it. Laws without supporting moral conventions invite crime, but much more importantly, they spur the growth of an expedient, amoral attitude.

A society that is in its higher circles and on its middle levels widely believed to be a network of smart rackets does not produce men with an inner moral sense; a society that is merely expedient does not produce men of conscience. A society that narrows the meaning of 'success' to the big money and in its terms condemns failure as the chief vice, raising money to the plane of absolute value, will produce the sharp operator and the shady deal. Blessed are the cynical, for only they have what it takes to succeed.

2

In the corporate world, in the political directorate, and increasingly in the ascendant military, the heads of the big hierarchies and power machines are seen not only as men who have suc-

"Look, Nixon's no dope. If the people really *wanted* moral leadership, he'd give them moral leadership."

ceeded, but as wielders of the patronage of success. They interpret and they apply to individuals the criteria of success. Those immediately below them are usually members of their clique, of their clientele, sound men as they themselves are sound. But the hierarchies are intricately related to one another, and inside each clique are some whose loyalties are to other cliques. There are personal loyalties as well as official ones, personal as well as impersonal criteria for advancement. As we trace the career of the individual member of various higher circles, we are also tracing the history of his loyalties, for the first and overshadowing fact about the higher circles, from the standpoint of what it takes to succeed within them, is that they are based upon self-co-optation. The second fact about these hierarchies of success is that they do not form one monolithic structure; they are a complex set of variously related and often antagonistic cliques. The third fact we must recognize is that, of any such world, younger men who would succeed attempt to relate themselves to those in charge of their selection of successes.

Accordingly, the American literature of practical aspiration—which carries the great fetish of success—has undergone a significant shift in its advice about 'what it takes to succeed.' The sober, personal virtues of will power and honesty, of high-mindedness and the constitutional inability to say 'yes' to The Easy Road of women, tobacco, and wine—this later nineteenth-century image has given way to 'the most important single factor, the effective personality,' which 'commands attention by charm,' and 'radiates self-confidence.' In this 'new way of life,' one must smile often and be a good listener, talk in terms of the other man's interests and make the other feel important—and one must do all this sincerely. Personal relations, in short, have become part of 'public relations,' a sacrifice of selfhood on a personality market, to the sole end of individual success in the corporate way of life.[4] Being justified by superior merit and hard work, but being founded on co-optation by a clique, often on quite other grounds, the elite careerist must continually persuade others and himself as well that he is the opposite of what he actually is.

It is the proud claim of the higher circles in America that their members are entirely self-made. That is their self-image and their well-publicized myth. Popular proof of this is based on anecdotes; its scholarly proof is supposed to rest upon statistical rituals whereby it is shown that varying proportions of the men at the top are sons of men of lower rank. They have already seen the proportions of given elite circles composed of the men who have risen. But what is more important than the proportions of the sons of wage workers among these higher circles is the criteria of admission to them, and the question of who applies these criteria. We cannot from upward mobility infer higher merit. Even if the rough figures that now generally hold were reversed, and 90 per cent of the elite were sons of wage workers—but the criteria of co-optation by the elite remained what they now are—we could not from that mobility necessarily infer merit. Only if the criteria of the top positions were meritorious, and only if they were self-applied, as in a purely entrepreneurial

manner, could we smuggle merit into such statistics—from any statistics—of mobility. The idea that the self-made man is somehow 'good' and that the family-made man is not good makes moral sense only when the career is independent, when one is on one's own as an entrepreneur. It would also make sense in a strict bureaucracy where examinations control advancement. It makes little sense in the system of corporate co-optation.

There is, in psychological fact, no such thing as a self-made man. No man makes himself, least of all the members of the American elite. In a world of corporate hierarchies, men are selected by those above them in the hierarchy in accordance with whatever criteria they use. In connection with the corporations of America, we have seen the current criteria. Men shape themselves to fit them, and are thus made by the criteria, the social premiums that prevail. If there is no such thing as a self-made man, there is such a thing as a self-used man, and there are many such men among the American elite.

Under such conditions of success, there is no virtue in starting out poor and becoming rich. Only where the ways of becoming rich are such as to require virtue or to lead to virtue does personal enrichment imply virtue. In a system of co-optation from above, whether you began rich or poor seems less relevant in revealing what kind of man you are when you have arrived than in revealing the principles of those in charge of selecting the ones who succeed.

All this is sensed by enough people below the higher circles to lead to cynical views of the lack of connection between merit and mobility, between virtue and success. It is a sense of the

---

[4] Cf. Mills, *White Collar*; (New York: Oxford University Press, 1951), pp. 259 ff.

immorality of accomplishment, and it is revealed in the prevalence of such views as: 'it's all just another racket,' and 'it's not what you know but who you know.' Considerable numbers of people now accept the immorality of accomplishment as a going fact.

Some observers are led by their sense of the immorality of accomplishment to the ideology, obliquely set forth by academic social science, of human relations in industry;[5] still others to the solace of mind provided by the newer literature of resignation, of peace of mind, which in some quietened circles replaces the old literature of frenzied aspiration, of how to get ahead. But, regardless of the particular style of reaction, the sense of the immorality of accomplishment often feeds into that level of public sensibility which we have called the higher immorality. The old self-made man's is a tarnished image, and no other image of success has taken its once bright place. Success itself, as the American model of excellence, declines as it becomes one more feature of the higher immorality.

3

Moral distrust of the American elite—as well as the fact of organized irresponsibility—rests upon the higher immorality, but also upon vague feelings about the higher ignorance. Once upon a time in the United States, men of affairs were also men of sensibility: to a considerable extent the elite of power and the elite of culture coincided, and where they did not coincide they often overlapped as circles. Within the compass of a knowledgeable and effective public, knowledge and power were in effective touch; and more than that, this public decided much that was decided.

'Nothing is more revealing,' James Reston has written, 'than to read the debate in the House of Representatives in the Eighteen Thirties on Greece's fight with Turkey for independence and the Greek-Turkish debate in the Congress in 1947. The first is dignified and eloquent, the argument marching from principle through illustration to conclusion; the second is a dreary garble of debating points, full of irrelevancies and bad history.'[6] George Washington in 1783 relaxed with Voltaire's 'letters' and Locke's 'On Human Understanding'; Eisenhower read cowboy tales and detective stories.[7] For such men as now typically arrive in the higher political, economic and military circles, the briefing and the memorandum seem to have pretty well replaced not only the serious book, but the newspaper as well. Given the immorality of accomplishment, this is perhaps as it must be, but what is somewhat disconcerting about it is that they are below the level on which they might feel a little bit ashamed of the uncultivated style of their relaxation and of their mental fare, and that no self-cultivated public is in a position by its reactions to educate them to such uneasiness.

By the middle of the twentieth century, the American elite have become an entirely different breed of men from those who could on any reasonable grounds be considered a cultural elite, or even for that matter cultivated men of sensibility. Knowledge and power are

[5] Cf. Mills, 'The Contribution of Sociology to Industrial Relations,' Proceedings of the First Annual Conference of the Industrial Relations Research Association, December 1948.

[6] James Reston, The New York Times, 31 January 1954, section 4, p. 8.

[7] The New York Times Book Review, 23 August 1953. But see also Time, 28 February 1955, pp. 12 ff.

not truly united inside the ruling circles; and when men of knowledge do come to a point of contact with the circles of powerful men, they come not as peers but as hired men. The elite of power, wealth, and celebrity do not have even a passing acquaintance with the elite of culture, knowledge and sensibility; they are not in touch with them—although the ostentatious fringes of the two worlds sometimes overlap in the world of the celebrity.

Most men are encouraged to assume that, in general, the most powerful and the wealthiest are also the most knowledgeable or, as they might say, 'the smartest.' Such ideas are propped up by many little slogans about those who 'teach because they can't *do*,' and about 'if you're so smart, why aren't you rich?'* But all that such wisecracks mean is that those who use them assume that power and wealth are sovereign values for all men and especially for men 'who are smart.' They assume also that knowledge always pays off in such ways, or surely ought to, and that the test of genuine knowledge is just such pay-offs. The powerful and the wealthy *must* be the men of most knowledge, otherwise how could they be where they are? But to say that those who succeed to power must be 'smart,'

is to say that power *is* knowledge. To say that those who succeed to wealth must be smart, is to say that wealth *is* knowledge.

The prevalence of such assumptions does reveal something that is true: that ordinary men, even today, are prone to explain and to justify power and wealth in terms of knowledge or ability. Such assumptions also reveal something of what has happened to the kind of experience that knowledge has come to be. Knowledge is no longer widely felt as an ideal; it is seen as an instrument. In a society of power and wealth, knowledge is valued as an instrument of power and wealth, and also, of course, as an ornament in conversation.

What knowledge does to a man (in clarifying what he is, and setting him free)—that is the personal ideal of knowledge. What knowledge does to a civilization (in revealing its human meaning, and setting it free)—that is the social ideal of knowledge. But today, the personal *and* the social ideals of knowledge have coincided in what knowledge does *for* the smart guy—it gets him ahead; and for the wise nation—it lends cultural prestige, sanctifying power with authority.

Knowledge seldom lends power to the man of knowledge. But the supposed, and secret, knowledge of some men-on-the-make, and their very free use thereof, has consequence for other men who have not the power of defense. Knowledge, of course, is neither good nor bad, nor is its use good or bad. 'Bad men increase in knowledge as fast as good men,' John Adams wrote, 'and science, arts, taste, sense and letters, are employed for the purpose of injustice as well as for virtue.'[9] That was in 1790;

---

* Bernard Baruch, an advisor to Presidents, has recently remarked, 'I think economists as [a] rule . . . take for granted they know a lot of things. If they really knew so much, they would have all the money and we would have none.' And again he reasons: 'These men [economists] can take facts and figures and bring them together, but their predictions are not worth any more than ours. If they were, they would have all the money and we would not have anything.'[8]

[8] *Hearings Before the Committee on Banking and Currency*, United States Senate, Eighty-fourth Congress, First Session (U.S. Government Printing Office, Washington, 1955), p. 1001.

[9] John Adams, *Discourses on Davila* (Boston: Russell and Cutler, 1805).

today we have good reason to know that it is so.

The problem of knowledge and power is, and always has been, the problem of the relations of men of knowledge with men of power. Suppose we were to select the one hundred most powerful men, from all fields of power, in America today and line them up. And then, suppose we select the one hundred most knowledgeable men, from all fields of social knowledge, and lined them up. How many men would be in *both* our line-ups? Of course our selection would depend upon what we mean by power and what we mean by knowledge—especially what we mean by knowledge. But, if we mean what the words seem to mean, surely we would find few if any men in America today who were in both groups, and surely we could find many more at the time the nation was founded than we could find today. For, in the eighteenth century, even in this colonial outpost, men of power pursued learning, and men of learning were often in positions of power. In these respects we have, I believe, suffered grievous decline.[10]

There is little union in the same persons of knowledge and power; but persons of power do surround themselves with men of some knowledge, or at least with men who are experienced in shrewd dealings. The man of knowledge has not become a philosopher king; but he has often become a consultant, and moreover a consultant to a man who is neither king-like nor philosophical. It is, of course, true that the chairman of the pulp writers section of the Authors' League helped a leading senator 'polish up the speeches he delivered in the 1952 senatorial campaign.'[11] But it is not natural in the course of their careers for men of knowledge to meet with those of power. The links between university and government are weak, and when they do occur, the man of knowledge appears as an 'expert' which usually means as a hired technician. Like most others in this society, the man of knowledge is himself dependent for his livelihood upon the job, which nowadays is a prime sanction of thought control. Where getting ahead requires the good opinions of more powerful others, their judgments become prime objects of concern. Accordingly, in so far as intellectuals serve power directly—in a job hierarchy—they often do so unfreely.

The democratic man assumes the existence of a public, and in his rhetoric asserts that this public is the very seat of sovereignty. Two things are needed in a democracy: articulate and knowledgeable publics, and political leaders who if not men of reason are at least reasonably responsible to such knowledgeable publics as exist. Only where publics and leaders are responsive and responsible, are human affairs in democratic order, and only when knowledge has public relevance is this order possible. Only when mind has an autonomous basis, independent of power, but powerfully related to it, can mind exert its force in the shaping of human affairs. This is democratically possible only when there exists a free and knowledgeable public, to which men of knowledge may address themselves, and to which men of

[10] In *Perspectives, USA,* No. 3, Mr. Lionell Trilling has written optimistically of 'new intellectual classes.' For an informed account of new cultural strata by a brilliantly self-conscious insider, see also Louis Kronenberger, *Company Manners* (Indianapolis: Bobbs-Merrill, 1954).

[11] Leo Egan, 'Political "Ghosts" Playing Usual Quiet Role as Experts,' *The New York Times,* 14 October 1954, p. 20.

power are truly responsible. Such a public and such men—either of power or of knowledge—do not now prevail, and accordingly, knowledge does not now have democratic relevance in America.

The characteristic member of the higher circles today is an intellectual mediocrity, sometimes a conscientious one, but still a mediocrity. His intelligence is revealed only by his occasional realization that he is not up to the decisions he sometimes feels called upon to confront. But usually he keeps such feelings private, his public utterances being pious and sentimental, grim and brave, cheerful and empty in their universal generality. He is open only to abbreviated and vulgarized, predigested and slanted ideas. He is a commander of the age of the phone call, the memo, and the briefing.

By the mindlessness and mediocrity of men of affairs, I do not, of course, mean that these men are not sometimes intelligent—although that is by no means automatically the case. It is not, however, primarily a matter of the distribution of 'intelligence'—as if intelligence were a homogeneous something of which there may be more or less. It is rather a matter of the type of intelligence, of the quality of mind that is selected and formed. It is a matter of the evaluation of substantive rationality as the chief value in a man's life and character and conduct. That evaluation is what is lacking in the American power elite. In its place there are 'weight' and 'judgment' which count for much more in their celebrated success than any subtlety of mind or force of intellect.

All around and just below the weighty man of affairs are his technical lieutenants of power who have been assigned the role of knowledge and even of speech: his public relations men, his ghost, his administrative assistants, his secretaries. And do not forget The Committees. With the increased means of decision, there is a crisis of understanding among the political directorate of the United States, and accordingly, there is often a commanding indecision.

The lack of knowledge as an experience among the elite ties in with the malign ascendancy of the expert, not only as fact but as legitimation. When questioned recently about a criticism of defense policies made by the leader of the opposition party, the Secretary of Defense replied, 'Do you think he is an expert in the matter?' When pressed further by reporters he asserted that the 'military chiefs think it is sound, and I think it is sound,' and later, when asked about specific cases, added: 'In some cases, all you can do is ask the Lord.'[12] With such a large role so arrogantly given to God and to experts, what room is there for political leadership? Much less for public debate of what is after all every bit as much a political and a moral as a military issue. But then, from before Pearl Harbor, the trend has been the abdication of debate and the collapse of opposition under the easy slogan of bipartisanship.

Beyond the lack of intellectual cultivation by political personnel and advisory circle, the absence of publicly relevant mind has come to mean that powerful decisions and important policies are not made in such a way as to be justified or attacked; in short, debated in any intellectual form. Moreover, the attempt to so justify them is often not even made. Public relations displace reasoned ar-

[12] Charles E. Wilson, quoted in *The New York Times*, 10 March 1954, p. 1.

gument; manipulation and undebated decisions of power replace democratic authority. More and more, since the nineteenth century, as administration has replaced politics, the decisions of importance do not carry even the panoply of reasonable discussion, but are made by God, by experts, and by men like Mr. Wilson.

More and more the area of the official secret expands, as well as the area of the secret listening in on those who might divulge in public what the public, not being composed of experts with Q clearance, is not to know. The entire sequence of decisions concerning the production and the use of atomic weaponry has been made without any genuine public debate and the facts needed to engage in that debate intelligently have been officially hidden, distorted, and even lied about. As the decisions become more fateful, not only for Americans but literally for mankind, the sources of information are closed up, and the relevant facts needed for decision (even the decisions made!) are, as politically convenient 'official secrets,' withheld from the heavily laden channels of information.

In those channels, meanwhile, political rhetoric seems to slide lower and lower down the scale of cultivation and sensibility. The height of such mindless communications to masses, or what are thought to be masses, is probably the demagogic assumption that suspicion and accusation, if repeated often enough, somehow equal proof of guilt—just as repeated claims about toothpaste or brands of cigarettes are assumed to equal facts. The greatest kind of propaganda with which America is beset, the greatest at least in terms of volume and loudness, is com-mercial propaganda for soap and cigarettes and automobiles; it is to such things, or rather to Their Names, that this society most frequently sings its loudest praises. What is important about this is that by implication and omission, by emphasis and sometimes by flat statement, this astounding volume of propaganda for commodities is often untruthful and misleading; and is addressed more often to the belly or to the groin than to the head or to the heart. Public communications from those who make powerful decisions, or who would have us vote them into such decision-making places, more and more take on these qualities of mindlessness and myth which commercial propaganda and advertising have come to exemplify.

In America today, men of affairs are not so much dogmatic as they are mindless. Dogma has usually meant some more or less elaborated justification of ideas and values, and thus has had some features (however inflexible and closed) of mind, of intellect, of reason. Nowadays what we are up against is precisely the absence of mind of any sort as a public force; what we are up against is a disinterest in and a fear of knowledge that might have liberating public relevance. What this makes possible are decisions having no rational justifications which the intellect could confront and engage in debate.

It is not the barbarous irrationality of dour political primitives that is the American danger; it is the respected judgments of Secretaries of State, the earnest platitudes of Presidents, the fearful self-righteousness of sincere young American politicians from sunny California. These men have replaced mind with platitude, and the dogmas by which they are legitimated are so widely accepted that no counter-balance of mind prevails against them. Such men as these are crackpot realists: in the name of realism they have constructed a paranoid reality all their own; in the name of practicality they have projected a utopian image of capitalism. They have replaced the responsible interpretation of events with the disguise of events by a maze of public relations; respect for public debate with unshrewed notions of psychological warfare; intellectual ability with agility of the sound, mediocre judgment; the capacity to elaborate alternatives and gauge their consequences with the executive stance.

4

Despite—perhaps because of—the ostracism of mind from public affairs, the immorality of accomplishment, and the general prevalence of organized irresponsibility, the men of the higher circles benefit from the total power of the institutional domains over which they rule. For the power of these institutions, actual or potential, is ascribed to them as the ostensible decision-makers. Their positions and their activities, and even their persons, are hallowed by these ascriptions; and, around all the high places of power, there is a penumbra of prestige in which the political directorate, the corporate rich, the admirals and generals are bathed. The elite of a society, however modest its individual member, embodies the prestige of the society's power.* Moreover, few indi-

viduals in positions of such authority can long resist the temptation to base their self-images, at least in part, upon the sounding board of the collectivity which they head. Acting as the representative of his nation, his corporation, his army, in due course, he comes to consider himself and what he says and believes as expressive of the historically accumulated glory of the great institutions with which he comes to identify himself. When he speaks in the name of his country or its cause, its past glory also echoes in his ears.

Status, no longer rooted primarily in local communities, follows the big hierarchies, which are on a national scale. Status follows the big money, even if it has a touch of the gangster about it. Status follows power, even if it be without background. Below, in the mass society, old moral and traditional barriers to status break down and Americans look for standards of excellence among the circles above them, in terms of which to model themselves and judge their self-esteem. Yet nowadays, it seems easier for Americans to recognize such representative men in the past than in the present. Whether this is due to a real historical difference or merely to the political ease and expediency of

* John Adams wrote in the late eighteenth century: 'When you rise to the first ranks, and consider the first men; a nobility who are known and respected at least, perhaps habitually esteemed and beloved by a nation; Princes and Kings, on

whom the eyes of all men are fixed, and whose every motion is regarded, the consequences of wounding their feelings are dreadful, because the feelings of a whole nation, and sometimes of many nations, are wounded at the same time. If the smallest variation is made in their situation, relatively to each other; if one who was inferior is raised to be superior, unless it be by fixed laws, whose evident policy and necessity may take away disgrace, nothing but war, carnage and vengeance has ever been the usual consequence of it . . .'[13]

[13] John Adams, op. cit. pp. 57–8.

hindsight is very difficult to tell.* At any rate it is a fact that in the political assignments of prestige there is little disparagement of Washington, Jefferson, and Lincoln, but much disagreement about current figures. Representative men seem more easily recognizable after they have died; contemporary political leaders are merely politicians; they may be big or little, but they are not great, and increasingly they are seen in terms of the higher immorality.

* In every intellectual period, some one discipline or school of thought becomes a sort of common denominator. The common denominator of the conservative mood in America today is American history. This is the time of the American historian. All nationalist celebration tends, of course, to be put in historical terms, but the celebrators do not wish to be relevant merely to the understanding of history as past event. Their purpose is the celebration of the present. (1) One reason why the American ideology is so historically oriented is that of all the scholarly community it is the historians who are most likely to create such public assumptions. For, of all the scholarly writers, the historians have been the ones with the literate tradition. Other 'social scientists' are more likely to be unacquainted with English usage and moreover, they do not write about large topics of public concern. (2) The 'good' historians, in fulfilling the public role of the higher journalists, the historians with the public attention and the Sunday acclaim, are the historians who are the quickest to re-interpret the American past with relevance to the current mood, and in turn, the cleverest at picking out of the past, just now, those characters and events that most easily make for optimism and lyric upsurge. (3) In truth, and without nostalgia, we ought to realize that the American past is a wonderful source for myths about the American present. That past, at times, did indeed embody quite a way of life; the United States has been extraordinarily fortunate in its time of origin and early development; the present is complicated, and, especially to a trained historian, quite undocumented. The general American ideology accordingly tends to be of history and by historians.[14]

[14] Cf. William Harlan Hale, 'The Boom in American History,' *The Reporter*, 24 February 1955, pp. 42 ff.

Now again status follows power, and older types of exemplary figures have been replaced by the fraternity of the successful—the professional executives who have become the political elite, and who are now the *official* representative men. It remains to be seen whether they will become representative men in the images and aspirations of the mass public, or whether they will endure any longer than the displaced liberals of the 'thirties. Their images are controversial, deeply involved in the immorality of accomplishment and the higher immorality in general. Increasingly, literate Americans feel that there is something synthetic about them. Their style and the conditions under which they become 'big' lend themselves too readily to the suspicion of the build-up; the shadows of the ghost writer and the make-up man loom too large; the slickness of the fabrication is too apparent.

We should, of course, bear in mind that men of the higher circles may or may not seek to impose themselves as representative upon the underlying population, and the relevant public sectors of the population may or may not accept their images. An elite may try to impose its claims upon the mass public, but this public may not cash them in. On the contrary, it may be indifferent or even debunk their values, caricature their image, laugh at their claim to be representative men.

In his discussion of models of national character, Walter Bagehot does not go into such possibilities;[15] but it is clear that for our contemporaries we must consider them, since precisely this reaction has led to a sometimes frenzied and always expensive practice of what is known as 'public relations.' Those who

[15] See Walter Bagehot, *Physics and Politics* (New York: D. Appleton, 1912), pp. 36, 146-7, 205-6.

have both power and status are perhaps best off when they do not actively have to seek acclaim. The truly proud old families will not seek it; the professional celebrities are specialists in seeking it actively. Increasingly, the political, economic, and military elite—as we have seen—compete with the celebrities and seek to borrow their status. Perhaps those who have unprecedented power without the aura of status, will always seek it, even if uneasily, among those who have publicity without power.

For the mass public, there is the status distraction of the celebrity, as well as the economic distraction of war prosperity; for the liberal intellectual, who does look to the political arena, there is the political distraction of the sovereign localities and of the middle levels of power, which sustain the illusion that America is still a self-balancing society. If the mass media focus on the professional celebrities, the liberal intellectuals, especially the academic social scientists among them, focus upon the noisy middle levels. Professional celebrities and middle-level politicians are the most visible figures of the system; in fact, together they tend to monopolize the communicated or public scene that is visible to the members of the mass society, and thus to obscure and to distract attention from the power elite.

The higher circles in America today contain, on the one hand, the laughing, erotic, dazzling glamour of the professional celebrity, and, on the other, the prestige aura of power, of authority, of might and wealth. These two pinnacles are not unrelated. The power elite is not so noticeable as the celebrities, and often does not want to be; the 'power' of the professional celebrity is the power of distraction. America as a national public is indeed possessed of a strange set of

idols. The professionals, in the main, are either glossy little animals or frivolous clowns; the men of power, in the main, rarely seem to be models of representative men.

Such moral uneasiness as prevails among the American elite themselves is accordingly quite understandable. Its existence is amply confirmed by the more serious among those who have come to feel that they represent America abroad. There, the double-faced character of the American celebrity is reflected both by the types of Americans who travel to play or to work, and in the images many literate and articulate Europeans hold of 'Americans.' Public honor in America tends now to be either frivolous or grim; either altogether trivial or portentous of a greatly tightened-up system of prestige.

The American elite is not composed of representative men whose conduct and character constitute models for American imitation and aspiration. There is no set of men with whom members of the mass public can rightfully and gladly identify. In this fundamental sense, America is indeed without leaders. Yet such is the nature of the mass public's morally cynical and politically unspecified distrust that it is readily drained off without real political effect. That this is so, after the men and events of the last thirty years, is further proof of the extreme difficulty of finding and of using in America today the political means of sanity for morally sane objectives.

America—a conservative country without any conservative ideology—appears now before the world a naked and arbitrary power, as, in the name of realism, its men of decision enforce their often crackpot definitions upon world reality. The second-rate mind is in command of the ponderously spoken platitude. In the liberal rhetoric, vagueness, and in the conservative mood, irrationality, are raised to principle. Public relations and the official secret, the trivializing campaign and the terrible fact clumsily accomplished, are replacing the reasoned debate of political ideas in the privately incorporated economy, the military ascendancy, and the political vacuum of modern America.

The men of the higher circles are not representative men; their high position is not a result of moral virtue; their fabulous success is not firmly connected with meritorious ability. Those who sit in the seats of the high and the mighty are selected and formed by the means of power, the sources of wealth, the mechanics of celebrity, which prevail in their society. They are not men selected and formed by a civil service that is linked with the world of knowledge and sensibility. They are not men shaped by nationally responsible parties that debate openly and clearly the issues this nation now so unintelligently confronts. They are not men held in responsible check by a plurality of voluntary associations which connect debating publics and the pinnacles of decision. Commanders of power unequaled in human history, they have succeeded within the American system of organized irresponsiblity.

QUESTIONS FOR DISCUSSION

1. Do you agree with Professor Commager that Watergate was basically a moral problem, rather than a political or constitutional problem?
2. What are some recent examples of government officials acting with a high moral sensibility?
3. How can extremism in morality be a vice?
4. Does the concept of a "power elite" continue to be relevant in contemporary America?
5. Is it fair to criticize law schools and the legal profession in general because so many of the indicted Nixon aides were lawyers?
6. If Watergate was the result of a breakdown in societal morality, how can our moral climate be improved?
7. Is American politics inherently immoral? Is it possible for young persons to participate in politics without acquiring a "blunted moral sensibility"?
8. How does the ethical behavior of members of Congress and executive officials compare with that of business executives and professionals such as doctors and teachers?
9. What can the elementary and secondary schools do to help raise the level of morality among young persons?
10. The president of Johns Hopkins University has stated that in this secular age the only remaining transmitter of values is history. He proposes requiring broad study of history for all Johns Hopkins students. What is your reaction to this idea?

"So The Last One Collapsed — Get In There And Try It Again"

chapter two

Political Parties and Elections

IDEOLOGICAL DIFFERENCES BETWEEN DEMOCRATS AND REPUBLICANS

Rates of voter turnout in recent federal elections have been very low. In 1974, the national average was a 38 percent turnout—the lowest off-year congressional percentage since 1946. In 1972 the turnout was 55.3 percent—the lowest presidential turnout since 1948.

A common explanation for low voter participation is that voters believe, "No choices of action on the issues are offered, so why bother to vote. What difference will it make?" Paradoxically, in spite of this widespread attitude, the political parties seem to be offering more clear-cut choices on issues as they veer apart ideologically. Democrats are becoming more liberal and Republicans are becoming more conservative. The *Congressional Quarterly* reported that in 1973–1974 a majority of Democrats opposed a majority of Republicans on 39 percent of the roll call votes. This reflects a continuing annual increase, up from 33 percent in 1960–1970.

Political columnist David Broder suggests that progressive Republicans, who dominated GOP presidential conventions from 1928 through 1960, have lost control. In part this has been due to the losses of moderate Republican gubernatorial candidates and to the election of conservative House Republicans from the South. On the other hand, northern liberals have reached an all-time high among the total House Democrats. At the same time, many southern Democrats, whose constituencies now include large numbers of blacks and white working-class people, are becoming more liberal. Journalist Jack Bass notes that since the Voting Rights Act became effective in 1968, "Every new Democrat elected to Congress from the South has been a moderate and damn near every Republican has been a conservative."

The University of Michigan Center of Political Studies reports that the 1972 election drew the ideological lines between Democrats and Republicans more sharply than any other election they had ever measured. From this, Broder concludes that just as American voters are becoming free from party identification (more likely to be ticket-splitters), the two major parties may finally achieve their own separate identities.

DEMOCRATIC ELECTORAL STRATEGY

In spite of this ideological division between the parties, major internal friction remains. For the Democrats, strategy in 1976 and beyond depends

Drawing by Reilly; © 1975 The New Yorker Magazine, Inc.

"Rhetoric aside, who do you think will *really* do most for the little people—George Wallace, Fred Harris, Jimmy Carter, Scoop Jackson, or Mo Udall?"

in large part on an examination of their 1972 defeat. A common explanation for McGovern's loss has been that his campaign was badly run and that he appeared too left-wing for white, working-class voters. However, these reasons have been rejected by several political analysts[1] who suggest that working-class persons are becoming more, rather than less, liberal on many issues. Their explanation for McGovern's loss is that McGovern and his supporters deserted the working class by concentrating too heavily on issues such as busing, abortion, and amnesty while ignoring the economic needs of average Americans. Lanny Davis suggests that McGovern lost because he "seemed to represent an elitist, moralistic constituency" whose "arrogant snobbery" was responsible for alienating white working-class

[1] See Lanny Davis, *The Emerging Democratic Majority* (New York: Stein and Day, 1974); Andrew Levison, *The Working Class Majority* (New York: Coward, McCann, and Geohegan, 1974); John Stewart, *One Last Chance* (New York: Praeger, 1974); and Ben Wattenberg, *The Real America* (Garden City, N.Y.: Doubleday, 1974).

and middle-class voters. The general conclusion of these authors is that Democrats cannot afford to alienate a large portion of their traditional supporters without suffering in a presidential election. An equally complicated problem for Democrats remains on the right—how to accommodate George Wallace within the party.

The 1972 election also highlighted the pitfalls of primary elections as that process becomes more open and more competitive. On the Democratic side, although the centrist views of Edmund Muskie were well suited for a general election campaign against President Nixon, they overlooked the realities of winning the nomination in a multi-candidate primary. Since primaries draw low turnouts, a small band of workers can often be successful in getting their candidate a plurality of votes. Thus while McGovern drew support from his New Politics constituency in the primaries and thereby secured his party's nomination, this narrow focus was damaging during the general election.

REPUBLICAN ELECTORAL STRATEGY

A basic strategy for Republicans in the 1970s was developed by Kevin Phillips in his book *The Emerging Republican Majority.* Phillips saw major Republican strength in the Rocky Mountain states, the farm states, and suburbs, combined with support from white southerners and white ethnic voters in industrial states. In 1974, the Republican party lost strength at each point. Among southerners, in a post-civil rights era, Democrats have successfully appealed to populist concerns such as tax reform and the role of oil companies. Issues concerning environmental protection and the energy crisis were used effectively by Democrats to help win 1974 elections in Wyoming, Colorado, and Montana. Economic concerns and the effect of Watergate on the law and order issue have weakened Republican support among blue-collar ethnics in northern cities.

Moreover, Republican conservatives are rising against the Ford administration policies of detente and deficit spending. They are unhappy with Ford's appointments of liberals to executive positions and with Ford's unwillingness to act tougher on Vietnam. A dump Ford–Rockefeller effort is likely in 1976. Even more ominous for the Republican party is the growing prospect of the creation of a new conservative party. Some right-wing leaders argue that because of Watergate and runaway inflation the Republican party is dead. They point out that while only 18 to 23 percent of the American voters describe themselves as Republicans, 62 percent classify themselves as conservatives. Thus they conclude that something obviously is wrong with the Republican label and image. Moreover, persons such as Kevin Phillips continue to believe that there is an authentic conservative majority. This line of reasoning holds that conservatives are not just the wealthy or Orange County, California voters. Rather, conservatives are lower- and middle-class individuals across the country who resent busing, high taxes, inflation, crime, and a general permissiveness in American society.

Although Watergate has been viewed as a Nixon problem, not a Republican party responsibility, its fallout has damaged the party badly. An early 1975 poll taken by Market Opinion Research found that while 44 percent of the respondents said they trusted the Democrats, only 25 percent said they trusted the Republicans. The conclusion of the researchers was that unless President Ford is able to re-establish the party's reputation for trustworthiness and competence, Nixon will haunt the Republican party. In 1974, of the 10 Republicans on the House Judiciary Committee who opposed impeachment on each televised roll call, four were defeated and one retired. In the congressional elections, Republicans lost 43 House seats and 3 Senate seats.

One of the earliest reforms to follow the Watergate scandal was the 1974 campaign finance bill which set up public financing of presidential campaigns. The finance legislation created a Federal Election Commission charged with administering the 1974 law. Although due to begin operation on January 1, 1975, the commission had not even been formed as Democratic hopefuls announced their candidacy in early 1975. Without anyone to answer questions and enforce the law, scandals appeared inevitable.

READINGS

In the article that follows, Stephen Hess outlines a series of proposals aimed at improving the presidential election process. Like many other reformers, Hess would seek ways of strengthening the political parties in order to counterbalance the power of the presidential candidate to control campaigns.

John Stewart examines reform of the Democratic party during the period 1969–1972. In responding to the question "What went wrong?" Stewart suggests that reforms, to be workable, cannot be viewed as ends in themselves. Stewart notes that many of the reforms were appealing to "casual Democrats" (those who seldom vote on Election Day), but they turned off the traditional activist Democrats (those who attend precinct caucuses and state conventions) whose support was vital in the general election.

Eugene McCarthy, former senator and presidential candidate, argues against the 1974 federal campaign finance law. That law created public financing of presidential campaigns and new regulations for congressional campaigns. McCarthy believes the law is unconstitutional. He is particularly concerned because he believes that the law discriminates against minor parties in presidential elections. McCarthy also criticizes the law for protecting incumbent members of Congress and providing loopholes for the wealthy.

The Presidential Campaign

Stephen Hess

DID "THE SYSTEM" FAIL IN 1972?

The events of Watergate, as they related to the presidential selection process, included the wiretapping and burglary of the Democratic National Committee (organized and executed by operatives of the Committee to Re-elect the President); a series of Nixon campaign efforts to sabotage contenders for the Democratic nomination (presumably designed to increase George McGovern's chances of being nominated); and illegal contributions to and expenditures by the Nixon organization. Other events, of even greater consequence to the governance of a democratic society, become enmeshed in the scandal but are outside the scope of an inquiry into how Americans choose their Presidents.

President Nixon in his April 30, 1973, address to the nation rejected the contention that Watergate represented the bankruptcy of the political system. "It was the system that has brought the facts to light and that will bring the guilty to justice—a system that in this case has included a determined grand jury, honest prosecutors, a courageous judge, and a vigorous free press." Successful prosecution of the guilty, it should be noted, does not necessarily mean that the political system is working well. Assuming, however, that the way Presidents are chosen is much the

same as it has been through history, the case for Watergate as an aberration, rather than a condition caused by something inherent in the system, is that Watergate is totally unprecedented in the American experience. "Politicians have played tricks on each other since politics was invented," Stewart Alsop wrote.[1] But in 185 years of presidential elections there had never been campaign corruption on this scale.

Ultimately, I believe, Watergate will be explained primarily as a failure of individuals who should have been conscious of acting illegally and should have known the possible consequences of their actions. That these were men who held high trust and upon whom society had lavished honor might cause us to ask how representative they are of the nation that produced them. If indeed they are like us, then we must find ways to contain ourselves. But a free society pays a price for assuming its own immorality. "Should we have a law against red wigs? A law compelling search of all suitcases for $100 bills?" asks Meg Greenfield. "[T]here are certain limits to what we can expect the written laws to do for us and certain dangers in trying to write laws that will cover and control every possible aspect of human malfeasance."[2] The events of Watergate were prohibited by existing law; they were committed by people

From *The Presidential Campaign: The Leadership Selection Process After Watergate*, pp. 93–116, by Stephen Hess. Copyright © 1974 by the Brookings Institution, Washington, D.C.

[1] Stewart Alsop, "War, Not Politics," *Newsweek* (May 14, 1973).

[2] Meg Greenfield, "A Trust Was Broken," *Washington Post*, May 18, 1973.

who knew the law. The prescription to prevent future Watergates is not likely to be additional laws or even stiffer penalties. Stiffer penalties will reflect the seriousness that society attaches to aberrant behavior, but there is little assurance that this would have deterred those involved in the crimes of 1972. Society prescribes a negative code of conduct—"thou shalt nots"—and enforces prohibitions through its legal system. The legal system is not designed to reward those who keep the law, nor can it in most cases prevent those who wish to from breaking the law. Still, it is incumbent upon us to examine the system in the light of Watergate and to consider ways to cleanse presidential selection politics.

Even if Watergate is viewed as a failure of men, it may be that politics can cause people to act more immorally than they might in other pursuits. There is no reason to believe, for example, that the bright young men who appeared before the Ervin Committee in 1973 were not good husbands or good parents, or otherwise failed to conduct themselves in an exemplary manner. Jerry Bruno, a leading Democratic advance man, once wrote, "[W]hen you're part of a political campaign, the stakes are as high as they come. . . . I think sometimes it's what fighting a war or playing a pro football game is like."[3] The analogies are apt. Modern warfare is often a suspension of morality, often in the name of morality; pro football is a sport in which infractions of the rules are penalized by loss of yards, rarely by banishment, so that breaking the rules becomes a calculated risk rather than an act of depravity. Moreover, it is in the nature of the ad hoc staffing arrangements of presiden-

tial campaigns to temporarily remove the participants from their "real" worlds in which they individually abide by the codes of conduct of whatever occupations engage them. This does not mean that all citizens leave their morality at home when they enter a presidential campaign; only a very small number do. But, almost without exception, they do see the world of politics as different, less enduring. And for some this makes a difference in their conduct.

Under the existing system, as I said earlier, candidates seeking a presidential nomination propose themselves, raise their own funds, and build their own organizations. When a person wishes to run for President, he must very quickly recruit a staff from among friends and others who are in a position to drop what they are doing and devote themselves to his cause for periods of up to a year. People are often "loaned" by corporations, law firms, advertising agencies, newspapers, labor unions, and trade associations. The rich often loan themselves. The young are available and do not cost much. After the conventions, the winning candidates' personal staffs become the nuclei of the campaign organizations. These people, who are responsible for conducting the most important free election campaign in the world, are generally amateurs in that politics is not their profession, despite varying degrees of experience. It is worth recalling the statement of Richard Neustadt, made in a somewhat different context: "The Presidency is no place for amateurs."[4]

The process of conducting a presidential campaign raises questions about individual and group ethics in an election system that lacks a professional mem-

[3] Jerry Bruno and Jeff Greenfield, *The Advance Man* (Morrow, 1971), p. 29.

[4] Richard E. Neustadt, *Presidential Power* (Wiley, 1960), p. 180.

ory. Professionalism, by definition, includes a set of standards by which one is judged and upon which depends one's status. High standards of conduct are strengthened by, if not dependent upon, continuing relationships. Yet continuity is exactly what is absent from the organization of presidential campaigns.

Instead the American system tends to divorce the presidential candidates from the political parties they represent. Television has encouraged this. So have election laws. So have legions of campaign consultants, who now can supply candidates with the services that they once received from their party organizations. So too has the predominance of foreign affairs, a special concern of Presidents but traditionally one that has been treated with bipartisan detachment. Primarily, though, this is a product of a prevailing American attitude. We have scorned the professional politician and glorified a form of political Cincinnatus, the citizen-soldier who drops his plow to wage war for his candidate. Running as a Republican or a Democrat is no longer an unalloyed asset, and so, in many cases, the candidates have chosen to turn their backs on their parties. "I'm not going to ask anybody here to vote on November the 8th because of the party label that I happen to wear," said Richard Nixon in 1960.[5] One by-product of this attitude is that the permanent party committees at the national level are anemic creatures, little more than the caretakers that keep the files, convene the conventions, and dispense routine services.

The grand irony of Watergate is the way in which Watergate will prevent future Watergates for a decade, perhaps

[5] *The Speeches of Vice President Richard M. Nixon*, S. Rept. 994, 87 Cong. 1 sess. (1961), Pt. 2, pp. 81–82.

a generation. Not because it will inspire corrective legislation—though it will—but because politicians rarely make the same mistake twice. (Nixon never repeated the error of waging a fifty-state campaign, as he did in 1960. The meaning of Muskie's 1972 campaign, in which his commitment to enter all state primaries stretched his resources to the diminishing point, is that future candidates will be highly selective, where possible, in choosing their fields of battle. The labor union elements in the Democratic Party, after their defeat by the McGovern forces, will no longer rely on playing a broker's role at future conventions but can be expected to become involved in nomination fights on the precinct level—indeed, it may be that some analysts in 1976 will bemoan the advantages that the party's rules give to the old lib-lab coalition with its shop stewards reaching into every community.) Thus the immediate lesson of Watergate for politicians will be that they must conduct themselves with a cleansing scrupulousness—at least until Watergate sounds as musty as Teapot Dome. While political scientists propose reforms on the basis of yesterday's deficiencies, politicians will be making instant adjustments. Yet there are proposals that professional students of politics should make as their contribution to improving the presidential selection process. The next section of this chapter is one attempt at setting the agenda.

PARTY CONTROL OF THE PRESIDENTIAL SELECTION PROCESS

Watergate provides a sorrowful reminder of how much we miss by not having a strong two-party system with a professional code of ethics for those who participate in the political process. Running presidential campaigns under the centralized control of the parties' national committees will not produce the millennium. American parties practice a type of accommodation politics that is not well suited to injecting creativity into public debate. But it is highly unlikely that the Republican National Committee would seriously consider breaking into the Democratic National Committee, or vice versa, if only for the reason stated by David S. Broder in *The Party's Over*: "Our political parties are old, and they expect to be in business a long time. Neither of them has any great temptation to kick down the walls, or to pursue tactics when temporarily in power that will invite revenge from the opposition when it (inevitably) returns to power."[6]

In is doubtful that the political parties can ever regain the central position in the American system that they held in the nineteenth century. Government has replaced the parties as dispenser of social services, patronage is no longer an attractive enough lure to recruit political workers, other forms of entertainment and voluntary associations now compete with the parties on unequal terms, and television gives the voters increased opportunities to get information and judge candidates outside the party context. But the parties do have it within their power to regain control of presidential campaigns. For they have one lever without which no candidate can expect to become President—a major party line on the voting machines. (Another important lever would be party control over campaign funds.)

The place to begin to assert control is

[6] David S. Broder, *The Party's Over* (Harper and Row, 1972), p. 179.

the quadrennial national conventions. Although thought of primarily as the places where presidential candidates are nominated and platforms written, the conventions also are the governing bodies of the political parties. It is at the conventions that the parties' rules are adopted and the national committees memberships are ratified. In theory the national committees are subordinate to the national conventions. The conventions' potential to act as the parties' supreme authority was evident at the 1972 Democratic meeting. Under the McGovern Commission guidelines, the convention excluded Mayor Daley's delegation, a graphic demonstration of its power to discipline even the most mighty local party organization. The same convention also approved increasing the size of the Democratic National Committee in an attempt to come to grips with the question of constituent group representation and voted to convene a 1974 conference, which will consider proposals for restructuring the party apparatus. The Republican Party in recent years has been less willing to seek ways to revitalize its organization, but it cannot allow itself to lag too far behind if the Democratic Party changes win popular acceptance.

Every fourth year the Republican and Democratic national conventions confer upon two individuals the right to seek the presidency. Whether the nominees feel any obligations in return is a question for students of psychology. But there should be obligations. The honor of running for President as a major party choice should be based on past conduct and future expectations. The parties should decree that their nominations will be given to persons who abide by certain rules of conduct while seeking their parties' endorsements and will

Drawing by Ashley; © 1975 The Toledo Blade

"Of course I have malpractice insurance!
Why do you ask?"

conduct their election campaigns along prescribed lines. As the keepers of the party seal—with the intrinsic power to refuse it as well as confer it—the national conventions (or their delegated agents) should consider the following types of actions:

Pre-convention Conduct

Any person seeking the party's nomination should have to submit financial records to periodic audit and agree to abide by a specific code of conduct; who in the party is authorized to press charges against a candidate for code violations should be spelled out in the party's rules; hearings on code violations should be conducted by a designated body; recommendations for sanctions should be voted upon by the full national committee; various penalties could be imposed, including denial of the party's nomination.

General Election Conduct

Candidates for the nomination should agree to wage their general election campaign under the aegis of the party's national committee. They also should agree that all monies will be raised and spent by the national committee. The nominee must have the right to choose his own campaign manager, who would be in charge of those aspects of the canvass that directly relate to the candidate—his schedule, the logistics of his travels, personal staff, and that part of the media budget that solely promotes the presidential candidate. All other operations should be controlled by the national chairman. No longer should a presidential candidate be able to make a unilateral decision to over-

finance his campaign while the rest of the ticket goes underfinanced. Surplus funds (as in the 1972 Nixon campaign) or other assets (as in the case of McGovern's mailing lists) automatically should be the property of the national parties.

Once the parties asserted control over the presidential selection process, a chain reaction might take place. The national committees, with new and important duties, might begin to attract different sorts of people; instead of being a resting place for ancient political warriors or financial angels, membership might go to those who are willing to fight for the right to participate in making decisions that affect the future of the party. The national chairmanship might be viewed as a legitimate career goal, the top position in the political party profession, rather than a part-time job for a busy public official, or a consolation prize for having been passed over for a vice-presidential nomination, or a symbolic reward for a representative of some constituent group. The national chairman even might begin issuing annual "state of the party" messages, which would report on the progress of platform implementation, fund raising, party programs, and staff activities. Television, commercial or public, could allot time to the parties for this purpose. The national conventions should become ongoing bodies to be reconvened two years after the selection of the presidential nominee to consider the health of the party; delegates should be ex officio members of their states' central committees, with election as a delegate implying a four-year obligation to work on party affairs. Such a scheme would create out of the national conventions and national committees a sort of two-chamber structure for the legislating of party concerns. If Americans are willing to work to rebuild the political parties, there is no shortage of imaginative proposals on ways to accomplish this goal.[7] The wisdom of having political parties long ago ceased to be debatable; they are essential to the governance of free societies.

. . .

PLATFORMS

The party platform (as David Truman has written) is "generally regarded as a document that says little, binds no one, and is forgotten by politicians as quickly as possible."[8] Why then do delegates to presidential conventions, practical people all, engage in such bloody battles over them? One answer, amply documented by Gerald M. Pomper, is that the record is not nearly so dismal as has been commonly assumed. "Perhaps most comforting to those who believe in party integrity," Pomper concludes, "is that only a tenth of the promises are completely ignored."[9] Still another reason why the writing of platforms is not mere finger exercises is that, more than trying to tell the voters what the parties will do for them, the drafters are engaged in a collective bargaining process over the composition of the party. The resultant document allows each group to decide whether it can remain within the coalition.

[7] See John S. Saloma III and Frederick H. Sontag, *Parties* (Knopf, 1972).

[8] David B. Truman, *The Governmental Process* (Knopf, 1951), pp. 282–83.

[9] Gerald M. Pomper, *Elections in America* (Dodd, Mead, 1970), p. 159. (Pomper stresses the same point on pp. 186–87.) See also Judith H. Parris, *The Convention Problem* (Brookings Institution, 1972), pp. 109–14.

Defining the perimeters of the parties' composition in terms of issue positions could be more usefully performed at the mid-term party conferences, proposed earlier. If such documents were on hand when the presidential selection process began, the candidates would be expected to indicate areas of agreement and disagreement during their preconvention campaigns. In a sense, the parties, rather than the candidates, would set the agenda for debate. The burden of proof would be on those candidates who argued for different goals and programs. Their selection, of course, would be proof that they had "won" their arguments. The national conventions then would be freed to concentrate on choosing presidential standard-bearers, with perhaps the additional duty of approving short, revised statements of principles.

COMMUNICATIONS

A number of thoughtful suggestions have been put forth for improving media coverage of the campaigns:

• Minow, Martin, and Mitchell in *Presidential Television* propose, "The national committee of the opposition party should be given by law an automatic right of response to any presidential radio or television address made during the ten months preceding a presidential election."[10] The purpose served by this "response time" proposal would be to neutralize the incumbent's usual advantage.

[10] Newton N. Minow, John Bartlow Martin, and Lee M. Mitchell, *Presidential Television* (Basic Books, 1973), p. 161. The authors also propose giving free prime TV time to major presidential candidates during the month before the election.

• Section 315 of the Communications Act of 1934—the equal time provision —should be repeated so that radio and television stations will have one less reason for denying free time to major party candidates.

• Fred W. Friendly, the former president of CBS News, has proposed a weekly TV broadcast during campaigns and suggests the title "Whose Ox Is Gored?" He sees this as "a venting mechanism" to "supply a place where all the politicians who feel that their ox has been gored by newspapermen or television and radio men get to meet that person and *vice versa* . . . [where] pollsters come in and report how they did their work . . . where those thirty-second commercials . . . [are] played and somebody says, 'Now let's . . . examine what that says and doesn't say.'"[11] This suggestion recognizes that there are more players than the candidates in presidential selection politics and that the voters need some method of assessing the products of the others—journalists, pollsters, advertising specialists—who also contribute to the outcomes of elections.

Separate studies of television and newspaper coverage of the 1972 campaign independently conclude that there was a strong bias against dealing with the substance of issues and in favor of treating politics as a horserace. The reporter wants to know who is going to win. Handicappers concentrate on such factors as the state of the track, performance in earlier races, conditioning, and the weight of the jockey. All have parallels in political campaign reporting.

Issues primarily are considered as they relate to possible outcomes. James Perry, for example, finds that though McGovern announced his "tax reform and redistribution of income" proposal on January 13, 1972, it was not given serious press attention until April 27 (*Wall Street Journal*) and May 7 (*Washington Post*).[12]

The corrective for newspapers in handling campaign stories is to make greater use of reporters with specialized knowledge (economics, foreign policy, and so on), to rotate reporters more often, and to give more attention to cross-candidate coverage, which would focus on how particular issues are being dealt with by all candidates rather than treating the candidates as if each existed in his own space capsule. The problem for television is more systemic. A prime prerequisite for network news is that an event should contain visual conflict. But, to paraphrase a former Vice President, "When you've seen one crowd (or demonstration), you've seen 'em all." The style for visual presentation of campaigns instead of heightening public interest has become a cliché. The definition of conflict should include the conflict of ideas. The complexities of a presidential campaign require longer stories and reportage that relies less heavily on moving pictures. In short, the networks should accept a less patronizing posture toward their viewers: Some pictures are not the equivalent of a thousand words. It is hard to overstate the importance of the news media. They are out greatest leverage for forcing candidates to inject substance into politics.

---

[11] "Government Information: The Media and the Public," transcript of a symposium sponsored by the Woodrow Wilson International Center of Scholars, Washington, D.C., May 20, 1971, pp. 158–60.

[12] James M. Perry, *Us & Them: How the Press Covered the 1972 Election* (Clarkson N. Potter, 1973), pp. 144–45.

SEPARATE FEDERAL AND STATE/LOCAL ELECTIONS

The U.S. system of government is complicated enough without commingling federal, state, and local elections on one ballot.[13] A variety of campaign spending abuses creeps into the process because of a failure to separate the various levels of elections. Of greater importance, the lumping together makes it difficult for voters to deal with their concerns in an appropriate and systematic manner. A more constructive way of conducting elections would be to hold contests for federal offices in even-numbered years and for state/local offices in odd-numbered years. This division could lead to a simplified ballot for President, senator, and member of the House of Representatives. The end result might promote party discipline; it certainly would promote a more rational dialogue.

DIRECT POPULAR ELECTIONS

Whether or not to abolish the Electoral College has been the longest-standing debate in American political science. Excellent books have been written on both sides.[14] Many alternatives have been proposed. Without attempting to review all the arguments, it is only necessary to add in an essay on the presidential selection process that I find no convincing evidence that the direct popular election of President would have any significant impact on the way campaigns are waged. It would not materially change the allocation of a candidate's time, the nature of his appeals, or the type of two-party competition that presently exists.

The Electoral College system almost had a mischievous effect on two recent presidential elections. That it did not is hardly a compelling reason to retain it. Had George Wallace been a mite more popular in 1968 and thus been able to transfer the electoral decision to the House of Representatives, we would have had a President chosen in a highly inequitable manner. That people called Electors have been able to cast ballots for President in ways that have nullified the wishes of the voters cannot be defended on any grounds. That different groups gain an advantage through the existence of the Electoral College might be reason for the advantaged to fight to keep what they have, but their arguments must be based on other than equity. That minor parties have less influence under the Electoral College system than if the vote was direct should give reformers pause, if true—but at least one scholar of third-party movements in presidential politics contends that the reverse would be the case.[15]

What the direct election of Presidents would do is replace a complicated, difficult to understand, and potentially divisive system with one that is elegantly simple, provides for a basic equality among voters, and ensures that the winning candidate will be the one

[13] See Committee for Economic Development, *Modernizing State Government* (New York: CED, 1967), pp. 21–22; CED, *Financing a Better Election System* (1968), p. 30.

[14] For a defense of the Electoral College, see Wallace S. Sayre and Judith H. Parris, *Voting for President* (Brookings Institution, 1970). The case for direct elections is presented by Neal R. Peirce, *The People's President* (Simon and Schuster, 1968), and Lawrence D. Longley and Alan G. Braun, *The Politics of Electoral College Reform* (Yale University Press, 1972).

[15] Daniel A. Mazmanian, *Third Parties in Presidential Elections* (Brookings Institution, 1974), p. 114.

who receives the most votes. In a presidential selection process that must be widely believed fair in order to legitimate its outcomes, this would be no small achievement.

Some of these proposals are meant to correct flaws in the system. Others are intended primarily to simplify ways that we now operate. A few are framed in response to the abuses of Watergate, understanding, however, that to the degree Watergate was not caused by mechanistic defects, so too incidents like it cannot be prevented solely by mechanistic improvements, only made less likely.

One effect of Watergate, at least until we can view it with some detachment, is that it tends to overshadow all that came before it. Watergate is our most recent history, and Americans have been accused, quite rightly, of having a short historical memory.

But it is not enough to say that the system has worked because the country has been generally well served by Presidents in the past, at least in times of crisis. Perhaps we were lucky. Perhaps something has changed or will change. Perhaps there is something about the office that lifts men to greatness, in which case almost any system would produce great Presidents. Still, all our Presidents have not been great. Some of the information the electorate might wish to have to help predict presidential fitness can never be discovered beforehand. There are times when no outstanding candidates are available. No matter how much information is on hand, some Presidents will surprise us, favorably as well as unfavorably. There can be no guarantee that voters will always act wisely, even when the facts are known. Rather we should ask whether

the way we go about picking chief executives gives us the knowledge we need to make the best decisions possible.

For this purpose I have attempted here to state the essence of presidential qualities, independent of time and ideology; those qualities—personal, political, and executive—without which a President could not properly function. The executive qualities, the ability to organize and manage large enterprises, are not tested significantly by the system. The political qualities, primarily the ability to gauge public opinion and the skill to win approval for one's programs, are well tested, as we should expect in a system where electoral success depends on the welding of so many diverse groups and interests. It is hard to imagine a President getting elected without having mastered the intricacies of politics. (The problem is that, once elected, he may ignore them.) Observers will differ on whether the system does as well at testing personal qualities—the ability to perform as a public person, honesty and courage, physical stamina, a style that is acceptable to most Americans, the ability to inspire public trust, and a sense of history, meaning "personal loyalty to democratic values." My own view is that, though our method falls short of what we desire, alternative systems would be equally flawed.

Yet my contention is that the process is more than a testing ground. It is equally a training ground. It tells the electorate things they need to know about the candidates, and it teaches the candidates things that will be useful in the White House. In 1960, when campaigning for the Democratic nomination, Kennedy spent a month in West Virginia. This experience, wrote

Schlesinger at the time, "gave his social views a new concreteness. He had read a good deal about poverty, but . . . he had never seen fellow countrymen living the way unemployed miners and their families are living today in West Virginia; and the sight struck home with peculiar force." [16] The West Virginia presidential primary, directly and indirectly, produced the Area Redevelopment Act, the Appalachian Regional Commission, and a governmental response to strip mining.

Functioning as a system of personnel selection, the presidential campaign, a long and arduous method of exposing candidates to public scrutiny, has taken on certain aspects of a presidency simulation and—exactly because it is an ordeal—gives the people much necessary data with which to measure politicians, as well as the time to make an assessment.

The system limits our mistakes to four years, allowing us to judge chief executives retrospectively and take corrective action if needed. As a mechanism for policy formulation, the campaign is not creative, precise, or intellectually rigorous; but if it does not bring forth new initiatives, it often grinds fine those that are already in the public arena. The constant repetition of the candidates' basic themes provides information on what they consider important, and through the interaction between candidates and electorate, they get some information on what the voters think is important. The campaign no longer entertains us, as it once did, but it is questionable whether this is any longer a worthwhile function.

The nature of the campaign has

[16] Arthur M. Schlesinger, Jr., *Kennedy or Nixon: Does It Make Any Difference?* (Macmillan, 1960), p. 27.

changed remarkably little in the twentieth century. It still produces the same types of candidates; basically it is a screening process for professional politicians. Other professions may produce persons of greater intelligence, integrity, or executive ability, and they should be tested, too. But it is doubtful that they would as closely fit the unique—if unattractive—set of personal and political qualities that are the presidential "constants." Television—the most notable addition to the tools of communications—must have long-term consequences on the viewers' expectations, acceptance of public officials, and menu of issues, but it has had surprisingly little impact in the short run on who gets nominated or elected. After two decades of experience, we are no more "manipulated" than we were before TV campaigning. Television and other factors add to the cost of running for the presidency. This has not deterred any otherwise viable candidates from seeking the office; nor, on the other hand, has any candidate been able to "buy" a nomination or election. Campaign financing raises troubling and serious problems; fortunately, however, they are susceptible to corrective legislation.

Besides the need to create a rational system of campaign financing, the most pressing need at this time is for a more disciplined party structure to contain the selection process. This does not mean that many of the other persistent criticisms of the system are necessarily wrong so much as that they are often esthetic rather than political judgments. The remedy, as Justice Holmes said about evils in general, may be "to grow more civilized." Yet this is not a matter that can be imposed by statute. Moreover, some of the proposals for change might be good esthetics and bad democratic procedure. Efforts to shorten the campaign, for example, would reduce the boredom while further handicapping the underdog candidate (usually the challenger) and those voters who need the most time to reach a decision (usually the underclass). More serious is the concern over the platitudinous nature of political discourse. Herbert Stein, an adviser to President Nixon, once said that during election campaigns "there is a certain depreciation of the verbal currency which goes on, which everyone seems to understand and discount and which apparently does no harm." [17] He is mistaken in saying that it does no harm. Voting must depend on "the verbal currency," and candidates constantly must be reminded that we hold them accountable. Here, as I have indicated, the press deserves some of the blame: fascinated by the political maneuverings of the candidates, newspaper and television reports have been distracted from adequately analyzing the candidates' stands on issues.

It is therefore possible to agree with many of the criticisms of the way Presidents are chosen—it is vulgar, it does debase the language, it is costly and wasteful and chaotic, it is a bore—and still conclude that the system provides a remarkably thorough way to learn those things that are learnable about the people who seek the presidency. It may be that campaigns show candidates at their worst. We would also like to know their best. But if we cannot know both, it is more useful to know the worst. At a time when national disillusion is becoming a minor art form, it is instructive to remind ourselves that this is considerably more than cold comfort.

[17] James L. Rowe, Jr., "Stein Sees Need for Big Economic Planning Agency," *Washington Post*, Dec. 30, 1973.

The Reform Imperative

John Stewart

The years of disintegration of the Democratic Party's majority presidential coalition have coincided, in large measure, with the party's efforts to open doors to a constituency even broader than FDR's. The reform agenda that com-

From *One Last Chance: The Democratic Party 1974–76* by John Stewart, Copyright © 1974 by Praeger Publishers, Inc., New York. Excerpted and reprinted by permission.

manded priority attention within the party from 1969 to 1972 was justified, at least in part, as being the most reliable way to recruit a new generation of Democrats, thereby ensuring the party's majority status in the closing decades of the century.

But if one takes the presidential returns of 1972 at face value, it is not off the mark to conclude that years of dedicated effort to open the Democratic Party to a broader constituency ended with the largest exodus of Democrats in generations. One is even tempted to suggest that, if the party opens its doors any further, it might vanish completely.

It is, of course, neither that simple nor that obvious. The Democratic presidential coalition, for example, has been in trouble for many years. But it is equally necessary to recognize the coincidence between the achievement of significant internal reforms and the massive defections of traditional Democrats in the contest for the Presidency. If the party seriously intends to build a winning presidential coalition in 1976 and subsequent elections, it cannot avoid taking a hard look at the motivation, ideology, and consequences of party reform. This, in turn, means a hard look at the impact of the Vietnam War on the party's actions and decisions for the past decade. For the frustrated antiwar activism of the late 1960s was the seedbed of the "New Politics" that ultimately failed in the 1972 general election.

REALITY OF REFORM

Social critics who specialize in wringing their hands about the imperviousness to change of American institutions should be mightily puzzled by what has been taking place within the national Democratic Party for the past eight years. The cynical assumption that powerful political leaders would never permit any dilution of their authority and control is contradicted by the facts. Whether one looks at the written rules and procedures that governed the Democratic presidential nominating process in 1972 or at the delegates who were chosen by

the process, the evidence of decisive change is clear and unmistakable.

At the 1968 Democratic National Convention, for example, women comprised 13 percent of the delegates, blacks 5.5 percent and youth (under thirty-one) 3 percent; 67 percent of the 1968 delegates were attending their first convention. In 1972, following the promulgation and implementation of the delegate-selection reforms, the percentages of blacks and women attending the Democratic National Convention in Miami Beach nearly tripled and the percentage of young delegates increased more than five times. Women accounted for 40 percent of the delegates, blacks 15 percent, young people 24 percent, and 83 percent of the 1972 delegates were attending their first national convention.

The incidence of change can be illustrated in other ways: Lawyers provided 30 percent of the delegates in 1968 but only 12 percent in 1972. In fact, *housewives* were the largest occupational group at the 1972 Democratic National Convention (369 delegates), followed by lawyers (360), teachers (346), and government officials (288). Officeholders, however, were fewer in number: In 1968, twenty-three out of twenty-five Democratic governors were delegates at Chicago; in 1972, only nineteen out of thirty made it to Miami Beach. Two-thirds of the Democrats in the U.S. Senate were delegates in 1968, but this fell to less than one-third in 1972.

In 1968, nearly 13 percent of the delegates were selected by committees of party officials, the procedure most removed from the influence of rank-and-file Democrats. Even though the reformed rules permitted a maximum of 10 percent of a state delegation in 1972 to be selected by party committees, only 1.7 percent of the delegates were actually selected in this manner. To put it another way, 98.3 percent of the delegates to the 1972 convention were elected by primary or open caucus or convention procedures. Whether or not these changes were beneficial in every respect will be considered later, but there can be little argument that important changes did, in fact, occur.[1]

The most fundamental change of all took place on February 19, 1971, when the Democratic National Committee adopted the eighteen guidelines for delegate selection originally promulgated by the Commission on Party Structure and Delegate Selection (the McGovern-Fraser Commission) and included them as part of the Preliminary Call for the 1972 Democratic National Convention. By establishing specific procedural criteria that state Democratic parties would have to meet in choosing delegates for the national convention, the national party achieved an unprecedented degree of control over the actions of state parties. Although the guidelines acknowledged that delegate-selection procedures could vary from state to state, the imposition of minimum standards in the operation of these procedures forced every state party to make significant changes in rules, traditions, and, in some instances, state law.

The reforms were not limited to the procedures for selecting the delegates who would go to Miami Beach. A sec-

ond Democratic Party commission, the Commission on Rules, recommended an equally comprehensive set of changes in the organization and conduct of the national convention itself. The commission's chairman, Republican James O'Hara of Michigan, set the tone at the first meeting: "We have the right and duty to turn things upside down, around or sideways if by so doing we will ensure the kind of participation in party affairs toward which we are striving."[2]

Democratic National Chairman Lawrence F. O'Brien summed up the national party's commitment to its reform agenda at the conclusion of a Democratic National Committee meeting in October 1971: "We have steadfastly maintained the course charted by the 1968 National Convention in the area of party reform. We have taken the '68 mandate and implemented it. . . . Never has a political party so totally changed its way of doing business in such a short period of time. . . . And there will be no turning back."

The reality of reform in the delegate-selection process and in the operation of the national convention itself makes it more necessary to find specific answers to one critical question: How could the Democrats do so many of the "right" things—as defined by an impressive collection of political commentators and practitioners—and end up so poorly on Election Day? Perhaps no question is more central to the Democratic search for a presidential majority to match the party's continuing successes in Congress and in gubernatorial and state legislative contests.

---

[1] Statistics on the composition of the 1968 and 1972 Democratic National Conventions are drawn from *Mandate for Reform: A Report of the Commission on Party Structure and Delegate Selection* (Washington: Democratic National Committee, 1970), and from a report, "The Delegates of '72," prepared by Martin Plissner, political editor, CBS News.

[2] *Call to Order: A Narrative Report by the Commission on Rules of the Democratic National Committee* (Washington: Democratic National Committee, 1972), p. 11.

The great leap forward in Democratic Party reform took place between 1969 and the 1972 Democratic National Convention, a direct outgrowth of the bitter and divisive struggle for the party's presidential nomination in 1968 and the disunity that plagued Hubert Humphrey through the general election campaign. But these steps can be more clearly understood—and their strengths and shortcomings more accurately evaluated—if they are viewed as part of a reform process that has been gaining momentum with the Democratic Party throughout the entire post-Roosevelt era.

The issue that dominated the pre-1968 Democratic conventions, apart from the quadrennial battle for the presidential nomination, was, of course, civil rights. At times the issue arose in the context of the platform, as in 1948, when adoption of the minority civil rights plank resulted in a mass exodus of Southern delegations and the creation of the Dixiecrat ticket in the general election. At other times, such as the 1952 convention, the issue remained in the background but was nonetheless at the root of the "loyalty oath" controversies in which the Northern and Western wings of the party attempted to compel Southern delegates to pledge their support of the Democratic ticket in the presidential campaign.

In those earlier conventions, however, the split over civil rights never led the national party to question the procedures followed by the state parties in selecting their national convention delegates. It was simply a matter of securing the loyalty to the national ticket of those Southern delegates who were chosen.

This pattern changed abruptly in 1964. At Atlantic City a group of Mississippi Democrats, predominantly black and loyal to the national party, challenged the credentials of the regular Mississippi delegation on the basis of alleged discrimination and exclusion in the delegate-selection process. At a convention where the only other item of undecided business was President Lyndon Johnson's selection of his running mate, the Mississippi Freedom Democratic Party's challenge dominated the nation's television screens and raised the possibility of a Southern walkout if credentials were denied to the regular Mississippi delegation. Needless to say, the prospect of a split convention did not exactly match President Johnson's expectations of what the delegates in Atlantic City were supposed to be doing.

The moving testimony of Fanny Lou Hamer and other Mississippi Democrats before the Credentials Committee left little doubt of the intimidation, violence, and outrageous procedures that had been used systematically to deny their participation in the delegate-selection process. At the same time, however, the regular Mississippi delegates and their Southern supporters pointed to the lack of any national standards by which the delegate-selection process could be judged—in Mississippi or anywhere else. They argued that to seat the challengers solely on the basis of discrimination they allegedly had suffered in the past would be arbitrary, unfair, and without precedent in Democratic Party history.

On direct orders from President Johnson, a negotiating team led by Senator Hubert Humphrey and UAW President Walter Reuther began seeking some form of compromise that, above

all else, would hold the convention together. Under the compromise they
finally drafted, the Mississippi regulars
were required to sign a stringent loyalty
oath; the Mississippi Freedom Democratic Party challengers were awarded
two at-large delegate seats; language
was adopted for inclusion in the Call to
the 1968 Democratic National Convention guaranteeing "that voters in the
States(s), regardless of race, color, creed
or national origin, will have the opportunity to participate fully in Party
affairs"; and a Special Equal Rights
Committee of the Democratic National
Committee was created to assist the
states in meeting these new requirements.

Both contending parties—the regulars
and the loyalists from Mississippi—
rejected the compromise. But the convention adopted it enthusiastically
and the feared Southern exodus was
averted. Of longer-term significance, the
basis now existed for the national party
at future conventions to reject any delegation selected by discriminatory or
exclusionary procedures.

Two points should be underscored.
First, the focus in 1964 was to remedy
racial discrimination in the delegate-
selection process, not the exclusion of
rank-and-file Democrats generally.
Second, the Atlantic City compromise,
although it brought the national party
directly into the delegate-selection process for the first time, was fundamentally
an extension of the process of gradual
adjustment and accommodation at earlier conventions in dealing with the civil
rights issue. The preservation of a
united party that could go into the general election at maximum strength
remained the principal motivation in
reaching the compromise. The goal of
opening the party nominating processes

to broad-scale grassroots participation
was to await the arrival of the Vietnam
War as the Democrats' most divisive
issue.

. . .

POLITICS OF REFORM

The struggle within the Democratic
Party over the Vietnam War lifted the
issue of party reform to a new plateau of
activity and commitment. Unlike 1964,
when the scope of the proposed reforms
was restricted to what was needed to
preserve a fragile unity within the party,
the post-1968 objective of democratizing
internal party procedures became, for
many persons, an all-consuming end in
itself. Such an environment was not
conducive, to say the least, to the kind
of pragmatic compromises and more
gradual accommodations that had
worked in the past.

There did emerge, however, a
rationale for the reform effort that
stressed the long-term political benefits
that supposedly would accrue to the
country and the Democratic Party if it
remained faithful to the reform mandate. This theme runs through all the
basic speeches of the reform advocates
and the principal reform documents.
Mandate for Reform, the report of the
Commission on Party Structure and
Delegate Selection, closed with these
words:

We believe that popular participation is
more than a proud heritage of our party,
more than a first principle. We believe that
popular control of the Democratic Party is
necessary for its survival. . . . If we are not
an open party; if we do not represent the
demands of change, then the danger is not

that people will go to the Republican Party; it is that there will no longer be a way for people committed to orderly change to fulfill their needs and desires within our traditional political system. It is that they will turn to third and fourth party politics or the anti-politics of the street.[3]

Fred Dutton, an ideologist of the New Politics and a member of the McGovern-Fraser Commission, emphasized the new sources of political power that were available to a political party with the imagination to attract them. In his *Changing Sources of Power*, Dutton said:

The large number of new voters and the high level of independence among them reinforce the probability that a critical passage in the politics of this country is at hand. . . . A clear-cut coalescing within this large sector even close to that of the New Deal generation could give it a significant measure of political power not only for the 1970s but well beyond. It is only a coincidence that this group will be moving into the electorate just as the New Deal generation's ranks are thinning and its public influence is slackening . . . there could be a quite literal passing of the political torch from one cornerstone generation to another.[4]

Democratic National Chairman O'Brien expressed this view in his year-end report for 1971. He said:

If significant numbers of young people, women, minorities, and others alienated by traditional political institutions are actively involved in the nominating process, a re-

vitalized and recharged Democratic Party almost surely will emerge in the general election campaign. I have no doubt that these votes—when combined with more traditional sources of Democratic strength—could spell the difference between victory and defeat in November 1972.

A number of assumptions—largely unstated and unquestioned—were buried beneath these assertions. It was assumed, for example, that millions of Americans, dissatisfied and unhappy in their daily lives, distrustful of their political leaders, were eagerly awaiting only the chance to recapture, as it was usually said, "control over their own destinies" through direct political action. More specifically, it was assumed that the 25 million first-time voters in 1972 would jump at the opportunity to begin remaking the society and the political system that repelled so many of them. Finally, it was assumed that the new grassroots Democrats attracted by the reality of an open party could simply be grafted to the established Democratic coalition, thereby assuring the party's majority position for the foreseeable future.

These assumptions were open to question. As was noted in the last chapter, the political chemistry of alienation, for many persons, did not always respond to McGovern's advocacy of reform. Not only did a majority of those who believed the system was rigged in favor of the special interests prefer Nixon over McGovern, but they also held relatively hard-line views on issues such as race and permissiveness that were offended by McGovern's brand of populism.

These assumptions were fed, no doubt, by many poll findings. In May 1968, for example, the Gallup Poll found

[3] *Mandate for Reform,* p. 49.

[4] Frederick G. Dutton, *Changing Sources of Power: American Politics in the 1970s* (New York: McGraw-Hill, 1971), p. 26.

that 33 percent of the public (and 41 percent of those under thirty years of age) said they would be "willing to work as a volunteer" for their political party in the coming campaign. Gallup later reported that 14 percent of college students surveyed said they had worked for a political organization in the 1970 congressional elections: 8 percent for the Democratic Party, 4 percent for the Republicans, and 2 percent for other parties. As the 1972 elections approached, it appeared that a vast army of volunteers could be mobilized if even a tiny fraction of the 15 percent of McGovern's backers nationwide who said they planned to "work for a party or a candidate in this election" actually followed through.

In the primaries, McGovern recruited an impressive force of volunteers, particularly in California. After Miami Beach, however, antagonisms between McGovern's lieutenants (both in Washington and in the states) and local political leaders frequently reduced the impact of the volunteer army that re-enlisted for the general election. Of most importance, McGovern's lack of credibility as a President created a barrier that no amount of organizational expertise could surmount.

Beyond McGovern's organizational problems was the mistaken assumption that an overwhelming majority of the new voters in 1972 would automatically respond to McGovern's brand of the New Politics. A special analysis by the Gallup Poll in July 1972 (see Table I) revealed that Nixon, not McGovern, held the advantage with unregistered persons between eighteen and twenty-four years of age. Although McGovern was favored among registered voters under twenty-four years, Nixon was

preferred by those who had not yet registered.[5]

Table I

	Percentage Favoring:		
	Nixon	McGovern	Undecided
Registered	41	57	2
Unregistered	46	43	11

And even among the college students, presumed to be the vanguard of the New Politics, the trend was *against* McGovern as the campaign wore on. In the spring of 1972, the Gallup Poll found college students dividing 61-35 percent in favor of McGovern, with 4 percent undecided. By early October, however, the split had narrowed to 49-47 percent in favor of the senator, with 4 percent undecided.

It is revealing that the only persons to question any of these assumptions during the McGovern-Fraser Commission's debate over the new delegate-selection guidelines were state Democratic chairmen, such as Will Davis of Texas and George Mitchell of Maine, men who had personally experienced the difficult problems of organizing and maintaining an effective party on the state level.

If the rationale supporting reform had not prevailed so totally in the post-1968 period, at least among those Democrats with the responsibility for carrying out

[5] The high showing of McGovern among registered 18-to-24-year-olds is explained by the strong preference in the spring of college students for McGovern and the fact that there are twice as many college students who are registered as unregistered:

	Nixon	McGovern	Undecided
College	35%	61%	4%
Noncollege	48	44	8

the convention's mandates, it might have been possible to approach the assignment with a more discerning eye to the critical organizational problems that inevitably were part of the reform equation. And this kind of hard questioning and probing, in turn, might have produced a more balanced effort that sought, on the one hand, to remedy the admitted inequities in the process without, on the other hand, sacrificing the valuable perspective and experience of established Democratic leaders, particularly on the state level. As it turned out, however, it took a brave and resilient Democrat to suggest that the party's reform effort did not represent the most propitious combination of Jacksonian democracy and political opportunity to come along since the early days of the New Deal.

. . .

CREDENTIALS CONTESTS

Despite widespread implementation of the reforms, the 1972 Credentials Committee still had to resolve eighty-two challenges in thirty-one state delegations. Twenty-one of the states faced challenges that related to the composition of delegations under A-1 and A-2. Many of those challenges were initiated by the Women's Political Caucus or the National Youth Caucus in the interests of women and young people. But in a large number of cases this had the operational effect of challenging non-McGovern delegates with persons who—if seated—intended to vote for McGovern. It soon became clear that most of the challenges, in result if not in initial motivation, were distinctly candidate-oriented—an effort by one

presidential contender to win additional delegates on the basis of alleged violations in the selection of his opponents' delegates. The reforms, in other words, became an offensive weapon in the battle for the nomination, as distinguished from an effort simply to democratize and open the Democratic Party to grassroots sentiment. That this development was fully predictable made it no less a departure from the wording and spirit of the recommendations of the McGovern-Fraser Commission.[6]

This intense *candidate*, as opposed to *party*, orientation carried over into the deliberations and decisions of the Credentials Committee and, subsequently, to the floor of the national convention. The Commission on Rules had designed what essentially was a judicial model for the settlement of credentials disputes, stressing the building of a factual record and the guarantees of procedural due process for the contending parties. This model was uniquely ill suited to a situation where decisions would be made, in large part, on whether they enhanced or reduced a candidate's delegate count.

As a consequence, the Credentials Committee evolved a procedure that looked to informal negotiations among the contending parties as the most realistic way of settling most of the disputes. Challenged delegates were certified, replaced, or, in many cases, reduced to half-vote status in conjunction with the addition of half-vote delegates

[6] It was also a departure from the agreement reached between the major Democratic contenders and Democratic National Chairman Lawrence F. O'Brien to "eschew frivolous challenges" and to refrain from using "credentials challenges as a tactic in pursuit of delegate support." The agreement was signed on July 14, 1971, in Washington, D.C.

from among the challengers on the basis of voting strength that the contending parties could muster among the Credentials Committee members. Deals were cut, compromises designed, and alliances established in very much the traditional manner. The ABM (Anybody But McGovern) alliance that initially defeated the McGovern forces on the California challenge, for example, arose out of a common desire among the other contenders to block his nomination and out of a shared sense of frustration and outrage over the seemingly endless challenges over the numbers of women and young people on their delegations.

It is beyond the scope of this book to recount the details of the credentials battles that unfolded before network television cameras at the Credentials Committee meetings in mid-June and subsequently on the floor of the national convention. But it is clearly our responsibility to ask this question: How did this final step in the reform process look to the nation at large and, especially, to the millions of viewers who considered themselves Democrats?

The evidence is conflicting and seemingly contradictory. On the one hand, the Harris Survey reported surprising levels of public support for the Democratic Party's efforts to open its doors and to bring new groups into the nominating process. Harris told the National Press Club three days after the presidential election that

. . . majorities of 70–19 percent liked seeing greater representation for young people, by 81–13 percent liked giving women more delegate seats, by 76–17 percent liked giving blacks and the Spanish-speaking a greater role, and agreed, 73–19 percent, that the Democratic Convention was more "open than any before."[7]

These data would appear to illustrate the positive side of a growing public unhappiness with institutions that appear unwilling or unable to respond affirmatively to popular pressures for greater access and influence at the individual level. No one who witnessed the Democratic Party's credentials disputes could doubt the reality of change in the composition of delegations that collectively represented the national Democratic Party. Its capacity to change old traditions and procedures in order to achieve greater responsiveness to a segment of the Democratic rank-and-file should be counted as a solid achievement, and according to Harris it was so recognized by the public.

On the other hand, it is impossible to dismiss reports from Democratic leaders in all sections of the country of a strong negative reaction to the apparent imposition of quotas in determining the composition of some delegations. The notion of a person's sex, age, or race as the determining factor in winning delegate status collided with the deep-seated, conventional belief that a person should make it on his or her own in free and open competition. The Illinois challenge—in which popularly elected delegates were unseated in favor of a carefully balanced slate of challengers—was the most dramatic example of what appeared to be the outright perversion of the democratic process in the name of party reform.

Without question, the goal of opening the nominating process to new groups and new faces stimulated a generally

[7] Speech by Louis Harris, National Press Club, Washington D.C., November 10, 1972, p. 17.

favorable public reaction. But the achievement of this goal produced considerable disaffection among party leaders and allied interest groups, especially segments of organized labor, on whom the Democrats traditionally relied in the general election campaign. And, to the extent that some of these new faces appeared through the operations of a *de facto* quota system instead of through the open competition that the reforms were instituted to achieve, this positive public reaction was diluted. This was especially true among the more traditional "casual Democrats,"[8] who encountered on television a greatly changed, if not unattractive, Democratic Party gathered in Convention Hall at Miami Beach.

CONVENTION REFORM

The work of the Commission on Rules was carried off with less controversy and less impact on the party itself, except as the party exists in the period of the national convention. But this fact does not blunt the basic conclusion about the commission's work: The largest national nominating convention in American history, with a daily agenda filled to overflowing with controversial items, functioned in an orderly and sensible, if lengthy, manner—in stark contrast to the chaos and disorder that had prevailed in Chicago four years earlier.

The commission's most controversial duty concerned the apportionment among the states of the 3,000 delegates to the national convention. From the outset, it was obvious that the populous

industrial states—the base of Democratic strength in the general election—were grievously underrepresented on the basis of past apportionment formulae. To remedy these inequities, the Commission on Rules recommended to the Democratic National Committee a formula that allocated half of the delegates among the states in accordance with each state's population in the 1970 census, the other half to be allocated among the states in direct ratio to each state's Democratic presidential vote in the last three elections—1960, 1964, and 1968. States such as New York, Pennsylvania, California, Michigan, New Jersey, and Illinois stood to gain a significant number of delegates at the expense of smaller and Southern states. (For example, New York's delegation would increase from 190 out of 2,622 in 1968 to 301 out of 3,000; Tennessee's would drop from 51 out of 2,622 to 49 out of 3,000.)[9]

After hours of heated debate, the Democratic National Committee on February 19, 1971—the same meeting that unanimously adopted the delegate-selection guidelines as part of the 1972 Call—modified the Commission on Rules' recommended formula. Electoral College strength was substituted for raw population in the allocation of 53 percent of the delegates, and the commission's proposal for using the presidential vote of the past three elections was retained as the basis for distributing the remaining 47 percent of the delegates. The change caused a small increase in the number of delegates for the less populous states and was not quite as harsh on Southern states that had voted Republican or American Inde-

[8] Representative James G. O'Hara suggested the term "casual Democrats."

[9] *Call to Order,* pp. 49–51.

pendent in the last three presidential elections. A group of reform Democrats filed suit in the federal courts challenging the constitutionality of the amended formula, but the courts eventually upheld the National Committee's decision.

Apart from the apportionment formula, the burden of the Rules Commission's work dealt with designing fair and sensible procedures for all aspects of the convention's work toward the goal of making the convention "representative, open, deliberative, and fair." [10] Some of the proposals reformed the planning and management of the convention: an elected, instead of an appointed, convention manager; an elected arrangements committee that included nonvoting representatives of all presidential candidates; the designation of hotel accommodations by lot; and the installation of extensive communications equipment available to all convention participants.

Other recommendations dealt with the operations of the convention's committees: specific administrative procedures for filing and deciding credentials challenges; regional public hearings by the platform committee; proportional voting strength among the states on the major convention committees; and the printing of the major committee reports ten days in advance of the convention to facilitate greater understanding of the proposals among the delegates and the general public.

Finally, the commission made a number of recommendations dealing with the conduct of the convention itself: a set of written convention rules (for the first time in Democratic Party history); abolition of the motion to table, so that delegates would have to vote on

[10] James G. O'Hara, "The New Convention," *FACT*, October 29, 1971, p. 2.

the substance of issues; a ban on motions offered from the floor (except under suspension of the rules that required a two-thirds vote), so that the delegates would not be forced to vote on unexpected and often poorly understood motions; floor seating of delegations and the roll of the states determined by lot; the elimination of favorite-son nominations; a strict time limit on nominating and seconding speeches; and the elimination of staged floor demonstrations.

Despite the length of the convention sessions and the controversial nature of many issues that came to the floor for final disposition, the delegates generally knew what was going on and why. They stayed in their seats—right through the night on two occasions—and maintained the deliberative character of this 3,000-plus delegate assembly. To be sure, the delegates didn't always agree with everything that happened, but the charges of unfairness and arbitrary action were at a minimum. [11]

WHAT WENT WRONG?

What, then, is one to make of this unique effort to change the rules, procedures, and behavioral patterns of the oldest political party among Western democracies? How, indeed, could the Democrats do so many of the "right" things and end up so poorly on Election Day?

[11] The only major exception to this conclusion arose out of the dispute over the number of delegate votes that would constitute a majority in settling the South Carolina and California credentials challenges on the convention floor. Temporary Convention Chairman Lawrence F. O'Brien ruled that the 151 challenged California delegates could not vote on any roll call involving that challenge

Part of the answer, of course—one that we have already explored in the previous chapter—is that the Nixon landslide was partially a creation of George McGovern, and it would be unfair, not to mention wrong, to blame delegate-selection and convention reforms for his disastrous presidential campaign. But, for several reasons, this cannot be the whole answer.

The ideology and rhetoric of party reform—the stirring declarations about participatory democracy and giving the people a greater voice in their own destiny—masked a much more traditional and basic struggle: Who runs the Democratic Party? One need not belittle George McGovern's commitment to opening the Democratic Party to greater rank-and-file involvement by pointing out that a large number of the new Democrats who took advantage of the reforms were enthusiastic McGovern supporters. McGovern's success in helping establish delegate-selection reform as the priority concern

of the national party—apart from his considerable skill in using the reformed rules and procedures to advantage in the actual competition for delegates—stands as a political achievement of considerable dimension. George McGovern was not handed the Democratic Party's presidential nomination on a silver platter; he won it in the primaries and state conventions by amassing more votes than his competitors. Although it has been learned subsequently that the Nixon forces did their best to disrupt the primary campaigns of McGovern's principal rivals—Muskie, Humphrey, and Jackson—there is no evidence that these activities, however outrageous, had a decisive effect on the eventual outcome of the nominating process.

But McGovern's considerable achievement could not negate the reality that the Democratic Party, in 1972, found itself in a frustrating dilemma of legitimacy, one that must be resolved before 1976 if winning the Presidency is to be a realistic goal. Those Democrats who had felt themselves most abused by the nominating process in 1968 looked to the success of the delegate-selection reforms as the only way the party could earn their loyalty in 1972. In this sense, the full implementation of the reforms, including criteria of the A-1 and A-2 guidelines, became the party's principal weapon in forestalling the mass defection of antiwar activists, New Politicians, and others generally dismayed by the traditional nominating procedures.

But a price was paid for that success. The gradual evolution of a strong desire to open the party to women, minorities, and young people via a *de facto* quota system that guaranteed their presence, in combination with the elimination of the traditional procedures by which

and that not 1,509 (an absolute majority of the 3,016 delegate votes) but a simple majority of those *eligible* to vote would be sufficient to decide the challenges. This ruling was bitterly opposed by the Humphrey, Muskie, Jackson, Mills, and Wallace forces, who argued that an absolute majority was required and charged that O'Brien had capitulated to the McGovern forces. O'Brien took the position that the rules clearly stated that a delegate could not vote on his or her challenge and that permitting the 151 challenged California delegates to vote would be tantamount to giving them an automatic "no" vote at the outset. In the end, both the South Carolina and California challenges were decided by more than the absolute majority of 1,509 (the McGovern forces lost South Carolina and won California), so the impact of O'Brien's ruling remains speculative. Some persons contend it effectively gave the nomination to McGovern; others argue that McGovern had already secured sufficient votes to win the nomination regardless of the ruling.

most elected Democratic leaders became delegates, resulted in the serious under-representation of another important constituency, the "casual Democrats"—the nonactivists who rarely attend precinct caucuses or state conventions and often don't even vote in primaries. But these are also the people who, on Election Day, usually can be counted on to vote Democratic, and these are the Democrats George McGovern lost by the millions—because they either voted for Richard Nixon or just stayed home.

Democrats who hold elective office—public or party—traditionally speak for these casual Democrats. They are best equipped to sense their moods and attitudes since they comprise a significant portion of most Democratic constituencies. The early and unexpected collapse of the Muskie candidacy left a number of prominent governors, senators, House members, and party leaders embarrassed, politically exposed, and gun-shy. But the restrictions on the *ex officio* designation of delegates meant that these Democratic leaders had to compete actively for a delegate's seat at Miami Beach. In these circumstances, a large number of Democratic leaders who otherwise might have exerted considerable influence on the contest for the nomination and in writing the platform simply stepped to the sidelines rather than compete for delegate status with a new and unpredictable collection of political activists, many of whom possessed the seeming advantage of being female or black or under thirty-one years of age.

This withdrawal of elected Democratic leadership from the nominating process left a void that was never filled at the national convention and contributed to a void that persisted throughout the presidential campaign itself. It is not just coincidence that the flight of Democratic politicians from Miami Beach and the presidential campaign occurred in a year when certain of the delegate-selection reforms made their involvement less than easy and, in some cases, nearly impossible.

The Democratic Party, in other words, fought the battle of legitimacy in its reform effort and achieved a legitimate result in terms of the rules laid down by the two reform commissions. But this same effort acquired a distinctly illegitimate flavor for many casual Democrats—an essential element of a winning presidential coalition—through the operation of what they perceived as *de facto* quotas and the peculiar absence of Democratic leaders who traditionally have been their spokesmen and advocates.

The diminished role of elected Democrats in the 1972 nominating process had one additional grave consequence: It reinforced the intense candidate orientation of the participants and lessened the concern that was exhibited for the party itself. To put it bluntly, a proportion of George McGovern's most enthusiastic supporters would have severed all Democratic ties if their man had failed to win. The candidate, in the final preconvention weeks, did little to discourage this attitude. He said in a *Life* magazine interview:

. . . if a bunch of old established politicians gang up to prevent me from getting the nomination, because I didn't come to them for help . . . then I will not let them get away with it. There's been so much hard work and emotion poured into this campaign by so many thousands of people—it would be such as infuriating, disillusioning experience for them all—that I would repudiate the whole process. I would run as an independent or support somebody else on an independent ticket.[12]

As we have seen, the reforms from the outset were justified primarily as a way to preserve not only the Democratic Party but the two-party system. And yet, in the closing week before Miami Beach, the party was almost forgotten in the bitter struggle between the McGovern and Humphrey forces. It even appeared at times that many of McGovern's most ardent supporters—if not McGovern himself—saw winning the nomination, and not the subsequent run for the Presidency, as their principal objective. Having been turned away and defeated at Chicago, the new generation of Democrats who came to Miami Beach wanted to win, to nominate their man and write their platform, largely as vindication of their earlier, unsuccessful effort. Where the Democratic Party fitted into these designs was never totally clear.

Because important elements of the year-round Democratic Party were nonparticipants in the nominating process, it is not surprising that these same elements exhibited a minimum interest in the presidential campaign during the postconvention period. The same cry could be heard in all sections of the country: "The McGovern people were good enough to win the nomination, they ought to be good enough to run the campaign without my help." As a result, George McGovern waged one of the most lonely—and most courageous—campaigns in memory.

This chapter is not intended to argue, in any sense, for a return to the nominating system that existed prior to 1972. The positive image of the Democratic Party as open and responsive to popular involvement, clearly detected by pollster Louis Harris, should be seen as an extremely valuable asset to be used in 1976 and subsequent presidential years. But it does suggest that wisdom lies in recapturing some of the pragmatic common sense that characterized the earlier reforms adopted at Atlantic City in 1964, which frankly recognized unacceptable practices and proposed a remedy that (a) laid the foundation for future progress and (b) stopped short of sacrificing the broad support of party leaders and workers needed in the general election. It does suggest that reforms, to be workable, cannot become an end in themselves but must remain one element in the much broader effort to win the Presidency. This means developing procedures more likely to produce an outcome that is viewed as legitimate not only by highly motivated activists—the people ready to take full advantage of an open nominating process—but also by the segment of the party that comprehends, and communicates with, the millions of casual Democrats without whose support victory in the general election is impossible.

[12] *Life,* July 7, 1972, p. 31.

Campaign Dollars and Sense

Eugene J. McCarthy

Does the campaign finance reform act go far enough? The question is not whether it goes far enough, but whether it goes in the right direction.

Advocates of the measure generally hold that money is the root of all political evil—money rather than stupidity, inordinate desire for power, or concern about one's place in history (formerly called pride).

Had the campaign finance act been in force in 1972, one defender of the law has said, Watergate would not have happened. Why not? Would Richard Nixon have been defeated in 1968 if the campaign finance law had been in effect? Would the Nixon campaign committee of 1972 have hesitated to spend money derived from the tax check-off to finance the Watergate activity, any more than they hesitated to use money collected either legally or illegally in 1972?

The passage of the campaign finance bill is one more indication of the thoughtlessness of the Congress, of its lack of sensitivity to the function of ideas and of institutions in American democracy. It may be the most serious, following after (1) its approval of the Twenty-Fifth Amendment, an ill-conceived and badly-written amendment; (2) the approval of the so-called volunteer army, which act insures an unrepresentative and undemocratic, mercenary army; and (3) the passage of

From *Commonweal*, January 17, 1975, pp. 322-325. Reprinted by permission of Commonweal Publishing Co., Inc. and of the author.

the revenue-sharing act, under conditions of panic and pressure from state governments and under the conditioning force of the economists who predicted unlimited economic growth and, consequently, a miraculous increase in federal revenues which could best be distributed to the states for their disposal.

The passage of the campaign finance act and its approval and support by the Democratic and Republican parties raises further questions as to the reliability of those parties and of their leaders as defenders of the Constitution and of democratic ideas.

A Republican supporter of the law commented on the floor of the House just before its passage: "I believe within this conference report there are at least 100 items questionable from a constitutional standpoint. Any time we pass legislation in this field we are causing constitutional doubts to be raised. I have many myself. . . ." The Democrat who managed the bill in the House said: "I do not know whether it is constitutional or not." And President Gerald Ford, upon signing the bill into law, released a statement in which he said: "And although I do have reservations about the First Amendment implications inherent in the limits on individual contributions and candidate expenditures, I am sure that such issues can be resolved in the courts."

Leaders of both parties were thus willing to evade the serious constitutional problems involved in the bill and to pass those problems on to the courts, which are already overburdened with challenges to other bad laws.

The founding fathers did not want the Congress or the President to evade responsibility in this fashion. In fact, the Presidential oath of office—including the pledge to "preserve, protect and defend the Constitution of the United States"—was written into the Constitution itself. The early Presidents took most seriously their role as guardian of the Constitution; they exercised the veto power more often because of constitutional doubts than for any other reason. The Constitution also provides that members of the Congress "shall be bound by Oath or Affirmation, to support this Constitution"; and the wording of their oath of office is prescribed by statute. The traditional reluctance of the courts to strike down Congressional legislation—even when the justices have grave doubts as to the constitutionality of a law—should make members of the Congress more keenly aware of their own responsibility to the Constitution.

Why, then, did the legislative and executive branches of the government evade their responsibilities in the case of the campaign finance law? One reason was that various reform groups exerted great pressure for passage of the law. Abuses revealed in the Watergate hearings moved many citizens and organizations to support reform of any kind. While their concern was justified, some of them supported cures that are worse than the sickness.

A second reason for passage of the bill was suggested by President Ford in the formal statement released at the time he signed the bill: "I am pleased with the bipartisan spirit that has led to this legislation. Both the Republican National Committee and the Democratic National Committee have expressed their pleasure with this bill, noting that it allows them to compete fairly."

It is assumed that if a proposal has bipartisan support, it is good. Why?

In any case, the two party committees were right in expressing pleasure. The new law may not provide fair competition between the two of them, but it effectively limits competition from any new group.

Anyone who has watched the two parties operate on a state level should not be surprised when they act as a trade association on the national level. The two have long cooperated in passing state laws which discourage Independent candidates and new parties from presenting effective challenges. The new campaign finance law is a logical extension, at a higher level, of the trade association's prior activities.

The new law's discrimination against Independent candidates and other outside challengers is most clearly apparent in the provisions for Presidential elections. The law provides public funding, through the tax check-off system, of $2 million for the next Democratic national convention and $2 million for the next Republican national convention. The rationale for this is that it will prevent the temptations presented by the old system of financing conventions by selling to large corporations advertising space in convention program books. The major parties, having committed some rather major sins, are to be protected from temptations rather than tested and held responsible.

What the law defines as a "minor party" would be entitled to a smaller convention subsidy; but no existing party meets the law's definition of a "minor party." That definition includes only a party which won at least 5 percent of the votes in the last Presidential election. None of the smaller parties which competed in the 1972 Presidential election won that high a percentage of the vote.

The Presidential nominee of each major party will receive $20 million in public funding for the general election campaign in 1976. Minor parties could receive a smaller subsidy—if there were any minor parties. The law's careful provision for non-existent minor parties may have been patterned on a scene from *Alice's Adventures in Wonderland:*

"Have some wine," the March Hare said in an encouraging tone.

Alice looked all round the table, but there was nothing on it but tea. "I don't see any wine," she remarked.

"There isn't any," said the March Hare.

Theoretically, an Independent Presidential candidate or the candidate of a "new party" (one that has just formed or one that received less than 5 percent of the vote in the last Presidential election) might be eligible for some public funding—but not until after the general election, and even then would be eligible only if he or she had obtained at least 5 percent of the vote, and even in that case would not be eligible for the same amount received by major-party candidates unless winning the average of their vote. An Independent or third-party candidate could in fact run second in a three-way race and receive a smaller share of federal funds than the privileged party candidate who had run third.

Quite apart from the deeper issue of discrimination is the question of whether public financing of campaigns is a good thing. There is a basic conflict and danger in having the government itself strongly influence the political process by which it is chosen.

A proposal to have the federal government finance political activities—especially party activities—would have lasted about five minutes at the Constitutional Convention. It would have been rejected as a repudiation of the basic theory of democracy. One-hundred and eighty-seven years later, the proposal is still contrary to the theory of democracy—and also, I believe, unconstitutional. As noted previously, even Democrats and Republicans in the Congress—and President Ford—seemed to be worried about its constitutionality.

The new law also discriminates against those citizens who wish to challenge incumbent members of the Congress. (There is no public funding for Congressional candidates, but there are severe limits—beginning in 1975—on campaign spending by such candidates.) This is a special problem in the case of House incumbents. The law initially limits House candidates to spending $84,000 in a primary election and $84,000 in a general election. An inflation escalator clause raises the initial limit; and a provision allowing political party contributions in general elections raises the limit even higher. Yet the final limit is low enough to prevent effective challenges in some districts. Consider a liberal candidate who is running in Manchester, New Hampshire—the city of the *Manchester Union Leader,* which day after day supports conservative officeholders and candidates.

Representatives who are running for re-election are given no handicap—despite their built-in advantages of Congressional staff, district offices, Library of Congress research service,

Editorial cartoon by Pat Oliphant; © Washington Star. Reprinted with permission Los Angeles Times Syndicate.

"More?? You want more?!"

government-supported newsletters, and so forth. Incumbents can spend as much for direct campaign costs as can their challengers; the plain effect of this is discrimination against challengers.

Even some members of the Congress who supported the bill as a whole expressed serious reservations about its favoritism toward incumbents. Senator James Buckley of New York, who opposed the bill, called it the "Incumbent Protection Act of 1974" and said, "To offer this bill in the name of reform is an act of unprecedent cynicism." The conservative Buckley added, "It is particularly disturbing that Senators who had heretofore been considered civil libertarians have rushed to support this measure without considering alternative means, less drastic in their scope, of accomplishing their purposes." Alluding

to the Constitution's guarantee of free speech, Buckley said that:

The fear of overly persuasive campaigns, particularly when expressed by incumbent members of Congress, strikes dangerously close to prohibited suppression of speech because of its content. It must certainly give the Supreme Court pause when they see officeholders with vested interests in remaining officeholders passing legislation that restricts the ability of potential opponents and average citizens alike to alter the political makeup of the Congress.

Although the discrimination against challengers is most evident in the case of House campaigns, it also appears in Senate campaigns and even in Presidential campaigns. The publicly-subsidized advantages of an incumbent President are rather obvious. Less obvious, but still significant, are the advantages of an incumbent Senator who runs for the Presidency. A recent *Atlantic* article on Senator Henry Jackson, a frontrunner for the Democratic nomination in 1976, said that Jackson's regular Senate staff, Interior Committee staff, and sub-committee staff amounted to 85 persons. The background research and the publicity that such staff people provide—at taxpayers' expense—is very great. And it is quite legal and proper for Senator Jackson to use them directly for his Senate duties and thus indirectly for his Presidential campaign. But a Presidential candidate who is not in public office must try to match this staff capacity with campaign money that is subject to strict limits. In realistic terms, Senator Jackson may well be 20–30 staff members ahead of any non-incumbent challenger. He is also well ahead of other incumbent Senators, since his seniority gives him control over many more staff people than most Senators have.

The new law also discriminates against poor and middle-income candidates. An individual can contribute no more than $2,000 to another person's campaign for federal office ($1,000 in the primary and $1,000 in the general election) and no more than $25,000 to all other persons' campaigns for federal office. Yet a wealthy Presidential candidate can contribute $50,000 to his own campaign; a wealthy Senate candidate can contribute $35,000 to his own campaign; and a wealthy House candidate can contribute $25,000 to his own campaign. The law thus includes class discrimination among its inequities.

Why shouldn't a non-wealthy candidate be permitted to receive from someone else one $50,000 contribution for a Presidential campaign; or one $35,000 contribution for a Senate campaign; or one $25,000 contribution for a House campaign? The argument for allowing a wealthy candidate to contribute more to his own campaign holds that such a person represents only himself. Yet elected officials are supposed to be representatives of their constituencies, as Gerald Ford suggested when he reportedly said of his record in the Congress: "Forget the voting record. The voting record reflects Grand Rapids." (On becoming Vice President and then President, he indicated that he was his own man. Subsequently, in his first address to the Congress, he suggested that he was everyone's man. And when he pardoned Richard Nixon, Ford referred to himself as "a humble servant of God.")

George E. Agree, who has studied campaign finances for the Twentieth Century Fund, notes another kind of class discrimination in the new law. Candidates running in Presidential primaries will be entitled to public funding on a matching basis once they have raised $100,000 in relatively small, private contributions from at least 20 states. Each private contribution up to $250 will then be matched by a government contribution. In a *New York Times* article of October 28, 1974, Agree remarked that this "enables a rich donor to trigger 250 times as much public funding as a poor donor who may only give $1. Twenty thousand rich people could command the same $5 million of tax money as five million poor people."

What the law defines as "multi-candidate committees" are also favored over individual citizens. While an individual may contribute only $2,000 to a Presidential or Congressional candidate, a group like the dairy committee, the AMA committee, or COPE is allowed to contribute $10,000 ($5,000 in the primary and $5,000 in the general election). Moreover, there is no limit on the total amount that a multi-candidate committee can contribute to all campaigns. This loophole is particularly interesting because some of the worst abuses in the 1972 campaign were connected with multi-candidate committees.

The Senate version of the campaign finance bill included specific provisions against voting fraud, which is the most direct kind of political corruption. The conference committee deleted those provisions and gave no explanation for its action.

The conference committee emerged with the worst of all possible worlds: It underwrote the two major parties at precisely the time when more and more voters deserve and want another alternative; it practically guaranteed that incumbents will remain incumbents; it provided special loopholes for wealthy candidates and for multi-candidate committees; it dropped the provisions against voting fraud; and it provided such severe restrictions on individuals' participation as to discourage many citizens from participating in politics at all.

The last feature of the new law is one of the worst. Voter participation in Presidential elections has declined steadily since 1960. Unfairness in the delegate selection process has discouraged participation in primaries by many citizens. State laws which discriminate against Independents and against new-party candidates have discouraged others. The new federal campaign law—as well as some of the more severe state laws on campaign finance—may well increase the barriers to citizen participation. The new federal law is over 40 pages long and very complex. It raises fines for violations up to $25,000. How many

volunteer treasurers for Congressional campaigns want to assume that kind of liability, in addition to the possibility of a one-year jail term? For that matter, how many challenging candidates want to assume that kind of liability? Anyone who must operate at all times with an accountant on the right hand and a lawyer on the left hand is likely to be discouraged from participation, to say the least.

Those who worry about citizen apathy should remember that fear is often a major component of apathy. Some people are afraid to speak out at public meetings because they think (often with good reason) that their neighbors will react with hostility. Some are afraid to write letters to editors for the same reason. Some are now afraid to become involved in any financial aspects of a campaign because of the increased complexity of the law—which makes unwitting violations far more likely—and because of the increased penalties for violations. And some now hesitate to contribute because of requirements for disclosure of relatively small contributions. Thus the Socialist Workers party recently sought exemption from a Minnesota disclosure law, citing past harassment of party supporters by the FBI.

Disclosure of large contributions can be defended in the public interest. But one might question the new California requirement that any contribution over $50 must be reported. Requiring disclosure of contributions is, in a sense, an invasion of the secret ballot. There are cases in which the public interest is sufficiently compelling to override one's private interest in the secret ballot, but I am not certain that $50 is the proper place to draw the line. The federal requirement (in both the old and the new laws) that any contribution over $100 must be disclosed seems more reasonable—although the suggestion that a candidate will sell out for $101 is an insult to his integrity.

Democracy involves some risk and some trust, especially in the election process. We have been warned against attempts at over-control by at least two poets. In the sixteenth century, William Shakespeare wrote in *Measure for Measure*, his greatest political drama:

Escalus: What news abroad i' the world?
Duke: None, but that there is so great a fever

on goodness, that the dissolution of it must cure it; novelty is only in request; and it is as dangerous to be aged in any kind of course as it is virtuous to be constant in any undertaking. There is scarce truth enough alive to make societies secure; but security enough to make fellowships accursed: much upon this riddle runs the wisdom of the world. This news is old enough, yet it is every day's news. . . .

And in our own century, William Stafford wrote in his poem "Connections":

And if we purify the pond, the lilies die.

QUESTIONS FOR DISCUSSION

1. Do you agree that "politics causes people to act more immorally than they might in other pursuits"? How much does the stress and strain of raising money contribute to this?
2. Should the political parties be strengthened? If so, how can this be accomplished?
3. Should we encourage the development of minor parties on the left and right? What might be some of the consequences of their existence?
4. How might the Democratic party reform movement have been more successful?
5. Is it possible to speak of an "emerging Democratic majority"?
6. What is the probable future role within the Democratic party for the followers of George McGovern?
7. How do you explain Nixon's landslide victory in 1972?
8. Do you favor either national primaries or the direct election of the President? What is your reaction to other electoral reforms such as staggered primaries, regional primaries, and uniform rules for all presidential primaries?
9. Can you make a strong argument in support of public financing of *all* federal election campaigns?
10. As an adviser to the Republican party, what recommendations would you make concerning techniques to help re-establish the credibility of the party?

"Hon, read me something from Jack
Anderson—blowing-the-lid-off-wise."

chapter three

Interest Groups, the Mass Media, and Public Opinion

REACTIONS OF THE AMERICAN PUBLIC

While Watergate brought trust in government to a low point, the scandal also had the effect of producing a new appreciation of the role of a free press in American society. Political opinion analyst Louis Harris (in *The Anguish of Change*) reports that in 1970, by 57 percent to 32 percent, a majority of Americans favored giving government authorities the right to "censor television, radio, newspapers, and the theater for unpatriotic or revolutionary content." In 1973, a 5 to 1 majority of the public believed that "in exposing the facts about Watergate, the *Washington Post* and other newspapers were an example of a free press at its best." By a 3 to 1 majority, they agreed that "if it had not been for the press exposés, the whole Watergate mess never would have been found out." Harris notes that Watergate has also produced a new demand for government at all levels to operate in the open.

By late 1974, public interest had turned from Watergate to the economy. Here too, confidence in government was low. Most people believed that neither government nor business was likely to provide the leadership to avoid an economic depression. A Yankelovich poll for *Time* magazine in the spring of 1975 showed that 77 percent of the respondents were pessimistic in reflecting confidence in the general political and economic future. An earlier Yankelovich poll indicated that economic preoccupation was leading to a growing isolationism. Only 2 percent of the respondents listed any aspect of foreign affairs as a major national concern. Fifty-five percent believed that inflation can be solved by domestic action alone. In summary, the nation's politicians face an electorate which feels helpless and depressed and has little confidence in government providing the leadership and solutions to improve conditions.

THE ROLE OF INTEREST GROUPS IN POLITICAL CAMPAIGNS

In spite of the fallout from Watergate, campaign spending in 1974 was at an all-time high for congressional races. While some "fat cats" were scared off by Watergate revelations, this loss was more than compensated for by contributions from special interest groups. With the 1974 campaign spending reform legislation opening up the field for the 1976 presidential race and placing strict limits on individual contributions, it is likely that contributions from interest groups will become even more significant.

It is estimated that special interest groups contributed 20 percent of the total campaign funds in 1974. For example, the American Medical Association's national political arm gave $100,000 in the last eight days of the 1974 congressional campaign to 43 candidates and it gave an additional $22,000 to 14 winners after the election. In total, AMA contributions were slightly over $1 million. AFL–CIO contributions also topped the $1 million mark. The United Auto Workers gave about $700,000 and the National Association of Manufacturers gave over $250,000. In the Indiana Senate race, loser Richard Lugar (Republican) spent over $1 million, while winner Birch Bayh spent about $860,000. Organized labor contributed about $150,000 to the Bayh campaign. The top 1974 campaign spender was incumbent Senator Alan Cranston (D., Calif.) with $1,336,202.

The Securities and Exchange Commission has charged the Gulf Oil Company with making contributions of $5.4 million to political campaigns during the period 1960–1974. Other companies have admitted making illegal corporate contributions to campaigns. They include Phillips Petroleum ($685,000) and Minnesota Mining and Manufacturing ($498,000) for gifts made during the period 1960–1974.

Seven of every 10 congressional races are won by the candidate with the most money and incumbents typically raise twice as much money as do challengers. Unopposed senatorial candidates Russell Long (D., La.) and Daniel Inouye (D., Hawaii) spent $160,000 and $250,000 in 1974. Even with campaign reform, representatives can spend up to $84,000 each in primaries and the general election, and senators in large states can spend over $1 million in the general election alone. Common Cause has reported that only 22 of the 810 major party House candidates and 16 of the 65 major Senate candidates in 1974 spent more than the limits to be imposed beginning in 1976 under the new federal election law. Special interest groups can give up to $15,000 in a primary, run-off, and general election campaign. In addition, these groups contribute a variety of services, such as registering voters, which are "free" to candidates. The charge that "Politics are bought out, the people sold out" does not help to increase our confidence in government.

THE MASS MEDIA AND OPENNESS IN GOVERNMENT

Clearly the press played a major role in exposing the Watergate affair. However, questions have been raised about why the story took so long to develop after the break-in occurred. More fundamental questions have been debated concerning the accuracy and fairness of the press. Some individuals continue to believe that a biased, liberal press was bent on revenge and used Watergate as a means to bring down an old enemy.

Drawing by Szep; © The Boston Globe

"We want the soap operas back on."

However, in the wake of Watergate, with public opinion supporting openness in government, the position of a free press has been strengthened. Still, the news media has a credibility problem to solve.

In 1974 the Supreme Court turned back a serious attack on the press. In a suit to compel Florida newspapers to give equal space to political candidates who had been criticized in print, the Court ruled 9 to 0 that the Florida statute was unconstitutional because of "its intrusion into the function of editors."

On another front, journalists have been helped by the passage of 17 amendments to the Freedom of Information Act. The original 1966 act permitted private persons to file complaints in federal courts to force government agencies to produce information they were withholding. The bill, however, did not work because the process was unduly costly and lengthy. Even the Senate Watergate Committee was unable to get the CIA to declassify its files on persons who had knowledge about Watergate. The new amendments, passed over President Ford's veto, give federal judges the authority to review in private classified political and national security information, at the behest of a private person, and to determine if it should continue to be classified. In addition, one amendment sets a strict timetable for the government's response to a request for information. While it remains to be seen how effective the new rules will be in providing freedom of information, they appear to have done a good job of balancing the people's right to know versus the government's need to protect legitimate secrets.

READINGS

In one of the articles in this section, Elizabeth Drew reports on an interview with John Gardner, founder and director of Common Cause. Since 1970, Common Cause has grown to a membership of about 250,000 and has been particularly successful in pressing for stricter campaign financing laws and control of lobbyists. Mr. Gardner discusses how citizens might organize for effective action in the area of governmental reform. The Krieghbaum article explores methods of monitoring the press through such means as media review boards and ombudsmen. Political analyst Ben Wattenberg examines the effects of the "New Politics Movement" on the 1972 presidential election and he discusses the nature of the current political mood in America.

Conversation with a Citizen

Elizabeth Drew

I interviewed Gardner recently in his office, on M Street, in Washington. It is a plainly decorated, linoleum-floored office, with photographs on its walls of James Bryant Conant, Abraham Flexner (whose report for the Carnegie Foundation for the Advancement of Teaching in 1910 revolutionized medical education in the United States), Lyndon Johnson, and Mrs. Johnson (with Gardner, inspecting a Headstart project), and of El Capitan, a dramatic cliff at Yosemite. On his desk there is a photograph of the Golden Gate Bridge; tucked in the frame is a slip of paper on which Gardner has written, in French, a quotation from the writer Jules Renard: "There are times when everything succeeds. Don't let it alarm you; it will pass."

Gardner has a perpetual tan, from working in the sun at home or in California. His right eyebrow seems constantly cocked in curiosity or amusement. As he talks, he waves his hands expansively, or move them in a molding fashion, as if he were literally shaping his answers. He speaks slowly.

I began by asking him about the relationship between his agenda of reform and Watergate.

"The agenda is about how to get responsive government, government that you can hold to account, government to which the citizen has access. Those underlie everything. All the Constitutional guarantees that have been vio-

lated by Watergate were attempts by the Founding Fathers to produce responsiveness, accountability, and access."

I asked him how close he thought we had come to losing the liberty that the Founding Fathers had attempted to guarantee.

"Frighteningly close. Some of the highest officials of this nation carried on a sustained and systematic attempt to destroy our form of government. It wasn't 'dirty tricks' within the system—it was an attempt to subvert the system, an assault on virtually all the checks and balances that protect our system. There were repeated attempts to undermine the judicial process, there was defiance of the Constitutional powers of Congress, intimidation of the media, invasion of the First Amendment rights of citizens, and systematic manipulation of the powers of government to reward friends and punish political opponents. It was about as broad an assault as we have ever seen. Delete the word 'about.' And with each month and each year that the events went undiscovered the possibility of pulling out of the danger must necessarily have been diminished. But I think we would have become aware sooner or later of what was happening. In fact, as you look back, we were in many ways aware that power was being abused. But our minds couldn't totally accept what our instincts told us. We couldn't accept the bits and pieces of the trouble that flicked before our eyes."

"Now that we have begun to discover, or face, what was going on, what are the remaining dangers?"

"There are several. It's not just that we have to stay angry long enough to make the changes that will prevent recurrence. We don't know if we will learn the wrong lesson and, in our unease and confusion, reach out for leaders to whom we will give even greater power. And, while we're on the subject of worries, keep in mind that there's an element in our populace that actually doesn't give a damn about the Constitutional guarantees that were endangered by Watergate. It's a larger element than we can be comfortable about. The danger is that in a time of economic panic or military crisis or political paralysis, the suspension of Constitutional guarantees might appear to be the quickest way to reëstablish order, and might even be welcomed. Watergate has raised some pretty rough questions about the American people. We let it happen. We neglected our instruments of self-government. We let the corruption develop. The big question now is whether we have the will to take tough remedial measures. The danger of apathy is there."

"Then to what extent can your own agenda of reform prevent such a basic assault on the idea of democracy?"

"I think we have to be pretty clear about what we think we can prevent. There isn't any possibility that we can make power less seductive. There isn't any possibility that we can banish from politics all those for whom the end justifies the means, or those who deceive the public 'for the public's good.' What we can do is to devise realistic arrangements that will make it much more difficult for officials to separate the citizens from the levers of power and much more difficult for a tightly knit inner

circle to monopolize those levers. Our Founding Fathers understood the problem very well. They did not place naïve confidence in those who found themselves in possession of power, and they surrounded the exercise of power with carefully fashioned constraints. But they presumed continuing vigilance on the part of citizens."

"So what you're talking about in your own agenda is bringing up to date the arrangements by which the public, if it chooses to be vigilant, might be able to watch more carefully—to hold accountable—the people who have their hands on the levers of power?"

"That's right. It's more difficult today for a citizen to know what is going on. It's vastly more difficult for him to be heard. It's hard for him to know his leaders. Manipulating information is much easier in an intricately organized society. So we have to bring up to date the constraints on power. We have to break through the skillful arrangements that insiders have devised to preserve control of the levers of power. The principles are the same. The means of making them work have to be freshened."

"It seems that a theme that runs through all the items on your agenda is secrecy, or, conversely, opening up the processes, opening up information to the public, whether it's through disclosure of campaign financing or through disclosure of contacts of lobbyists with the government or through having meetings of the executive and Congress open unless there are compelling reasons to have them closed. Is what you are basically trying to get, then, a breaking down of the secrecy with which decisions are made?"

"It is. People instinctively understand the power of money to corrupt the public process, but they understand less well the power of secrecy to corrupt that same process. Accountability is at the heart of free self-government. That's what it is about. Accountability. And there isn't any way for the citizen to hold his government to account if he doesn't know what is going on. What he doesn't know he can't object to. Secrecy cuts the link of accountability. It strikes at the very root of what our government is about. Yet the bad habit of doing the public business in secret runs from the Congress of the United States right down to the state legislatures and the school boards, and to the county board of supervisors where the chairman is handing a gravel contract to his brother-in-law. There are notable exceptions in some states and cities. But, taking government generally, we've got to open a lot of closed doors. You know, Mencken said, 'Conscience is the inner voice which warns us that someone may be looking.' Recent events have underscored some other things we have to do. In our federal government, we have to do something about the politicization of the Department of Justice. We have to take some exceedingly stern measures to regain control of covert police activities and intelligence activities. We must find ways to outlaw the outright subversion of the political process through espionage, forged documents, the use of *agents provocateurs*, and so on."

"If we did generally open up the processes, and increase access to the decision-making, how do you think that would affect the substance of what happens?"

"It would make government more responsive to citizens. You can foresee better consequences from that only if you have some confidence in the people."

"You mentioned the power of money to corrupt the public process. Do you think we will, or can, really curb this?"

"We've made some gains, but money is still the hydra-headed monster that will wreck our system if we don't chain it down. And the final answer is public financing of campaigns. In addition to campaign-financing laws we need, of course, tough lobbying-disclosure laws and conflict-of-interest legislation. Congress's lack of enthusiasm for such legislation is bottomless."

"Might not public financing of campaigns set up another manipulable federal instrument?"

"There isn't any final safety in any system. Obviously, there are hazards in public financing, and I would never rush into it impulsively. But it appears to be the only possible alternative to the immeasurable corruption of the present system. When you see the scandalous capacity of money for buying votes, buying politicians, buying political outcomes, and see the wreckage of public confidence produced by that process, public financing seems the best way out. We can try to surround it with safeguards, and we'll have to keep a close watch on it. I don't think our system can survive the corrosion of confidence produced by the present arrangements."

"You're proposing a substantial reform agenda. And yet if you look at the history of reform movements, or reforms, you might get discouraged. Some of the most decrepit institutions and agencies around Washington are the debris of what was once a glorious moment of reform. So how do you keep reforms alive?"

"In the long run, everything ends up as an object of curiosity to some future archeologist. Everything we create will end up as shards and items from the diggings. There's no way of guaranteeing eternal vitality. But I'd make a distinction between citizen organizations and the idea of citizen action. Any specific citizen organization will grow old and ineffective. But the idea of citizen action will continue. It's emerging in new forms. The type of citizen action we are trying to create is a new ingredient in the political process—highly organized, tough-minded citizen action to hold government continuously accountable, a means of voting between elections. The tasks of citizen action are never-ending. The battles are never over. Nothing is finally safe. There will always be issues of freedom and government."

"Are you, then, talking about a new definition of the role of the citizen who chooses to be interested?"

"Absolutely."

"How is this role to be different from what it has been in the past?"

"We now have a huge, intricately organized society. It's hard for individuals to understand the issues that affect their lives or the way government is organized to deal with those issues. They can't know what decisions are being made by some middle-level bureaucrat that will affect the way they pay their taxes or the way their children are educated. They need to organize with other citizens so that they can have the kind of information that will enable them to find the targets. They need to organize in order to know how to move in on those targets. It was easier in our early history for citizens not only to see the evils that were impinging on them but to express themselves. It's very difficult now."

"If you succeed in opening up government in the way you propose, there will be a staggering amount of information available to citizens. How will they absorb it, and what are they to do with it?"

"Of course, no one individual or group will attempt to absorb it all. The environmentalists will use the information pertinent to their concerns. So will the civil-rights groups, the better-government groups, the consumer groups, women's-rights groups, and so on. I think there will be a proliferation of citizen-action groups in special fields. As for what they will do with the information, they will have to become increasingly skilled in the proved techniques of public-interest lobbying. We are learning more and more about what these are."

"What are they?"

"The first requirement for effective citizen action is stamina. Arthur Vanderbilt said court reform is no sport for the short-winded. The same is true of citizen action. The special-interest lobbies never let up. The second requirement is an informed public. The special interests flourish in the dark. Officials begin to respect citizen action when they discover that citizens are watching and the media are reporting what the citizens see. The third requirement is focussed action. The gravest weakness of many high-minded citizens is random indignation. They must pick a few targets and mobilize strength, numbers, and money in order to have an impact. The fourth requirement is the creation of inside-outside alliances. An effective citizen group doesn't sit outside Congress, or any government body, lobbing mortar shells over the walls. There are ready allies inside for any forward-looking movement, and they have to be found. The fifth requirement is a professional cutting edge. It's a peculiar quirk of high-minded people to believe that only the wicked need good lawyers. Citizens must be prepared to match professional skill and knowledge with their opponents."

"That's a rather tall order. If a citizen wants to be involved and effective, does he have to belong to or organize a group with all those resources?"

"Not necessarily. He may be lucky. Some battles have been won on sheer enthusiasm or anger. But, if you're serious, don't depend on luck or the intensity of your caring. People often point to Ralph Nader as an example of the effective citizen acting alone. But the lessons learned from Nader that we can apply—you can't go around replicating his particular genius—relate to the points I raised earlier. He did his homework, he knew his facts, he understood the role of the press, he found his allies within; he was a match for his opponents in thoroughness and skill."

"All this is predicated on the idea that there are a great many citizens who want to know what is going on and would do something about it if they did know. How many such citizens do you think there are?"

"Nobody knows how many. There are in any population a lot of people who are very busy just living, just surviving, just getting through the day. It's hard enough to pay the bills and get the kids off to school without worrying about whether the House Ways and Means Committee is meeting in secret. I sympathize with that. But there is always a segment of the population that has the time and energy to worry about the community and the nation. You find these people in all parts of society—in the ghettos, in the labor unions, in the suburbs. Since you can't know where these vigorous, concerned citizens will

come from, you have to keep the channels of a free society open, so that they can step forward and make themselves felt."

"What is the difference between your movement and the more traditional reform movements?"

"I think the old-style good-government movements had two failings. First, they imagined that we might achieve a kind of static perfection of governmental processes and then we could all relax and be happy under a good government. They didn't understand that somebody always has too much power and somebody always has too little, and that if you drive the bad guys out of power the good guys who replace them will soon get accustomed to power and grow to love it and may eventually abuse it. So the struggle never ends. The other failing of the old good-government movement was that they felt themselves to be above politics. But politics is the only forum in which we can resolve our differences. As long as equally worthy people have incompatible goals, somebody has to mediate—unless you want things decided by the whim of a dictator or unless you want to shoot it out. The politicians are our mediators. We have to rehabilitate the whole notion of politics as the kind of free market in which we resolve conflicting purposes. It's always untidy. It will always be grubbier than we might want it to be. But we can't afford to scorn it."

"You are, therefore, as I understand it, describing an interconnection between citizen action and political action which in some way vitalizes, or revitalizes, politics and tries to keep it honest."

"That's right. There are all kinds of politicians. There are some extraordinarily good, resilient, effective people in politics. At the other extreme are the crooks and the exploiters. And in the middle are a lot of unheroic types who will respond to pressures, good or bad. Citizen action tries to work with the good guys, immobilize the crooks, and stiffen the spines of the unheroic."

Who's to Keep the Media's Conscience?

Hillier Krieghbaum

With all the oft-cited pressures on the media, who is to insure that the press does its job? Can reporters, editors, producers, publishers, and station owners patrol and police their own efforts? In short, who will keep the media's conscience?

As all communications come under mounting charges of bias and prejudice, of serving other than commonly accepted ideas and ideals, and of supposedly flawed and inaccurate performances, the fact looms increasingly large that competent observers (including intelligent, nonprofessional members of their audiences) may have to study and even to monitor the activities and then to ascertain who is right and who is wrong in the baffling welter of controversy over press actions or lack of them.

Many readers, listeners, and viewers feel that newsmen should not—possibly cannot—undertake this assignment of self-evaluation with real effectiveness. Most print and broadcast journalists

naturally have a deep involvement in their work and to expect them to be impartial would be asking for Solomon-like fairness. If mediamen were all angels, this might work, but some practitioners would not thus qualify. But I, for one (and I am sure I am not alone), would be reluctant to surrender the rights to censor and to suppress *my* reading matter or *my* broadcast programs to politicians, to lawyers and judges, or to any other special group.

Again, then, who is to keep the media on a proper track, assuming that "proper" can be meaningfully defined? What we may have to do is to borrow from some recent experimental press councils set up in smaller U.S. communities and from foreign countries' media supervision. Such an independent, impartial agency might be a media review board or one individual operating either as an ombudsman, such as in Sweden, a "resident critic," as now on the *Washington Post,* or a "readers' referee" as in Minneapolis. Charged with observing and evaluating what the press does and then issuing a report, such a group or person would use the methods of effective communications and, with some luck, there would be future improvements. This machinery would depend solely on the power of publicity, rather than any form of compulsion or penalty. It would not be a governmental commission with official powers. It would not be some other professional body trying to impose its own standards on the press.

Quite a few pluses are going for such an arrangement. For instance:

• By providing an institutionalized channel for considering the wide range of attacks on the press, a media review board or, possibly, an ombudsman would sort out the crackpot comments and the self-seeking propagandistic criticisms so that credible observations and objections would receive serious attention and be fed into the informational system. This would provide newsmen and the general public with the necessary data to evaluate criticisms and, if necessary, to act upon them.

• By establishing minimum standards for reporting, editing, and dissemination of news, such machinery could protect media from being tarred by the irresponsible actions of their own less reliable members and could guard the people from repetitions of such defects in the future—if publishers and station owners listened. General acceptance of such an operation would insure that attention would be paid to the findings.

• By repeatedly stressing the need for a free and responsible media, these new agencies would serve a useful educational function in telling readers, listeners, and viewers that they are the real losers when the media bow to outside pressures and serve not them but some special interest, be it governmental, political, industrial, or individual.

• By spreading truth, rather than current myths and fantasies, such an arrangement would improve the general level of press credibility. With a truly informed people, it would become increasingly difficult for the government to evade the First Amendment guarantees. Just what lengths a U.S. government official may strive to reach is illustrated by a 1971 order from Governor John M. Haydon, Jr., of American Samoa to deport the editor of a newspaper there which had been critical of the islands' administration.

Establishment of some kind of media review agency would bypass objections that some American editors and publishers have to organizing a group of their journalistic peers to monitor others in the field. Who, some of these objectors ask, is So-and-so that he should tell me how to run my newspaper or broadcasting station? Furthermore, these individuals argue, this smacks of violating the First Amendment guarantees (at least, for print). Nevertheless, some journalists probably would have to be members of any reviewing group to provide the know-how for sophisticated evaluations of what was taking place, why it was done, and of potential alternatives.

Such a media review board or ombudsman could borrow from the experiences of systems established in several Scandinavian countries and the United Kingdom. Also it could draw on recent experiments in this country so that it would not have to be an innovation untried in the United States.

. . .

On the *Washington Post*, starting in September 1970, Richard Harwood, with the title of assistant managing editor, became involved exclusively as the daily's "resident critic." A reporter or editor for more than two decades, Harwood saw his job as more than just an ombudsman or in-house representative of the readership and so criticized the news product regularly for the *Post*'s publisher, editors, and the staff. For example, a loud complaint from the Department of Justice brought a front-page apology to Attorney General John Mitchell who had been misquoted in a news item. In addition, Harwood kept up a stream of private memoranda to Mrs. Katharine Graham, publisher, and her associates. He said:

My job is mainly monitoring the paper for fairness, balance and perspective. If I see something wrong, and they agree with it, they put out a memo and fix it.

. . .

Too often, however, media operations have been business-as-usual. As a result a tinder pile of frustration, resentment, and anger among the mass audience has increased rapidly. Vice-President Spiro T. Agnew's criticism of both broadcasting and print ignited what already had been smoldering for some years.

Thus it was little wonder that Norman E. Isaacs wrote as follows in the *Columbia Journalism Review* (Fall, 1970):

If the polls are correct—and I do not challenge them—journalism can not continue to sweep the idea [of some sort of monitoring] under the rug. One fairly recent Gallup Poll reported that only 37 percent of the public feels newspapers deal fairly on political and social issues. Some 45 percent think newspapers unfair. Listed as not sure were 18 percent. It is significant that the more highly educated the person questioned, the stronger the feeling that newspapers were unfair. . . .

I considered and still consider the Agnew attacks a form of intimidation of the press. Though his more recent approaches stress "sensible authority," it is not inconceivable that a drive for "sensible authority" could be stretched to the creation of an overview agency by government ostensibly to preserve and protect the First Amendment freedoms. Far better, I hold, for the press to create its own protection. . . .

We needed to be rebuilding faith in the American press; the shrugging off of inaccuracy and slanting in news columns was the most dangerous course we could follow. An ethics or grievance committee—or, if you will, a press council—seemed to be an effective way to deal with the situation.

Fears, some legitimate and some seemingly fantastic, have been expressed about the proposals to form press councils in this country. There is no question that an effective operation would restrict an editor's freedom of action if only by making him more responsible for inaccuracies and slanting in the news he printed—and thus impelling him to do a better job. But that really is not the key objection, obviously, although some publishers and some editors seem to regard the First Amendment guarantees as granting to them rights to any kind of activity short of outright murder. Not very far in the background of such monitoring considerations are (1) the possibility of licensing newsmen and (2) the successful application of community pressure to cow editors into submitting to majority opinions.

Dr. W. Walter Menninger, psychiatrist and member of the National Commission on the Causes and Prevention of Violence, nullified much of the group's support for local press councils when he went to the National Press

Club in Washington early in 1970 and called for journalists to meet the same practices as doctors, lawyers, and educators: ". . . laws for licensure and certification assure the public that the practitioner has fulfilled minimum standards, met certain requirements for training and demonstrated competence in the profession." The prospect of regulating the profession in this way—of saying who could be a journalist and under what circumstances—raised totalitarian nightmares. Even Dr. Menninger in a later speech in his home town of Topeka, Kan., conceded that he might have chosen "the wrong word to emphasize a concern about professional standards in journalism" and that, given the First Amendment, there undoubtedly would be "many legal, constitutional, and procedural problems that would make certification or licensure of journalists by law well nigh impossible."

Certainly any licensing of journalists in the United States would have to be instigated over the limp bodies of many working newsmen and their bosses. One Midwestern editor commented:

American publishers approach the issue of self-sanitation as the reluctant bride faces her wedding night. The publishers want to be loved but they fear the process of pregnancy.

What may be accepted for doctors, lawyers, and educators does not automatically translate into good practice for newsmen. Journalists who work more in the fields of ideas and creativity—on occasion—should not be put in straitjackets.

Another objection to monitoring and evaluation centers around the idea that an editor of either print or broadcasting should have the chance and the courage to buck the majority of his own community. If there is no place at all for courage, even if only rarely utilized, then most editors might as well be replaced by computers programed to scan public opinion polls and utilize the results for playback in editorials, cartoons, opinion columns—and, where the greatest damage may be done in creating a democratic and informed public reaction, in the news coverage and its positioning.

J. Russell Wiggins, former executive editor of the *Washington Post* who quit his job to represent this country briefly at the United Nations, was concerned about the reinforcing effect that such local press councils would have in tightening the Establishment's hold, already not insignificant, on the local mass media. Such mechanisms, he properly pointed out, could easily become "channels through which the very worst special-interest groups would bring pressures to suppress or withhold news." These groups could make "the collective opinion of the community irresistible at the very moment when that opinion was the most misguided and most in need of contradiction and restraint." One has only to recall the actions of most German newspapermen and broadcasters under the lash of the Hitler regime to realize that editorial bravery can be a rare commodity, in scarcest supply when needed most. Institutionalization of criticism might stifle such independence as remains and, as Isaacs put it, "most middlesized and smaller newspapers are already, to some degree, prisoners of 'the establishment.' "

Already the philosophy that the First Amendment guarantees should be restricted and reinterpreted is in the arena of public discussion. Under this proposal, the communications complex would be converted into something like a public utility, such as telephone service or a community's sewage system. Most prominent of its advocates during the 1960's was Prof. Jerome A. Barron, who wrote a frequently cited presentation for the *Harvard Law Review* in 1967. He argued that media monopolization in the twentieth century and other contemporary trends demanded that an affirmative responsibility be imposed under the First Amendment if the "marketplace" theory was to operate in the present economic and communications environment. He wrote, in part:

What is required is an interpretation of the first amendment which focuses on the idea that restraining the hand of government is quite useless in assuring free speech if a restraint on access is effectively secured by private groups. A constitutional prohibition against governmental restrictions on expression is effective only if the Constitution ensures an adequate opportunity for discussion. Since this opportunity exists only in the mass media, the interests of those who control the means of communication must be accommodated with the interests of those who seek a forum in which to express their point of view. . . .

If the mass media are essentially business enterprises and their commercial nature makes it difficult to give a full and effective hearing to a wide spectrum of opinion, a theory of the first amendment is unrealistic if it prevents courts or legislatures from requiring the media to do that which, for commercial reasons, they would be otherwise unlikely to do. . . .

The changing nature of communications process has made it imperative that the law show concern for the public interest in effective utilization of media for the expression of diverse points of view. Confrontation of

ideas, a topic of eloquent affection in contemporary decisions, demands some recognition of a right to be heard as a constitutional principle. It is the writer's position that it is open to the courts to fashion a remedy for a right of access, at least in the most arbitrary cases, independently of legislation. If such an innovation is judicially resisted, I suggest that our constitutional law authorizes a carefully framed right of access statute which would forbid an arbitrary denial of space, hence securing an effective forum for the expression of divergent opinions.

With the development of private restraints on free expression, the idea of a free marketplace where ideas can compete on their merits has become just as unrealistic in the twentieth century as the economic theory of perfect competition. The world in which an essentially rationalist philosophy of the first amendment was born has vanished and what was rationalism is now romance.

Prof. Barron's arguments generally are opposed by media managers, both print and broadcast, but his idea may provide a rationale for imposing new ways on the dissemination of news, opinions, and ideas. Already the Federal Communications Commission has expanded its "fairness doctrine" to mandate airing of differing, rebuttal viewpoints over the airways. And minority groups, especially the blacks during the early 1970's, have been successful in moderating long-standing station policies (some of which definitely were racist) when they mobilized aggressively to complain at license hearings. Potential loss of authorizations worth multimillion dollars has proved a powerful prod to force ideological modifications toward better "marketplace" programing. The FCC's power to approve or to reject license applications presents an opportunity for evaluation of broadcasters' operations. For instance, the Commission does judge how well a station has lived up to its own promises to serve its home community, as outlined in its original application, and poor marks in this category have caused many anxious moments for those whose actions have not conformed to their pledges. The National Association of Broadcasters, too, has used a code for performance to govern station operations to a far greater degree than editors and publishers ever have done with any of the professional print credos.

The concept of an independent, outside monitoring and evaluating agency has implications for broadcasting and print that would be more palatable than imposition of any sort of A. T. & T. regulations by what might become the news division of a state or federal public service commission. A truly impartial evaluating agency, such as a media review board, would have far more pluses than minuses in comparison with public utility regulations, at least for the professionals and probably for the public as well.

Neither the motivations for journalistic procedures nor the procedures of such a media review board can be cleanly outlined like a series of rates for the regulated prices of natural gas or electricity. Too many subjective values are involved for such massive and exacting classifications. However, there is no reason why editorial judgments should not be studied and, yes, even evaluated. The media are not above criticism—and improvement—and if this is done intelligently, rather than emotionally and self-servingly, they and the public should both gain. In the fall of 1971, the first state review board, or press coun-

cil, was established for Minnesota and, if the anticipated pluses actually take place, this may well be a model for other such efforts.

Some media evaluations already are being done although the resulting findings are not widely disseminated outside professional circles. If they were, the information might help reduce the antagonisms toward the press. Among the publications which are doing this are the *Columbia Journalism Review*, which celebrated its tenth birthday in 1971; the *Chicago Journalism Review*, a professional fallout after the Chicago Democratic convention coverage; comparable publications in other sections of the country; *Nieman Reports*, put out by the journalism fellows of Harvard University; the almost inhouse studies of the Associated Press Managing Editors, an independently incorporated organization of representatives from members of the press association; occasional articles in Association for Education in Journalism publications such as *Journalism Quarterly* and *Journalism Monographs*; and infrequent federal and state inquiries into some special aspect of the communications operations.

However, there exists no wide channel for redress open to individuals or organizations that believe they have a substantial grievance against the media for alleged sloppy, incompetent, or vicious actions. Of course, a suit for libel is possible but, as pointed out in Chapter Twelve, during the 1960's this doorway was closed to keyhole size so that a court victory for an injured party now follows only the most flagrant form of journalistic malpractice.

If an ombudsman, with real independence and unintimidated, operates for the media, then anyone believing he has been injured may appeal to him. But, as noted earlier, only a few papers and no major broadcasters have established this procedure. If they had done so, then the need for another channel would be far lessened.

Media review boards could fill this gap. An individual with an objection against one or several of the media and who had tried unsuccessfully to solve his own problem could take his complaint to the review board, stating as many of the specifics as possible. Moreover, it should not be required that he hire an attorney and proceed as if this were a court case. An investigator from a media review board would try to find out all the relevant facts; probably he would (1) talk to the complainant for even further information, (2) obtain copies of the pages or pictures or, in the case of radio and television, tapes of the broadcast, (3) interview representatives of the publication or broadcast station, and, if necessary, (4) ascertain additional information from the probable news source or other informed witnesses. Most frivolous and inconsequential complaints should be filtered out before getting far in this four-stage inquiry.

If a valid case thus appeared to have been documented, then the investigator could suggest (this word "suggest" is mighty important because it never should be an order to media) to the print or broadcasting representative that an injustice seemed to have been done and that possibly the publication or station would want to correct the wrong with a retraction or apology. If this effort failed, then the media review board would set the time and place for a formal hearing with notices to both sides so that a full-dress discussion could be held. After these sessions, a finding or "decision" would be released to all the news channels and agencies and eventually to the general public. What the media did with these findings or facts or "decisions" would, of course, depend on their own operations and their own consciences.

If newsmen did not want to cooperate, the proceeding could move forward as *in absentia* trials are held in some foreign countries. This has a slight smack of antidemocracy, but then this machinery is outside the courts and even the legal system. It depends, as said previously, on that cardinal point of the media themselves: the power of publicity to change things after the people know the facts. Under such circumstances, probably, the publication or station concerned would not publicize the findings but many of the professional journals would, probably reprinting considerable excerpts from them. Certainly this "raw material" on media performance would have far greater usefulness than some of the highly subjective flotsam and jetsam that drift across the contemporary communications scene as supposed criticism. Thus the media could count on a better-informed general audience the next time around.

Should some type of compensation for damages be allowed? Probably not. If an individual wanted to recover with a cash settlement for alleged losses to his business, his reputation, or even his honor, let him proceed exclusively through the court system. There are laws and judges for just those kinds of cases. Why not use them—if money is the principal goal sought? Probably most Americans, if given the chance, would simply want to "see justice done" and would not try to establish a cash value for injured honor or reputation. Even the largely nominal and "symbolic" fines imposed by some of the foreign press councils could well be eliminated from any U.S. counterparts. Actual financial losses resulting from a news item might be something else again and it should be the function of the courts rather than the media review board system to determine damages. At least, that has been the trend overseas.

How would one go about organizing a system of media review boards for all the United States? Should there be a wide range of local operations, expanding into many communities—and especially into the larger metropolitan areas—as the Mellett Fund has been able to do in a very few towns? Or should Americans fit into the common tendency and set up a national superagency or nongovernmental conglomerate group in Washington or New York City to handle the misconducts of the country's communications system in all its parts?

As an initial tentative experiment, I would propose that boards be established on a series of levels, starting at the local scene:

(1) A local board for each area to handle those errors and mistakes that concern only a limited audience and have only, at most, regional distribution. These would be much like nonstaff ombudsmen or the Mellett-funded local press councils. Probably like these, they initially would feed back community opinion and thinking more than evaluate performance. Much of the initial efforts probably would have to depend on the cooperation and financial backing of responsible local media.

(2) A regional or state middle layer of review boards to treat those matters that were spread well beyond a single city or community.

(3) Some type of national organization for the most flagrant and widespread cases. A nationwide agency of some sort would appear desirable because some cases would have impact across the country. For instance, how would several dozen or more local media review boards handle a news item from Washington, D.C., which allegedly injured some individual and which was printed as a press association dispatch on most front pages of the nation and broadcast from most radio and television stations? Or the misconduct might be against a minority segment or a whole national group. For local boards to conduct repetitive inquiries would be wasteful, at best; self-defeating and confusing, at worst. However, inauguration of the national phase might well wait a couple of years until the merit of the review board idea has been proven first on the local, and then the regional, level.

If and when the three-level review boards were in operation, I would not propose that hearings, like cases in the U.S. courts, be appealable to a higher jurisdiction so that all the key cases would be heard eventually by the national review board. Let the complainant pick his level and, if justified, make him stay with it. These review boards should not be confused with the legal machinery; they are, in a way, the nonviolent equivalent of the old-fashioned system of dueling in that they are designed to satisfy one's honor and reputation, not to enrich one's pocketbook. A finding in an individual's or organization's favor by a local board would be vindication in the eyes of neighbors and acquaintances as much as a national finding.

Even a local media council decision may have far-reaching effects. For instance, the Honolulu Community-Media Council, which brings together a group of laymen with print and broadcast representatives, examined the use of such phrases as "Communist forces," "enemy," and "Reds" in news stories from Southeast Asia when more appropriate and accurate terms might have been "National Liberation Front," "Democratic Republic of Vietnam," "North Vietnamese," and "mainland China." A report from a "committee on euphemisms" in 1971 commented:

We are particularly concerned with the use of such terms as "Communist" and "enemy" which are too easily employed to refer to a wide variety of people and organizations in Indochina. These terms should be avoided as much as possible in favor of more descriptive terms which accurately designate the people and organizations to which they refer.

The council adopted the committee report unanimously and it was disseminated widely. Roger Tatarian, editor and vice-president of United Press International, which had been mentioned because of its greater use of "Communist" in preference to "North Vietnamese," cited the Honolulu council findings in a newsletter sent to UPI clients and employees. He wrote that "specifics are preferable to generalities and should be used wherever possible." Thus the Honolulu council's action became a basis for an international news service's policy revision.

All media review boards must keep their inquiries away from editorials and commentary. Any publication's or broadcasting station's right to state its subjective comments and opinions should not be called into accountability by such a group. Media review boards'

attention should center on the accuracy and validity of news reporting and on questions of ethics and responsible journalism, such as those involving calloused intrusions of privacy, for example, and not be concerned with whether editorials square neatly with local community mores. However, such exemption from inquiry of publications' and stations' editorial position does not imply that they will receive a free ride if they deny others a chance to express their viewpoints. In other words, letters to the editor columns and rebuttal guest editorials can not forever be closed to any sizable segment of a community. Obviously, this poses formidable problems for opinionated proprietors of media—but with a little diplomacy and skill in human relations a blatant case of suppression could be handled, I would suspect, without transgression of the conventional concept of freedom of the press. I would only hope that these would not be the first cases to come before members of a media review board; they could use experiences in the more conventional straight news field before they tangled in this region of opinion and commentary.

Membership of the media review boards poses a whole series of sticky problems.

Essential to any efficient and effective procedure is the requirement of enough journalists to supply technical information on how the media operate. Entirely civilian groups commenting on the press in the past have lost much of their thrust because they just did not know how news was gathered and disseminated. While too many newsmen on a board could bias decisions against complainants who have valid cases but presented them in such a way as to arouse journalistic chauvinism and defense mechanisms, too few newsmen could result in insufficient attention being paid to deadline pressures and other professional and mechanical circumstances, thus divorcing the whole operation from reality and thereby diluting its impact. Possibly individuals recently retired from print or broadcast assignments could supply both a background of know-how and an objectivity somewhat greater than working newsmen involved directly in cases like those under consideration. Again, communities with schools and departments of journalism and communications might tap these resources for board members.

Community leaders, always in demand for launching new projects, could provide the program with at least initial supportive recognition from the Establishment. Obviously, this would be a minus in some sections of the country and among some parts of the populace. To compensate for this, articulate (but probably, if the scheme is to obtain general support, not too abrasive) representatives of non-Establishment viewpoints as well as of any sizable minority groups in a community would have to be included. Obviously, again, it is easier to suggest this than to get such a cross-section to serve.

Recent chairmen in the relatively successful press councils of Britain and the Scandinavian countries have been intelligent laymen as far as media experiences were concerned. And, apparently, they have learned the requisite details about techniques in rapid style. It should be possible to follow the same approach in the United States. Yet some individuals with in-depth knowledge need to serve, even if not as board chairmen, in order to educate the other members.

Failing their outright support and membership participation, at least a guarantee of no violent opposition or sabotage will be necessary from the media managers. They and their associates have the power to block and thwart well-intentioned efforts that others may initiate and try to carry foward—unless, of course, the review system is enacted into law, which could well conflict with First Amendment guarantees. In any case, the whole concept of media review boards, as outlined here, rigorously tries to avoid even the slightest semblance of a powerful governmental bureau with enforcement and punitive authority. To attempt to ram findings of facts and "decisions" down throats of disapproving writers, editors, and broadcasters would negate most of the essential purposes of an impartial, informed board for considering alleged wrongs and, if they turned out to be that, for providing some non-monetary redress for those hurt. It is a matter of fair play and decency, not promulgating findings by fiat and authority.

Where will the spark for establishing these boards come from? That is a vital question and no easy answer is at hand.

The foundations, which have fueled so many innovative programs since World War II, have displayed, at least until recently, a distinct reluctance to affront publishers, editors, and broadcast executives. This is not without cause. After Sigma Delta Chi, professional journalism society, approved the idea for evaluating the 1956 presidential election coverage, interested foundations made their financing contingent on the approval and cooperation of the nation's newspaper publishers and editors. That group voted overwhelmingly—and vehemently on the part of some representatives—in the negative. The project withered and no wide-range, national study of that sort has ever been conducted. Change, however, is much in the air. Within the next several years, the people who control foundation allocations might be willing to earmark substantial funding for experimental media review boards. (Probably a requirement would be that the term "press council" not be mentioned in any proposal requests or in plans submitted to print or broadcast executives for comments. Such a phrase brings the same reaction as mentioning "socialized medicine" to almost any group of U.S. medical men.)

By participating honestly and actively in the review system, the media would gain substantial advantages in the marketplace of public opinion since much of the current resentment against them arises from the frustrated and angry feelings that one's chances of winning a battle with the press are even less than in the proverbial fight with City Hall. With some modest successes, the media review boards should damp down such sentiments to a substantial degree.

At least, that was the result of Houstoun Waring's several feedback procedures at the *Littleton* (Colorado) *Independent*, semiweekly of a Denver suburban community. In 1946, Waring, then the editor, established an Editorial Advisory Board, which six years later became an annual Critics Dinner. In November 1967, a Community Press Council was set up. Just before its fourth birthday, Waring wrote me:

"Our own Littleton Press Council, which offers criticism three times a year, has prevented any credibility gap here. I think our public image is the best in 83 years."

One argument that should have far greater impact with newsmen in the 1970s than before Vice-President Agnew and others began their current attacks on media is that such review boards might help to educate the general public about the procedures and techniques of print and broadcasting operations. This, alone, would be a tremendous benefit because it could provide what might be called "adult education" for the opinion leaders of each community in which such boards existed.

As Professor J. Edward Gerald, University of Minnesota journalism teacher, wisely explained, an effective media review board or press council would be "a two-phased educational institution," which benefited both public and journalists. To many individuals, including some public officials, it would represent a way of obtaining a public hearing of grievances. For journalists' benefit, it would force aggrieved individuals to think—possibly for the first time—about the importance of the media and to accept freedom of the press as a principle at once superior to private convenience and indispensable to political freedom.

Criticism and contentiousness from high government circles have alerted the more sensitive and perceptive media managers that they may have to act themselves to avoid regulations and restraints being imposed upon them from outside. It may be that print and broadcast professional organizations and even some individuals and affluent publications and stations—or networks— will agree that it would be far better for them (and for the public which are their audiences) to act now with some freedom of choice on how an evaluating or monitoring system is established than to have one imposed by the government, which undoubtedly would be the worst of all possible solutions. The media would even do well to consider underwriting the initial costs of setting up the system. Such expenditures might be the insurance premiums against governmental actions in which they would have a great deal to lose: probably the true essence of freedom of the press.

When the media do a good job, let them get full credit where all can see —as they would, with the open and full reporting of media review board findings. And when they do a poor job, under a review system they will merely receive public attention comparable to that editorial writers and other commentators have given politicians, private citizens, corporations, and social groups for several centuries.

The credibility gap between the media and their audiences should narrow when (1) the public realizes that newsmen do care about accuracy and fairness and that something can be done when individuals or groups suffer undue harm and (2) readers, listeners, and viewers develop more sophistication about how news is processed. When a majority of the population appreciates that most of those within media are men of good will and good intentions (although they do not always attain their goals), the appeals of the demagogues and others who whip the press for their own selfish reasons should diminish. This, in turn, would enable the media to get on with the business of reporting the news, the bad as well as the good, without fearing the frequent fate of the bearer of ill tidings. Just conceivably, with this improved popular understanding, the news of what is wrong with the world will have greater impact than ever before and more serious efforts will be made to solve the problems described.

The New Politics and Today's Politics

Ben J. Wattenberg

Who or what threatened morality? Who or what threatened values?

We arrive now at a critical point in the argument. There are many causes for the American malaise. It may well be that we will never really understand the phenomenon. But in *the public mind, it is apparent that one of the causes of the erosion*

of values, one of the causes of the erosion of moral standards, one of the causes of the resulting malaise, has been—call it what you will—the Cause People, the Movement, the Failure and Guilt Complex and their assorted camp followers, sub-species, promoters, drum beaters, faddists, apologists, spear carriers and political types, let alone parents who wanted their kids to think they were hip.

Further, this perception by the public is not just perception, it carries with it a dose of truth.

The charge is serious and must be documented and explained.

Consider once again the argument.

In the last decade or dozen years, life in America, in most measurable ways, has improved. The American middle class has grown to a massive majority. The life choices and life options available to ordinary citizens have grown inordinately. These changes, on balance, have been better by far than what they have replaced.

With these changes have come problems, which Americans recognize as the side effects of progress. They are major problems indeed, but not so major as to wipe out the progress itself. When asked, Americans feel that their lives, their communities, their jobs, their kids, their homes, their incomes are pretty good, even with the problems that exist.

Now, at roughly the moment that so many Americans are beginning to realize the fruits of their hard labors, they hear the earlier middle class derogate their labors, their values, their morality and their achievements. Consider again the thrust of the rhetoric of our time, as heard through the ears of many in the new middle class:

Want to send your kid to college?

Why bother—college is ossified, bureaucratic, irrelevant and unresponsive, a handmaiden of the death dealers of the military-industrial complex.

Want to move to a suburban home, with some green and some safety? Don't do it—suburbia is plastic and escapist. You're not thinking green, mister, you're thinking black. Suburbia is racist, a white noose constructed of plastic ticky-tack.

You think you've got a good job? Wrong again. You've got a *dehumanizing* job, a brutalized job, a boring, monotonous, meaningless and unfulfill-ing job. The fact that you're doing it is meaningful to *you*, that it means you can live in a nice house and send your kids to college—that doesn't count. And, remember, people on welfare shouldn't be demeaned, only people on work should be demeaned.

You think it's nice to have a car, a washing machine, a swimming pool, a vacation in the Rockies or in Europe, a second car, air conditioning and power steering? Nope, all that means is that you're a materialist, and worse than that you're a greedy polluter. You Americans are only 6% of humanity and you use up 30%, 40%, 50%, 60% of the world's resources—why aren't you kind to the planet like the Indian peasants or the black sharecroppers in the South? Black sharecroppers don't pollute, but you do!

You think it's important to have religion, to believe in moderation, in sobriety, in sexual responsibility, in abiding by the laws, in cleanliness, in family? That's square. God is dead, a rip-off is cute, pot is good, sex is a hang-up, pornography is chic, abortion is noble, family is a middle-class put-on, cleanliness is next to ugliness. Your values, your traditions, your culture, your law, your morality—are no good.

You think a woman can live a decent and dignified life by raising a family and providing a warm home? Wrong again; that's sexual repression.

You think it's important to worry about your family? Sorry—that's cultural Philistinism, that's apathy, that's me-first, that's wrong also. You have to worry about Vietnam, racism, women and ecology until the signal is given. Then, as soon as you hear the magic words "inward looking," then, and only then, start looking inward.

You think America is a great country? Wrong—America is imperialist, racist, fascist, genocidal, colonial and sexist. Amerika is the cancer of the world, and the white race is the cancer of civilization. And if Vietnam didn't prove it, look at Watergate—rotten, corrupt, fascist, repressive—and so natural in America.

These views, only mildly exaggerated here, are heard by the men and women of the Massive Majority Middle, and elicit two very different sorts of reaction. One is harsh, crisp and sometimes brutal—and has often resulted in a vote for George Wallace. The second is more in a spirit of sorrow than in bitterness, and is usually in the form of a question: *How can smart people be so stupid?* Here are our best and our brightest, *and they just don't understand,* and sorrowfully, in 1972, these questioners voted for Nixon or just didn't vote.

Americans look at the Cause People, at the Movement, at the Failure and Guilt Complex and they know that so many of the causes they helped publicize had a validity and a vitality that was hard to deny.

At the same time they reject— vehemently—the spirit of exaggeration, of guilt, of smugness, of elitism, of arrogance and of wrongheadedness, too. And that, Americans saw, is very much of a problem in its own right. Most Americans felt that these people, these Cause People, went beyond the pale and were destroying what was held dear. And that problem, the destruction of values, was often seen to be a worse problem than all the other problems that the value destroyers raise.

. . .

Which brings us to politics.

Ours is a highly responsive political system—elections mirror life in America—and anything and everything that concerns Americans usually ends up sooner or later on the political anvil.

If we are seeking evidence as to what kind of national problems we have, and what kind of national solutions we seek, we must look to our national elections as the ultimate national survey.

The 1972 election has been called "a referendum on the cultural revolution" and that's probably sound. Here is how Elizabeth Hardwicke, writing in the fall of 1972 in the *New York Review,* listed the reasons for Senator McGovern's low standing:

Revenge for the 1960s, for show-off students, for runaways, for attacks on the family and the system, for obscenity, for pot, for prisoner pity, for dropping out, tuning in, for radical chic, for store-front lawyers, for folk singers, for muggings, for addicts, for well-to-do WASPs grogged on charity binges.

The Democratic Convention in Miami in July of 1972 turned out to be a national trade show for the Movement. Just as automobile accessory manufacturers, or barge line operators, or discount store owners, or book publishing companies or oil companies have a convention, so too did the Movement. Just as every self-respecting widget manufacturer has to have a booth at the auto accessory show, so every self-respecting submovement of the supermovement came to Miami to display their wares and tout their candidate.

And the Failure and Guilt Complex did have a candidate, whether he knew it or not. The first phase of the McGovern candidacy involved capturing the Movement and its young, hard-working, collegiate shock troops—young men and women deeply concerned about peace, ecology, women, welfare, ZPG, racism, the new culture. In order to capture these dedicated young political workers, McGovern, in the first phase of his campaign felt that "my one unique position, with reference to the potential competition, is to be to the left of them all . . ."[1] As his strategist Rick Stearnes put it, "We would have to consolidate the left wing. . . ."[2]

McGovern captured the Movement by being "to the left of them all," by agreeing with some and seeming to be sympathetic to almost all Movement positions and, perhaps most important, by adopting so much of the shrill Movement rhetoric of failure. As late as September of 1972 McGovern told a reporter, "I have this feeling I'm working with a historical trend, history is going for me. This country is going to pieces."[3]

When the election was all over, McGovern's shrewd lieutenant Frank Mankiewicz looked back at the campaign for author Theodore White:

Mankiewicz reflected on what he considered the basic mistake of the campaign. Mankiewicz did not use the word "blackmail" but he expressed succinctly what he had learned. "We were always subject to this pressure from the cause people," said Mankiewicz. "We reacted to every threat from women or militants, or college groups. If I had to do it all over again, I'd learn when to tell them to go to hell."

And so, in July of 1972, the Movement came to Miami for its trade show in the flush of victory. The Peace Movement was there—"Stop bombing the dikes!" was their new rallying cry. The Welfare Rights group was there lobbying for a $6,500 welfare minimum—and a small army of black women chased Lawrence O'Brien out of one Democratic National Committee meeting. Women's Libbers were there demanding legalization of abortion. Gay libbers were there demanding legalization of homosexual marriage. Busing and amnesty planks were voted into the platform.

Long-haired mustached young men who were delegates denounced Richard J. Daley who was not. Young women who were delegates denounced congressmen, senators and governors who were not. And the rallying cry was: *Reorder priorities.*

It was good, exciting, theater—and the tens of millions of Americans who saw it on television enjoyed it as theater. As politics, however, it was catastrophic. For the Movement convention revealed to the American people with finality that it was George McGovern who was fronting for almost everyone they had come to disapprove of in the last five years. And the polls showed it. A Gallup survey taken immediately after the Democratic Convention revealed that George McGovern was running further behind Richard Nixon after the convention than before it. For the first time since the advent of American public opinion polling, the nominee of a major party had *lost ground* during the week of his greatest glory, his greatest accomplishment and his greatest exposure. Even in 1968, after the most bitter and bloody convention in recent American history, with blood literally flowing in the streets of Chicago, Hubert Humphrey had picked up 4 percentage points on Richard Nixon.

[1] Quoted in *The Making of the President, 1972*, p. 43, from the minutes of a July 1971 staff meeting.

[2] Ibid.

[3] Ibid.

But not in 1972. Cause People had identified their candidate to America and America made clear its feelings about the Cause People—which was negative. Having been tarred as the Movement's boy, McGovern spent four months trying to scrub the tar off, but to no avail:

Q. McGovern's ideas are impractical and too far out.

A. Agree completely   47% (!)
Agree partially   27%
Disagree   22%
Not sure   4%
(Yankelovich, October 1972)

Q. Do you consider McGovern a
Conservative   8%
Moderate   12%
Liberal   31%
Radical   31% (!)
Not sure   18%
(Yankelovich, October 1972)

Americans considered the Movement/McGovern view of America and said, in effect, "I see problems in America, too, but not the same ones nor in the same way as these people do." Americans decided that *mea culpa* was not their kind of a campaign slogan. And Senator McGovern became the only presidential candidate to give his acceptance speech at 3:00 A.M. and to concede in prime time.

Senator McGovern did not lose because he was an inept candidate; he was never an inept candidate in his other races nor is likely to be inept in any future ones. He is, in fact, a very able political man. McGovern lost because he became a symbol of a cause whose time had not come.

By election day, Americans understood, finally, the difference between "New Politcs" and traditional liberalism, a political movement which rarely loses elections by landslides. Traditional liberals—and many nonliberals too—say, "America is a great nation with great problems and the federal government can act to help solve those great problems." What the New Politics people said—picking up the intrinsic rhetoric of the F&GC, was something else: "America is a corrupt and sick nation teetering on the brink of failure, a nation that needs a domestic shock treatment." On November 8, 1972, Americans rejected that view. Not for the first time, his enemies helped to make Richard Nixon President of the United States.

As the 1972 election results were sifted and analyzed, as the 1973 off-year elections came and went, an important but little-noticed pattern of politics emerged. The New Politics disintegrated. And the old politics—economically oriented, hard-nosed, socially tough and programmatically activist—seemed again to be the wave of the future, not only for old politicians but for re-imaged new ones.

This transformation occurred for diverse reasons. To some large degree, as always, events were in the saddle. The American combat role in Vietnam ended. The draft ended, and with those terminations the morality-peace crusade also ended. As the professional peaceniks turned inward, the cutting edge of the New Politics blunted. A runaway food inflation in the mid-months of 1973 reminded politicians of the almighty power of the politics of the dollar. The Yom Kippur war in the Middle East reminded reorder-priorities ideologues that American military might still have a function, and the size of the defense budget no longer was issue number one for many New Politicos. The Arab oil boycott and the energy crisis took some wind out of the ecological windmills as Americans remembered that while a clean environment is good, materialism is also good, and sensible environmentalists and sensible materialists tried to figure out ways to have both. Of course, Watergate gave the Movement ideologues a new chance to explain how inherently corrupt is America, but with conservatives like Sam Ervin and John Sirica as the heroes and with traditional-liberal labor chief George Meany leading the fight for impeachment, it was somewhat less than a full measure of political pleasure for the New Pols.

But it was more than changing events that changed American politics. A changing awareness on the part of New Politicians moved them toward sometimes strange, new political turf. Senator Edward Kennedy thought it politically profitable to journey to Decatur, Alabama, on July 4, 1973, to say of formerly segregationist Governor George Wallace:

For if there is one thing George Wallace stands for, it is the right of every American to speak his mind and be heard—fearlessly and in any part of the country.

And Senator Walter F. Mondale, a leading Senate proponent of busing pre-1972, was seen and heard in this dialogue with columnist Robert Novak on "Meet the Press" in 1973:

MR. NOVAK: Let's try the question a different way from the specific. Senator McGovern was a strong advocate of forced racial busing in the school system. Are you?
SENATOR MONDALE: I have never been for busing as such. What I have been opposed to is a stand which would prevent the elimination of discrimination, which would deny the court the power it must have if it finds a discriminatory school district from taking steps to end it.
MR. NOVAK: You were known by some of your colleagues as "Mr. Busing" in the Senate. Do you think that is an unfair appellation; you are against busing now?
SENATOR MONDALE: I think you didn't hear my answer very well.
MR. NOVAK: I didn't understand it.

Even more interesting than what was being said about defense, inflation, energy and America's role in the world was what was *not* being said by those who are often America's most reliable weathervanes, the practicing pols. Where were the preachments for amnesty? Who went up front with a new plan for de-criminalizing marijuana? Who reminded his constituents that he had always believed busing to be one tool to help desegregate schools? Who was for political quotas? Who announced that law-and-order was a proto-fascist issue?

A rhetorical era had passed, and it had passed for an elemental reason. Politicians realized that the much heralded, much touted, much feared "new class"—the harbinger of New Politics—was a hoax. The idea that a new army of voters—well educated, well-to-do, white collared, often suburban, often young—would provide a nouveau-liberal tilt in a new era of American politics simply did not materialize in the voting booth. These new voters were indeed younger, more suburban, better educated, well-to-do and white collared but this Massive Majority Middle Class was not cast in the image of George McGovern. Nor of John

Editorial cartoon by Pat Oliphant; copyright, Washington Star. Reprinted with permission Los Angeles Times Syndicate.

"Anyone care to give again to Vietnam . . . ?"

Lindsay. Nor even of John Gardner. They were demographically new, but politically and attitudinally they were earthy "middle class," which has never been flamingly liberal in American political history. They were progressive, they wanted action from government, they accepted many halfway positions espoused by the New Pols and the Cause People, but they were not all-the-way or even most-of-the-way left ideological. Like most middle classniks all over the world, "stability" was high on their list of priorities. And when runaway inflation and long gas lines threatened that stability—they fumed. Insofar as they represented a "constituency for change," as pollster Louis Harris has called it, they wanted change *away* from crisscross school busing, *away*

from "soft" attitudes toward criminality, and change *toward* "values and morality." If the new class is so all-fired, change oriented why, as this book goes to press, are the polls showing that in the political pairing of Edward Kennedy versus Gerald Ford, the well-educated, well-to-do and white collarites tend toward Ford rather than Kennedy? And Kennedy aside, why are the well-to-do still more likely to vote Republican?

In fact, on most issues in American life today, there is relatively little differentiation of viewpoint when cross tabulations are run by region, occupation, income, age, sex and residence. Some issues, of course, do show important differences, and some patterns of minor gradations show up, but the general impression gained by scanning the standard Gallup list of thirty demographic cross tabulations shows general *similarity*, not wild *differentiation*.

And so, a funny thing happened as the New Politics disintegrated. The oft-mourned, oft-interred, oft-discussed "FDR coalition" showed that its vital signs were still strong.

Who won in the 1973 elections?

Nonpresidential-year elections are always difficult to assess and noncongressional odd-year elections are particularly difficult. A few governorships are up for grabs, a handful of mayoralties, some few state legislatures, and all these races are heavily influenced by local issues.

Still, look at some of the results:

In New York City, Abraham Beame, a sixty-seven-year-old regular Democrat beat off not one but two New Politics challengers (Herman Badillo and Albert Blumenthal) and was elected mayor with 57% of the vote in a *four*-man field, with no other candidate getting more than 16% of the vote. (The New York *Times* endorsed first Badillo, then Blumenthal.)

In New Jersey, a handsome Democratic judge named Brendan Byrne beat a New Politics candidate (Ann Klein) in the gubernatorial primary and won the election with a 68% majority. (The New York *Times* endorsed Ms. Klein.)

In Los Angeles, Tom Bradley, a black former police captain beat Mayor Sam Yorty, who had beaten him in 1969. This time Bradley didn't let anyone talk tougher than he about public safety. (The New York *Times* tut-tutted Bradley for his tough stance.)

In Minneapolis, Al Hofstede, a young man from the Hubert Humphrey wing of the Democratic-Farmer-Labor Party, turned out incumbent law-and-order Mayor Charles Stenvig.

In Virginia, Henry Howell, a self-styled "populist" with a tinge of New Politics coloration, dumped his earlier lukewarm pro-busing position and any other semblance of New Politicism— and came within .8% of beating former Governor Mills Godwin, who won by a whisker in a southern state allegedly now solidly Republican.

So who won? Surely, Democrats did well in the year of Watergate. But what kind of Democrats? With what kind of rhetoric? *Non-New Politics Democrats, with non-New Politics rhetoric.*

And there, again, was the FDR coalition, scourge of Republicans for three decades. The poor voted Democratic. The Jews voted Democratic. The ethnics voted Democratic. The big cities voted Democratic. The union members voted Democratic. The "working people," now well into the Massive Majority Middle Class, remembered that they were still working people even if they lived in suburbia, and worked at a desk, not a lathe—and voted Democratic. Of the old FDR coalition, only "the South" may prove to be out of reach for Democrats. But that will only be determined in 1976, and it will depend in large measure on who the Democrats nominate.

Galvanized anew by non-New Politics issues like inflation, recession and energy (as well as Watergate), the party of the little guy was on the march again.

And what of that vaunted great, growing, New Politics-oriented "constituency of change"? What of that "new class"?

The proper analogy comes from the near-final scene of *The Wizard of Oz*. Dorothy and her friends enter the great hall to see the Wizard and hear his powerful and echoing voice speaking mighty platitudes from behind a drape.

Awed, the visitors hang on the Wizard's every robust syllable. But Dorothy's dog beings tugging on the drape, and it falls. And there is the "Wizard"—an old faker speaking into an amplifying system. There was no Wizard. And when the drape was pulled aside, there wasn't much New Politics or new class either, just a fine amplification system.

Here, then, is the political progression:

Through 1972, Americans were by and large anti-anti-Establishment. They resented what they perceived to be the vehement New Politics attacks on America and the American way of life. The election of 1972 sounded the death knell of cultural politics.

But times are changing. Events are changing. People are changing. Politicians are changing. Inflation, recession, energy shortages, a dose of Watergate are turning many Americans into anti-Establishmentarians, or at least into anti-the-current-Administrationites. These switches are, by and large, based on economic judgments. Democrats generally win elections when they are phrased on economic rather than social or cultural grounds. This is generally understood now not only by "old liberals" (who knew it all along) but by most of the smarter "new politics liberals."

There is, then, a sense of coming together within the always-contentious Democratic Party. New politicos have sensed the dead end inherent in cultural politics. And old liberals are sensing that Americans have already made many synthesizing accommodations to the earlier social demands of the left. Cultural change *has* ensued; judgments have been made; and no one is looking to rub salt in any wounds. No one wants to call anyone radical. Within bounds, there is today the bare possibility of that favorite cliché of political writers: "a unified party."

There is only one danger. The new anti-Establishment sentiment should not be confused with the old. If some Democrats, feeling their oats from Watergate, think that Americans are now ready for what they rejected in 1972, that a campaign can be waged on the platform of "America Stinks," there will again be a risk of a sundered party and a Republican victory in 1976.[4]

[4] Democrats may also be legitimately nervous about a May 1974 Gallup poll showing that Americans who regard themselves as "Conservative" are at an all-time high—even though respondents also report all-time low levels of self-identification as "Republican." The mystery and the paradox of the 1974 congressional elections is this: How will voters respond to Conservative Republican candidates?

QUESTIONS FOR DISCUSSION

1. Discuss the current interest among students in journalism as a career. Has Watergate unfairly romanticized this profession?
2. Were some media persons out to "get" Richard M. Nixon? How fair has media coverage of the Ford administration been?
3. Would you support the idea of a "resident critic" for your college newspaper?
4. Is the New Politics Movement really dead?

5. How can we differentiate between the Movement and traditional liberalism?
6. At the present time, how do the political values and attitudes of younger people differ from those of persons over 30?
7. How effective have political interest groups such as Common Cause and the Nader organization been? Would you pay $15 for an annual membership?
8. Do enough people care about government to organize in the manner suggested by John Gardner?
9. Can the interests of either the radical left or radical right be accommodated within the framework of the Democratic and Republican parties?
10. Has government really become more open since Watergate?

Editorial cartoon by Pat Oliphant; copyright,
Washington Star. Reprinted with permission Los
Angeles Times Syndicate

chapter four

Congress

DECLINE OF CONSERVATISM

In ways unnoticed by many people, Congress has been moving away from the popular stereotype of passive conservatism. Reform has been occurring in an evolutionary manner since the late 1960s. While Congress has not emerged as a dramatically active, liberal body, there is considerable evidence to show that since Richard Nixon was elected president, Congress has been the most progressive of the three branches of government.

Conservative congressional power has declined as older, southern members have left office and big city representation has increased. Even before the 1974 assault on the seniority system, northern liberal Democrats were becoming chairmen of an increasing number of committees. During the Nixon years, the executive proposed little substantive legislation while Congress, relatively speaking, initiated a substantial number of major new programs.

Where the Nixon administration opposed continued and expanded federal programs in civil rights and education, it met costly defeat. Led by the Ervin and Rodino committees, the 93rd Congress (1973–1974) made history forcing Mr. Nixon's resignation. It also was the first Congress to use the 25th Amendment to fill a vacancy in the vice presidency. Mr. Ford's confirmation was followed by that of Nelson Rockefeller. In addition, its major achievements included enactment of the war powers bill, public financing of presidential campaigns, and budget reform.

Following Watergate, congressional elections gave the Democrats a 291 to 144 House majority. This included 75 freshmen who were unawed by the existing power structure and eager for reform. In 1975 when the Democratic Caucus voted 189 to 49 against aid to Cambodia, 68 new members of Congress voted with the majority. Even before the new session of Congress began, the House had forced Chairman Wilbur Mills to divide his Ways and Means Committee into four subcommittees with separate chairmen, thus weakening his power. By December 1974, Mills' adventures with stripper Fanne Foxe and his admitted alcoholism had forced the most powerful congressman to the sidelines.

Major reform came after the Democrats in the 94th Congress assigned the 24-member House Steering Committee the duty of nominating committee chairmen without relying mainly on seniority. The entire Democratic Caucus was given the right to vote on the Steering Committee's recommendations. As a result, three committee chairmen—Hebert (Armed Services), Poage (Agriculture), and Patman (Banking and Currency)—were deposed. Others, including Wayne L. Hays and George Mahon, were rejected by the Steering Committee, but survived close votes in the Democratic Caucus to retain their chairmanships. At the subcommittee level, several junior members have become chairmen. The Democrats also elected an aggressive liberal, Phillip Burton of California, chairman of the party caucus. With a full time staff and strong support from freshmen members, the caucus may be successful in taking power away from committee chairmen and from elected party leaders, including the Speaker.

On the Senate side, no committee chairmen have been deposed and the 10 new senators elected in 1974 have held to established chamber norms. Yet gradual change has been occurring because of a power shift within the Democratic party from southern conservatives to northern liberals. That liberals have gained control of the 19-member Steering Committee and have used their power to give the choicest committee assignments to other liberals is of particular significance.

After bitter debate, Senate liberals in 1975 succeeded in making it easier to choke off filibusters. Instead of requiring two-thirds of those present and voting, the new cloture rule requires the support of three-fifths of the total Senate membership to shut off debate. Even under the old rule, cloture was successfully invoked seven times in 1974.

Another agent for change has been consumer, environmental, and other special interest groups which began in the 1960s to rate members of congress by analyzing their voting records. In 1970 a group called Environmental Action began publishing a "dirty dozen" list of congress members who "are proven foes of the environment." In 1970, seven of the original "dirty dozen" were defeated; in 1972, four more, including the chairman of the House Interior Committee, were defeated; in 1974, eight were defeated in their bids for re-election. When Representative Edward Hebert (D., La.) was deposed as chairman of the House Armed Services Committee he blamed his defeat on a "vicious and reprehensible" campaign by Common Cause to depose him. John Gardner accepted this as a compliment. One congressional aide has noted, "In the last few years, we've seen more early retirements than ever before, mostly because the old guys who were used to doing business in private couldn't stand it in the open."

Along with procedural and strategic changes, Congress also has changed its focus from Watergate to the economy. Inflation, the energy crisis, and recession have dominated congressional deliberations since late 1974. Significantly, old pros Hubert Humphrey and Edmund Muskie have moved to the chairmanships of the Joint Economic Committee and the new Senate Budget Committee. Congress even opened a Geneva office to oversee international trade negotiations.

Leadership Vacuum

Columnist David Broder states that the entire thrust of reform efforts in the House has been to diffuse power as equally as possible among the new-comers and veterans. At the same time, the leaders in both houses—Speaker Carl Albert and Majority Leader Mike Mansfield—have an aversion to using power, and the president has taken steps to lessen executive power. Broder suggests that the American people have come to believe that strong leadership is bad leadership—the way to "keep the big boys honest" is to chop down their power. As a result we are faced with the problem of whether there is sufficient leverage left for anyone to lead; whether anyone can be said to be minding the store. Government appears bogged down with the president (and secretary of state) quick to place blame but unable to present creative policies.

After Lyndon Johnson left as Senate majority leader and House Speaker Sam Rayburn died, Congress seemed to welcome a retreat from aggressive leadership. Thus under Mike Mansfield and Carl Albert, Senate and House leadership has been characterized as *laissez faire*. While some have suggested that this period of weak leadership has bottomed out, there is a lack of clear evidence that Congress truly is beginning to reassert itself. Certainly, strong individual leadership has not yet emerged. Thus when President Ford in 1975 acted unilaterally to use American forces to rescue foreign nationals in Vietnam, Congress failed to act forthrightly to pro-scribe presidential war-making initiative. By its inaction and refusal even to provide *ex post facto* authorization for the Vietnam evacuation, Congress accepted another "inherent" presidential power.

Secrecy and Ethical Conduct

Congress long has been under fire for its secrecy and its failure to take action when its members are involved in unethical conduct. In the past few years both the House and Senate have moved to open committee meetings to the public. The House has changed its rule permitting nonrecorded "teller votes." Now, both votes in the House Committee of the Whole (where teller votes occurred) and at the committee "mark-up" stage are recorded and made a matter of public information.

In the area of ethical conduct, each chamber has a Select Committee on Standards and Conduct and conflict-of-interest statutes were revised in the early 1960s. All legislators are required to disclose sources of income from businesses engaged in "substantial" dealings with the federal government or under government regulation. Senators must report all lecture fees and honoraria in excess of $300. However, little action has been taken in recent years and Watergate has not spurred Congress to act beyond the new campaign finance bill to redefine conflict-of-interest or to enact disclosure statutes requiring members to make annual public reports on sources of outside income.

GUMS

Congress v. the President

In the spring of 1975, President Ford ordered the recapture of the merchant ship *Mayaguez* by force. A Marine contingent was ordered to an island off the Cambodian coast, and bombing raids on an airport and an oil depot on the Cambodian mainland were authorized.

The War Powers Act of 1973 calls upon the president to "consult" with Congress in "every possible instance" before ordering military action and to "report" to Congress within 48 hours when time does not allow consultation. The White House claimed that it did "notify" Congress within the specified time period. However, Senate Majority Leader Mike Mansfield said he was not informed. Regardless of the method of notification, the main goal of the War Powers Act was to make certain that presidential decisions involving the use of force would be subject to timely review by Congress. Impulsive presidential action was to be checked by a deliberate Congress. In the *Mayaguez* incident this did not happen.

With public opinion supporting the president's action, only a few congressmen were critical of the American military action. Coming shortly after the "loss" of South Vietnam, any show of strength in Southeast Asia was bound to have a positive effect on those tired of seeing Americans being "pushed around." Indeed, President Ford's popularity improved significantly following the safe return of the *Mayaguez* crew members.

Yet it was learned that the marines had landed first on the wrong island, casualties had been far heavier than initially reported, the biggest American non-nuclear weapon had been dropped on a patch of jungle, and a mainland Cambodian oil dump was attacked after the crew was released. In our outrage at being "pushed around" we forgot that we dropped 250,000 tons of bombs on Cambodia during the Vietnam War. Thinking basically in terms of power, the "realists" (led by Secretary of State Kissinger) won out over the "moralists" in determining American policy in Southeast Asia. Once again, Congress did not seriously challenge the military initiative of the president.

READINGS

In his article, political scientist John Johannes discusses executive-legislative relations during the Johnson, Nixon, and Ford administrations. In particular, he focuses upon Nixon's inability to deal effectively with Congress. Mr. Johannes suggests that the pendulum has swung to the side of Congress, but he is careful to note the existence of forces working against congressional dominance. Separation of powers (including executive privilege, impoundment, the budget, and war powers) has been a central issue in many of the post-Watergate reform proposals. It is noteworthy that Congress was very slow to assert itself and that these reforms are not likely to result in substantial limitations on the actual exercise of presidential power. Gary Orfield suggests that Congress has become increasingly progressive since the late 1960s. Orfield speculates that recent congressional "reform," for example, the election of committee chairpersons, may actually impede the progressive movement. In his two articles, Walter Pincus examines the proliferation of House and Senate subcommittees, with particular attention directed to their misuse of increasingly large sums of money.

From White House to Capitol Hill: How Far Will the Pendulum Swing?

John R. Johannes

Obscured by Watergate, *de facto* impeachment, and resignation, the more general state of presidential-Congressional relations during the Nixon Presidency has been tragically ignored. It was Pres. Nixon's inability to cooperate—or even to co-exist—with the Congress, and not his banishment from office, that reveals the condition of executive-legislative relations today and allows for speculation about the future. These relations are almost constantly in flux, although, most recently, the relative advantage has been held by the executive branch.

The record of Pres. Nixon's experience with the legislature, however, seems to indicate that the pendulum may be swinging—or may already have swung—back toward the Congress. How bad were the Nixon years in terms of presidential-Congressional interaction? What explains the apparent reversal of presidential dominance? How far can and will the pendulum swing? Finally, assuming that future occupants of the White House will heed the specific warnings of Watergate, will they learn the broader lessons of cooperation with Congress?

LEGISLATIVE-EXECUTIVE RELATIONS DURING THE NIXON YEARS

Impasse and tension characterized legislative-executive relations during the Nixon presidency, indicating that, as heir to the title "Chief Legislator," Richard Nixon failed. Compared to recent presidents, Nixon made very few requests of Congress. Yet, even on the basis of these modest demands, he recieved less from the legislature than any of his four predecessors.[1] Although Nixon secured some of his requests (such as the ABM system, the all-volunteer armed forces, a District of Columbia Crime Act, and general revenue sharing), he suffered serious notable reversals. These included defeats of his attempts to reorganize the executive branch, to reform the welfare system, to institute special revenue sharing, to develop the SST, to reduce and consolidate many domestic programs, and to enact energy legislation.

One mark of presidential power and compatibility with Congress is what *Congressional Quarterly* calls a "presidential support score"—the percentage of times a president's position on a Congressional roll call vote is upheld by Senators and Representatives. Nixon

From *Intellect*, March 18, 1975, pp. 356–360. Reprinted by permission.

[1] In his first five years, through 1973, Pres. Nixon made 882 specific legislative requests of Congress, an average of only 176 per year. The legislature gave him 300, for an over-all success score of 34%. These figures compare to Truman's 43% (73 requests annually, although *Congressional Quarterly* used a different scoring system then), Eisenhower's 52% success on an average of 195 annual requests, Kennedy's 39% of 351 requests per year, and Johnson's 57% success on an average of 380 proposals.

seldom took a position, but, when he did, he fared poorly. Congress upheld his position less frequently than it did those of Truman, Eisenhower, Kennedy, and Johnson.[2]

There were other indicators. Nixon met resistance in a number of attempts to secure senatorial confirmation of major appointments. Two Supreme Court nominees were rejected, and the Senate refused to confirm one Assistant Secretary of State, forced the withdrawal of several appointments, and delayed still others.

On his high-priority matter of government spending, Nixon lost more often than he won. On the one hand, his foreign and military aid recommendations were cut severely. On the other hand, although there were exceptions, Congress enacted domestic spending measures well in excess of what the Administration insisted was the maximum the country could afford. Frustrated, Nixon turned to impoundment and vetoes, only to have his withholding of appropriated monies reversed in some 25 of 30 court cases and to have Congress override five of his 40 vetoes—a record of veto futility unparalleled in the past 50 years. Pres. Ford, in turn, is finding that Congress is now flexing its muscles more often with its recent overriding of his vetoes.

Finally, Congress enacted, or came close to enacting, a number of measures designed to limit presidential powers. Laws were passed requiring senatorial confirmation of previously "untouchable" presidential assistants, such as the Director of the Office of Management and Budget and the head of the Council on International Economic Policy. Anti-impoundment legislation was enacted; Congress required that all executive agreements with foreign countries be sent to Congress—and seriously considered passing a bill calling for Senate ratification of such pacts; legislators ended the bombing in, and forbade the use of combat troops in and around, Southeast Asia; and, perhaps most significantly, Congress enacted the War Powers Act, limiting the President's authority to send troops abroad. These and similar measures, demonstrating a reassertion of Congressional prerogatives, constituted a frontal attack not only on Richard Nixon, but on presidential powers.

This litany of specifics, however, can not convey the sense of stress and frustration that marked legislative-executive relations during the late 1960's and early 1970's. To be sure, other presidents have alienated Congress but never in recent history has there been the degree of antipathy that was so noticeable on Capitol Hill whenever Pres. Nixon's name was mentioned. All of this happened to the supposedly "Imperial Presidency."

[2] The "support score" provides not only an indicator of presidential involvement and "courage" (*i.e.*, the frequency with which he chooses to take a stand), but also a measure of his "power." Risking little (he took a position on only 27% of the votes in 1973 and 10% in 1972, for example), Nixon fared poorly, with annual support scores of 74, 77, 75, 66, and 51%. The 74% for 1969 was the lowest for a first-year president since *Congressional Quarterly* began keeping score in 1953, and the 51% in 1973 hit an all-time bottom. Over-all, Nixon fared slightly worse than Eisenhower, and much worse than Kennedy and Johnson.

THE REASONS WHY

How to account for these goings-on constitutes a more complicated task than would appear at first glance. Do we blame the Nixon personality and style? Was it merely the Democratic Congress? Or are there longer-term forces at work which have set the stage for trouble between branches over and above that which is endemic to the constitutional system of separated institutions sharing powers? A balanced answer must take all these explanations into account.

The Legacy of Lyndon Johnson

Surely, the political environment of the late 1960's and early 1970's is responsible for much of the tension between the President and Congress, and much of that environment was the legacy of Nixon's predecessor. Lyndon Johnson bequeathed to Richard Nixon three crucial and interrelated problems. The first was Vietnam. Regardless of how Nixon chose to settle the mess in Southeast Asia, he was bound to meet resistance on Captiol Hill. More importantly, the very existence of the Vietnam problem meant that it would have to be his number-one priority, ineluctably displacing other matters and thereby creating doubts about Nixon's concern for problems many Congressmen saw as important. When the President chose to see Vietnam through to an "honorable" solution, despite the costs and frustration attached to such a strategy, the die was cast.

Johnson's second legacy was inflation, caused in no small measure by the expenses of the war and LBJ's reluctance to ask Congress for a tax to cover them until it was too late. Inflation created financial difficulties, forced the President into unpleasant alternatives, and further ate away at much of the popular support which new presidents have come to rely on and which this particular new president desperately needed to carry out his primary goals in foreign policy.

Third, Richard Nixon inherited a credibility gap, which he proceeded to widen further, depriving him of popular backing. That backing, had it existed, would have more favorably affected dispositions in Congress, much as it had during the 1950's in the case of the revered Eisenhower.

The foundation for Nixon's problems with Congress, therefore, had been set in place by his predecessor. There is a temptation to find significance in the linkage between one president and another—not just the spillover of issues, but something deeper, relating to the institution of the Presidency and its role in decision-making—for the choices leading to Vietnam, inflation, and credibility gap were peculiarly *presidential* decisions. They were decisions that emerged from an institution grown incredibly immense, important, and "imperial"—and one that had grown isolated as well, perceiving Congress as a roadblock to rational policy-making.

Democratic Preponderance

The politics of the last decade saw a continuation of Democratic preponderance in both the Congress and the nation at large. For a Republican president, conflict thus became unavoidable. Democratic dominance, of course, is a long-term factor, dating back to Franklin Roosevelt, but several relatively recent developments slightly altered the picture. First, voter identification with parties in general has decreased, and ticket-splitting has increased. Hardest hit by these phenomena have been the Republicans. When voters chose Nixon in 1968, they simultaneously backed Democrats for Congress. Despite—or, perhaps, because of—Nixon-Agnew efforts to the contrary, support for Democratic representatives and senators continued in 1970 and 1972. Second, although more conservative than their northern cousins, southern Democrats are becoming less so as Republicanism in the South provides a haven for many conservatives. Nixon's hopes for an ideological majority in 1970 and 1972 perished when the likes of Sen. Lloyd Bentsen (D.-Tex.) came to Washington. In short, today's Democratic majority in Congress may be far more "Democratic" than yesterday's. Third, the number and influence of *liberal* Democrats on Capitol Hill have grown over the past 15 years. Thus, although Eisenhower faced a Democratic Congress for six years, the nature of that Democratic majority and Eisenhower's popularity provided him with a measure of protection not available to Nixon and one that will not be available to Gerald Ford or other Republican presidents who face Democratic Congresses in the future. Furthermore, given the decrease in the voters' allegiance to Republicanism, and the obvious dangers for Republican candidates who too strongly associate themselves with the party label, there is built into Congress a new dynamic— Republicans may run risks by appearing to support a Republican president too loyally. They must, for their own survival, appear independent. The only exception would be if a tremendously popular Republican occupied the White House, but the likelihood of that seems minimal in these days of growing political cynicism and alienation.

THE INSTITUTIONAL FACTOR

Too great an emphasis on the political environment as an explanation of Nixon's problems, however, overlooks the institutional factor. The Presidency has become a monster of sorts. The causes are too numerous to list, but surely the enhanced position of the U.S. in international politics and the exaggerated domestic policy expectations of the populace carry most of the responsibility. Occupants of the White House develop an unreal view of their importance, and are inclined to deprecate "do-nothing" or "interfering" Congresses and to seek means of centralizing in the White House the decision-making that traditionally was spread out in departments and agencies. Accompanying this centralization of power has been the isolation of the president and the "swollen-head effect" of the man and his closest advisers. With decisions being made inside the Oval Office or in the offices of presidential assistants; with one strong president following upon another (Eisenhower excepted); with a president's flexibility increasingly constrained by his predecessor's actions; with presidents usurping Congressional powers; and with unpopular and often disastrous policies flowing from this process, it is no wonder that the institution of the Presidency lay exposed to attack—even before Watergate. As the noted constitutional scholar, Edward S. Corwin, pointed out two decades ago, presidential power follows a law of "ebb and flow"—sooner or later Congress gets even. To a large extent, Nixon happened upon the scene when the tide was going out. Or, to use another of the presidential metaphors, the president has only so much political capital in the bank. Nixon arrived just in time to see Lyndon Johnson make the last withdrawal.

The other institution in question is the Congress. Maligned by liberals during the Kennedy years for the "deadlock of democracy" it supposedly caused, roundly condemned by conservatives for its subservience as a "rubber stamp" to Johnson, and constantly criticized (erroneously) by everyone for never taking the initiative in policy-making, the national legislature had clearly had enough by the time Nixon was inaugurated. Leaving aside the question of party control, virtually all legislators experienced a change in attitudes by the end of the Johnson administration and the early part of Nixon's. Granted, Congress gave Johnson most of what he wanted (at least until 1967), but most of what he sought until 1967 he "borrowed" from lawmakers who had been pushing those same programs for years. At first, Johnson shared the glory, but he increasingly tended to seek the limelight for himself. Congressional politicians became jealous, and then mad.

The Rise of Liberal and Moderate Activists

Johnson's, and then Nixon's, practice of infringing on Congressional prerogatives, defying Congressional wishes, and ignoring and bypassing the legislature altogether in order to rule by fiat was too much to take. Simultaneously, the influx of activist Democrats in the 1960's set the stage for institutional reassertion and for internal change. Probably by 1968, and certainly by 1970, the balance of power within the Congressional Democratic Party had swung to the liberal and moderate activists.

These representatives felt that, *if* Congress really were to blame for not asserting itself on Vietnam and domestic policy, it was because the Congressional structure and processes created a disincentive to do so. There followed a series of moves that may prove vital in the future, especially the Reorganization Act of 1970 and the reformist actions of the House Democratic caucus in 1971 and 1973. These changes have democratized and decentralized power within Congress by weakening the power of committee chairmen, distributing authority to subcommittees, providing Congress with added staff and informational resources (further increased by the 1974 House reforms), and opening up the law-making process to the public.

THE BREAKDOWN OF INTERBRANCH COOPERATION

This combination of environmental and institutional developments presaged difficulties for whoever followed Lyndon Johnson into the Presidency. Were he a Republican, impasse was predictable. When it turned out that the president was Richard Nixon, interbranch warfare became certain.

Nixon's personality, style, and priorities inevitably led to discord with Congress. Withdrawn, shirking from face-to-face confrontations, and unsure of himself, Nixon chose to govern through a tightly organized staff system. Much of the tension with Congress was attributable to the increased centralization of power in the White House and in the presidential staff, effectively denying Congress access to decision-makers who were infinitely more important than cabinet members. Frequent informal use of executive privilege, although the administration claimed it formally invoked the doctrine less often than did previous presidents, made matters worse. However, what made a disaster of presidential-Congressional relations was Nixon's selection of men to staff this system—Haldeman, Ehrlichman, Kissinger, Zeigler, Flanigan, and Colson. Most members of the inner White House staff had little or no experience in dealing with Congress when they arrived in Washington.[3] When they tried to deal with legislators—which was seldom—they proved inept, and this ineptitude rapidly evolved into disdain and a superiority complex.

The President himself made few credible gestures toward Congress, and he failed to exude respect, or anything approaching it, for his elected peers. In one White House tape, Nixon referred to Congress as "irrelevant because they are so damned irresponsible." Others were more critical. When he could not get his way on proposals to consolidate categorical grant programs, he threatened, blustered, vetoed, and impounded. (On other matters, White House actions, at times, were more sinister.) Rather than take even leaders of his own party into his confidence, he opted for what one Senate Republican leader termed "government by surprise." Nixon's propensities for secrecy and control, his penchant for viewing adversaries as enemies, his insistence on perpetual "game plans" leading to

"victories," and, ultimately, his involvement in Watergate made unavoidable a Congressional revolt.

Normally, Congressmen feel themselves reasonably competent to act in cooperation with the President in domestic affairs while deferring to him on matters of foreign and defense policy. Yet, cooperation requires that a president look positively on domestic programs. Nixon's priorities, however, were in foreign policy. Congressional initiatives on domestic policy, when not opposed by the White House, were at least slighted. Frequently, the responsibility to deal with them was passed down to staffers who took seriously the President's view that the Kennedy-Johnson programs should be reduced or, like many Office of Economic Opportunities operations, dismantled despite demonstrable Congressional feeling to the contrary.

In short, Richard Nixon and his inner circle of advisers bear a good deal of the blame for the damage done to legislative-executive relations. The individual in the White House *does* matter, because of his priorities, his staff system and appointments, his style, and, most important, his personality.

THE SEEMING LACK OF CONGRESSIONAL INITIATIVE

Given Nixon's reticence to lead in domestic policy, and considering recent changes in Congress and in the electorate, what might strike observers as remarkable about the breakdown in interbranch cooperation is not that it occurred, but, rather, that the nation did not witness something akin to an attempt at Congressional government— particularly after the Watergate scandal

[3] Were its significance not so sad, one could chuckle over the (perhaps apocryphal) story about how former Congressman Clark MacGregor, when hired to take over Nixon's Congressional liaison operation, immediately passed out lapel buttons inscribed "I care about Congress" to the White House staff.

broke. Indeed, compared to the 1950's, when most of the New Frontier-Great Society program was conceived, proposed, and tested in Congress, there seemed to be relatively few successful Congressional policy initiatives. Why? Besides the obvious references to the size and power of the Presidency, there are other answers.

First, the lack of positive Congressional initiative is somewhat of an optical illusion. On the one hand, Congressional initiatives do not appear in a dramatic programmatic fashion resembling the president's annual shopping list presented in his State of the Union message. Congress does initiate, and Democrats did initiate during the Nixon years, but Congress does so episodically, quietly, and often tentatively. Bills were introduced, hearings held, and laws enacted, but they did not always grab the headlines. Much Congressional initiation is more properly policy incubation. On the other hand, in those policy areas that do attract attention (pollution, the economy, consumer protection), presidents retain institutional advantages. If need be, they can veto, or threaten a veto. More often, they can deny or impede Congress' access to executive policy-planners, at least at the highest levels. (Congressional subcommittees, of course, establish their own accommodations with lower-level officials in the executive branch.) More often still, when members of Congress propose popular new programs that are likely to pass, presidents incorporate those ideas into their own programs, endorse them in such a way as to take the credit, or offer counter-proposals in the name of "improving" or "making financially responsible" the legislators' initiatives. While devoting comparatively little attention to domestic affairs, Nixon used all of these tactics, with the resulting appearance that Congress did little except obstruct.

Second, to the extent that "Congressional government" really was absent, there may be good explanations. The most obvious is that Congress can not compete for leadership on a routine basis with the executive. Regular and coordinate leadership is impossible for two bodies of 535 "equals" divided up into five dozen standing, joint, and special committees and over 200 subcommittees. Indeed, leadership—except on specific items—probably *should not* be Congress' job. In the last analysis, Congress is primarily the arena for battling out political questions, and only secondarily a "back-up" to the better-prepared executive when it comes to legislative initiation.

Another reason for Congress' relative docility (if that it was) was that, compared to the 1950's and 1960's, there are fewer significant policy gaps to fill today, or, at least, those that need filling are less susceptible to definitive action than was the case in earlier years. Since many of the previously enacted solutions to problems of poverty, the environment, and social welfare have proved inadequate or even counterproductive, growing numbers of legislators have come to realize that policy gaps require longer and more sustained periods of policy gestation and incubation than did yesterday's "burning" problems. On many matters, that period of incubation *began* when Nixon took office, and some of those policies may be about ready to hatch. This sort of policy development gives the appearance of inaction.

A fourth explanation is that Congress, during the Nixon years, was too busy with other matters to assert itself forcefully and positively in new policy areas. A glance back at the points of contention between Nixon and Congress reveals a great deal about what the lawmakers were doing. Ending the Vietnamese war; defending Congressional prerogatives in foreign policy, budgeting, and spending; fighting over the continuation and generous funding (not initiation) of domestic programs; settling the Watergate affair—all these took up great amounts of time and effort. Two decades ago, Congress had little inclination or need to assert itself against presidential hegemony and to preserve programs it had passed previously (and had a hand in creating). Under Nixon, Congress was kept busy with such necessities and with much more. As mentioned earlier, Congress devoted considerable energy to "tooling up"—creating and expanding its resources and reforming its internal mechanisms and procedures, perhaps in preparation for an attempt at that elusive "Congressional government."

FORD AND THE CONGRESS—PROSPECTS

These observations have consequences for legislative-executive relations during the Ford Presidency. First, although the general tenor of relations between the branches will improve and much of the tension caused by the Nixon style should disappear, there will by no means be an extended honeymoon, let alone the "marriage" Ford asked for in his first address to the legislators. Packed with activist Democrats now in positions of power—having beaten one president, having improved its capabilities, and having asserted its prerogatives—Congress is more capable

of taking the offensive than at any other time in recent history.

Four factors, however, may inhibit any spectacular Congressional "blitz." One is the nature of the problems confronting the country. Not only are many of them related to the international arena (over which the U.S. has little control) and to shortages of raw materials, but the problems seem more complex. The law-makers are aware of this complexity. Second, the mounting political cynicism of the electorate is unlikely to furnish support for complicated new social and economic experiments. Third, the internal reforms enacted by Congress over the last five years will not automatically translate into policy initiatives or into a coordinated attempt to control the executive. Decentralizing power to subcommittees in the name of democratizing Congress may sound better than it actually is. Dividing authority and parceling out subcommittee chairmanships to more activist members undoubtedly makes possible more new ideas and policy initiatives. However, pulling them together, coordinating them across subcommittee and committee lines, enacting them, and supervising their implementation require some sort of centralizing authority. Given the weak condition of political parties, both on Capitol Hill and in the nation at large, what that authority will be remains unclear. What *is* clear is that, without such authority, Congress can not alter substantially the fragmented way in which it makes policy.

Finally, there remains the role of the President. Popular presidents are hard to buck. Pres. Ford's high popularity when he took office quickly dropped off, reflecting its shallowness—largely attributable to the way in which he became president, to the fact that he is a

Dave Simpson—Tulsa Tribune

"Sometimes we mule skinners have to give a little ground."

relatively unknown entity, and to his decision to pardon Nixon. Still, the Presidency retains immense resources and powers. To the extent that Ford is willing and able to use them, and to the degree that Ford's tight budget and fiscal conservatism strike a responsive chord among voters, legislators may find themselves in a bind. That bind typifies the dilemma facing Congressmen, especially activists. On the one hand, Congressmen like to be lawmakers. There is a positive incentive to introduce legislation and to push for its enactment, but Congressmen also like to be re-elected. If Ford can create a budget-cutting atmosphere—and he is in a far better position than his predecessor to do so—he can make Congress think twice about new programs. This dualistic nature of legislators (*i.e.*, legislate, but don't raise taxpayers' hackles)

is institutionalized in the Congressional separation of legislative committees that authorize programs from the more conservative appropriations and tax-raising committees. Perhaps the recent creation of the two multi-purpose congressional Budget Committees, along with a Congressional Budget Office to furnish expert staff assistance, is an attempt to solve this schizophrenia.

Congress today is in an interesting position—stronger than ever in absolute terms, faced with a president who constantly reminds everyone that at heart he still is a Congressman, and primed with activists seeking to solve problems. However, this does not mean an era of Congressional domination. At the least, it means that Congress' role as inventor and incubator of domestic policies will be enhanced, even if those policies are not immediately enacted. If Pres. Ford and the electorate say "no more spending," Congressmen will be wavering on the fence that separates solving problems via legislation from guarding the Treasury. Still, once the economic situation improves, and especially if a Democratic president succeeds Ford, the potential for dynamism is there.

Thanks both to the agonies of the Nixon years and to the longer-term forces discussed earlier, legislative-executive relations in the future will be more balanced. Congress will place greater restraints on the President in foreign affairs and—reversing the Kennedy complaint of the early 1960's— probably will take a more active role in domestic policy.

The pedulum has indeed swung back toward Congress, but it simply can not and should not go all the way. As Willmoore Kendall noted in 1960, the question is not which branch is more representative and which stands for what is best for the country. Rather, the question should be whether both branches—representing two ways of counting popular majorities and, thus, two slightly different versions of the good—can cooperate, one prodding and simultaneously restraining the other in a sort of dynamic tension. The prospects for such a relationship during the Ford years are better than they have ever been.

Would a Reformed Congress Be Progressive?

Gary Orfield

THE REFORM CRITIQUE

Most political scientists who have studied Congress belong to one of two major streams. The dominant group until the past generation were reformers, frequently focusing on themes similar to those first sounded in Woodrow Wilson's book. This tradition still has active and important spokesmen. More recently, however, most research on Congress has come out of the behaviorist movement. The preoccupation

From *Congressional Power: Congress and Social Change* by Gary Orfield, copyright © 1975 by Harcourt Brace Jovanovich, Inc. and reprinted with their permission.

of this group, which is committed to a more scientific study of politics through direct observation, survey techniques, mathematical analysis of roll call votes, and other statistical methods, is to find out how Congress really works. Whereas the older tradition emphasized the legislative process, the newer one focuses on explaining the underlying relationships and behavior of members of Congress through the application of a variety of social science concepts. While the adequacy of Congress as a central institution for the making of national policy was a basic preoccupation of the earlier students, it is usually ignored by the newer group, most of whom are committed to the role of value-free scientists describing processes rather than prescribing reforms. Since the Second World War we have been accumulating both a massive body of data on particular aspects of Congressional processes, and a series of general critiques showing little familiarity with the detailed studies. This book tries to provide more accurate and useful answers to important old questions through use of new data.

The growth of the Presidency and executive responsibilities during the Second World War, and the period of U.S. international leadership after the war, stirred deep concern about the effectiveness of Congress among political scientists still preoccupied with the traditional questions of institutional adequacy. During the war, political scientist Roland Young concluded that the President had taken "effective leadership of Congress." He alone had "the power and information necessary for formulating and co-ordinating a national policy."[1]

Congress itself was sufficiently worried to set up a joint committee on organization whose staff director, political scientist George Galloway, concluded that Congress had been in "gradual decline" for decades and was in danger of becoming a "mere ceremonial appendix to bureaucracy." During the period from the early 1900s through the war, Congress changed from a part-time assembly of a predominantly rural country isolated from world affairs and operating very few domestic social programs, to a full-time legislative body re-

sponsible for a vast array of social and economic legislation, serving an urban society with extremely heavy international responsibilities. Yet during this period Congress's major response had been simply to create more and more standing committees, with neither staff nor coordination. As they rushed from one endless subcommittee meeting to another, Congressmen, said Galloway, were "working with the tools and techniques of the snuffbox era."[2] His analysis of Congress would have sounded familiar to Wilson:

Its internal structure is dispersive and duplicating. It is a body without a head. Leadership is scattered among the chairmen of 81 little legislatures who compete with each other for jurisdiction and power. Its supervision of executive performance is superficial. Most of its time is consumed by petty local and private matters. . . . It lacks machinery for developing coherent legislative programs. . . . Its posts of power are held on the basis of political age, regardless of ability or agreement with party policies.[3]

The situation was serious enough to bring correction of some of the most obvious weaknesses in 1946. The number of committees was cut in half and, more important, staff resources were considerably improved. Although Congress ducked the hard issues of the seniority system, the lack of party leadership, Rules Committee power, the filibuster system, and others, the reforms that did pass strengthened it.

The critics weren't satisfied. The American Political Science Association issued major reports in this period call-

[1] Roland Young, *This is Congress* (New York: Knopf, 1943), pp. 38–39.

[2] George B. Galloway, *Congress at the Crossroads* (New York: Crowell, 1946), pp. v, 50–63.

[3] Ibid., p. 334.

ing for more centralized party leadership and strong organized majorities in Congress.[4] In *Congress on Trial*, James MacGregor Burns saw Congressmen as lobbyists for the "dominant economic enterprise" in their districts, responding to "the small but disciplined forces of the special interests." The President, he said, spoke for the "national interest."[5]

Later, in the 1960s, Burns's *Deadlock of Democracy* portrayed each party divided into two wings, a progressive Presidential wing and a conservative Congressional wing. The Presidential wing, he said, was responsible for nationally oriented innovation while the Congressional wing was the main obstacle to needed reforms.[6] In *Uncommon Sense*, published during the Nixon years, Burns said the central need was to "generate strong and steady political power" supporting basic social and economic change. He saw Congress as the "prime *institutional* reason for the lagging social progress of the 1950s and the upheavals of the 1960s."[7]

. . .

CHANGE WITHOUT REFORM

Ironically, while reformers were losing battle after battle, as the years passed Congress was somehow becoming less conservative. Although the structure

was the same, political and social changes altered the membership of each house, thus changing the policy impact of various rules and customs. When political scientists of the behaviorist school began to gather detailed information about the internal operation of Congress, it soon became evident that the reformers had oversimplified both their description of Congressional processes and the political meaning of various procedures.

Examined closely, for example, the description of the seniority system's inevitable magnification of the power of Southern reactionaries looked more like a comment about a particular set of political circumstances than an unchangeable rule. Recent critics of Southern power in the seniority system seldom noted the fact that liberal Democrats had long been the minority faction in a majority party traditionally dominated by Southern members. During 1947–56, for example, more than half the Democrats in each house were Southerners. During this same era the accumulation of Northern Democratic seniority was severely damaged by reverses in the 1946, 1950, and 1952 elections, each of which saw the loss of fifty of more House seats, almost all from the North. The political circumstances of the period were to be reflected in committee chairmanships in the 1960s, even as Southern strength in the Democratic Caucus was rapidly diminishing.[8]

Contrary to the argument of liberal critics that the seniority system is inherently conservative, the system is in reality inherently biased in favor of any fac-

[4] American Political Science Association, *The Organization of Congress* (1945); APSA, "Toward a More Responsible Two Party System," *American Political Science Review* XLIV (1950), Supplement.

[5] James MacGregor Burns, *Congress on Trial* (New York: Harper and Brothers, 1949), pp. 18–19, 31, 114.

[6] James MacGregor Burns, *The Deadlock of Democracy* (Englewood Cliffs, N. J.: Prentice-Hall, 1963).

[7] James MacGregor Burns, *Uncommon Sense* (New York: Harper & Row, 1972), pp. 114, 124.

[8] Barbara Hinckley, *The Seniority System in Congress* (Bloomington: Indiana University Press, 1971), p. 41; Congressional Quarterly, *Politics in America* (Washington: Congressional Quarterly, Inc., 1969), p. 121.

tion that had the most seats some years earlier and that wins reelection with little turnover. Until the mid-1960s, these circumstances worked clearly in favor of the South, but they no longer do.

From the mid-1950s to the early 1970s, political conditions became far more favorable to the accumulation of seniority power by moderates and liberals. Between the 1954 election and 1974, the Democratic majority in the House was never defeated. The two dramatic political tides of the period, in 1958 and 1964, swept liberals into Congress. The only substantial GOP gains, in 1966, were more a recovery from the Goldwater disaster than any significant threat to the steady growth of Northern seniority.

Even as Northerners were strengthening their position, Southerners were losing the easy comfort of certain reelection that they had once enjoyed. The Goldwater campaign and the GOP's aggressive "Southern strategy" of the following years brought real two-party competition into substantial portions of the South. In 1964 five of the eight Alabama Democratic Congressmen lost their seats and the first Republican Representatives since Reconstruction went to Washington from Georgia and Mississippi. South Carolina's Senator Strom Thurmond switched to the GOP. While growing numbers of historically "competitive" Eastern and Midwestern states were now consistently sending Democrats to Capitol Hill, things were changing in the South. By the end of 1972, for instance, GOP Senators had been elected from Texas, Florida, Tennessee, South Carolina, North Carolina, and Virginia. The Virginia House delegation had a Republican majority.

Intense ideological divisions among Democrats in some Southern states had effects similar to those produced by two-party competition. The political change in Virginia in 1966 provided a particularly drastic example of this. In 1965 Virginia conservative Democrats exercised vast power in Congress, holding the chairmanships of the Senate Finance Committee, the House Rules Committee, and the Senate Banking and Currency Committee. After the 1966 election all were gone as the Old Dominion lost a century of seniority. Senate Finance Chairman Harry Byrd resigned and his son barely fought off a tough primary challenge. Rules Committee Chairman "Judge" Howard Smith, longtime leader of Southern conservatives on the House floor, was defeated in a primary. Banking Committee Chairman Willis Robertson lost to a moderate contender, William Spong, who refused to join the Southern caucus after he was elected. In 1972 the conservative faction returned the favor by supporting Spong's extremely conservative GOP challenger, William Scott. Scott's victory again broke the cycle of seniority accumulation.

While much of the South has remained solidly Democratic in House elections, the Solid South is clearly shrinking and even the Southern Democratic Party is developing major ideological factions. The firm base of safe seats on which the South built its domination of Democratic Congresses is crumbling. An increasing number of Southerners are accumulating their seniority on the Republican side of the aisle, where it rarely counts for much.

The changes were particularly striking in the Senate, which had been described as a "Southern club" in William White's *Citadel*. Just prior to the 1958 election, there were only twenty-eight Democratic Senators from outside the states of the Old Confederacy. Most of them came from relatively conservative Border or Western states. In 1958 the Democrats gained seats in California, Connecticut, New Jersey, Maine, and such Midwestern states as Michigan, Ohio, and Minnesota. Fifteen new Democrats from the North and West tipped the numbers decisively against the Southern wing of the party. This was the precondition for future changes in the character of the Senate. Since it normally takes about a decade for a Senator to become a committee chairman, the key question was whether the Democratic seats won in the 1958 recession landslide could be held in 1964. The massive defeat of the Goldwater Presidential campaign helped consolidate the shift toward the left within the Senate Democratic delegation.

After a period of political circumstances favorable to liberals, the mere passage of time meant that the political consequences of the seniority system would become less conservative. The system did not become more democratic, but it did elevate growing numbers of progressives. Contrary to popular myth, there is significant turnover in committee chairmanships, and most chairmen do not see President after President come and go. The average chairman assumes his post at an advanced age and serves for less than seven years. This average, of course, masks wide variation, and the hardy senior citizens who dominate major committees for years are far better known than those who finally succeed to power after many years of apprenticeship, only to be cheated by political tides or the Grim Reaper.

Not only is the quantity of Southern seniority power diminishing, but the quality of Southern representation is undergoing some change as reapportionment reflects both the rapid urbanization of the South and the substantial migration of Northerners into the region. The changes have been particularly dramatic in Atlanta and Houston, where voters have elected the first Southern black Congressmen since Reconstruction. In Atlanta a very conservative GOP member, Fletcher Thompson, best known for his slashing assaults on federal civil rights programs, was replaced by Andrew Young, a leading figure in Martin Luther King's Southern Christian Leadership Conference. Although most young Southern Congressmen were still voting conservative in early 1972, those from the more urbanized districts have been more likely to support domestic social programs.[9] The 1973 voting records suggested that the new Southern Congressmen elected in 1972 were substantially closer to their Northern party colleagues than any earlier group of Dixie freshman members.

More importantly, Southern members of Congress are no longer either obsessed by or rigidly unified on the race question. Historically, the most dramatic impact of Southern power in Congress had been the insulation of Southern racial practices from federal power. The Southern stranglehold, enforced through Southern power on the House Rules Committee and the Senate Judiciary Committee, through the "conservative coalition" with Republicans, and through the Senate filibuster system, was finally broken in 1964. The 1964 Civil Rights Act ended segregation in public accommodations and greatly

[9] *Congressional Quarterly*, February 19, 1972, pp. 387–90; David R. Mayhew, *Party Loyalty among Congressmen* (Cambridge: Harvard University Press, 1966), pp. 81–87.

accelerated Southern school desegregation. With the passage of the 1965 Voting Rights Act, the change in Southern society was reinforced by a change in the politics of the Deep South, spurred by a rise in black registrations. When school desegregation was completed in much of the South, and politicians considered the reality of almost a million new black voters, some of the old equations of Southern politics changed.

V. O. Key's classic study, *Southern Politics*, showed that the heart of traditional Southern solidarity in both houses was unity on racial issues. In examining 598 roll call votes between 1933 and 1945, Key found only nine votes where at least 90 percent of the Southern Senators voted against majorities of Republicans and Northern Democrats. Seven of the votes concerned racial issues, most of them were against bills making lynching a federal offense. The others concerned school segregation and federal action against job discrimination. In the House seven out of eleven votes that isolated Southern Democrats during this period dealt with antilynching legislation and action against the poll tax, which restricted black voting.[10]

Changes in the South meant that there was less political benefit and more risk in playing racial politics. Once the issue of desegregation was decided and the law firmly settled, it became far more difficult to arouse hysterical fears of racial change or to credibly promise to stop it. Once substantial numbers of blacks were voting, there was a real incentive for candidates to find ways to appeal for black votes without losing white support. With the exception of

[10] V. O. Key, Jr., *Southern Politics* (New York: Vintage, 1949), pp. 349-52, 371-72.

the explosive busing issue, many Southern members now sought to avoid civil rights fights. Some Southern Senators even decided to vote for the 1970 bill extending the Voting Rights Act, and against the controversial Southern judges that Nixon futilely attempted to put on the Supreme Court.

There were, of course, crosscurrents in the South. If Democrats like Senators Ernest Hollings (S.C.) and Lawton Childs (Fla.) were moving toward the political center, the defeat of moderates in Tennessee, Texas, Virginia, and North Carolina in the 1970 and 1972 elections showed the continuing strength of the conservative tradition. The two new Southern Republican Senators sworn in in January 1973, Scott of Virginia and Helms of North Carolina, represented the far right wing of their party. While some Southern Democrats were espousing moderate positions, Southern Republicans seemed to be moving solidly into the Goldwater tradition. From the perspective of the seniority system, these complex changes meant that by 1973 almost a third of the Southern Senators were accumulating Republican seniority— power that would probably count for little, barring a major national political shift. This group included most of the intense conservatives. On the Democratic side, a number of the younger members were much closer to national party positions. Within the majority party, then, seniority was giving the South less power, and that power was less disruptive to realization of national party objectives.

The changing meaning of seniority was apparent first in the Senate, where fewer years of service are needed to attain power. Majority Leader Lyndon Johnson's rule giving new members important committee assignments intensified the impact of the liberal influx of 1958. By 1971 three of the liberals elected that year chaired committees. Others ran major subcommittees and were nationally known as sponsors of important legislation. In 1970 two Senators with only six and seven years of seniority, McGovern (D-S. Dak.) and Mondale (D-Minn.), became chairmen of widely publicized select committees on hunger and school desegregation.[11]

Less dramatic but important changes were underway in the House, where more seniority is required for chairmanships and few liberals had been named to some of the most important committees. By 1971 twelve of the twenty-one standing committees were chaired by non-Southerners, but Southerners still led the three most powerful—Ways and Means, Rules, and Appropriations.[12] By 1973 the South claimed only eight chairmanships and a liberal Northern member chaired the Rules Committee.[13] Almost two-thirds of the third, fourth, and fifth seniority rankings on the committees were held by non-Southerners, while the Southerners had their full share of the three lowest committee seniority ratings.[14] A considerable equalization of seniority power by region had taken place.

One interesting possibility was that the late 1970s might bring criticism of a different kind of overrepresentation through the seniority system. By 1974 the Rules and Judiciary Committees, two of the House's most important

bodies, were chaired by senior members from Gary, Indiana, and Newark, New Jersey. Five other House committees had big-city chairmen, and big-city members were second or third on the seniority ladder on such important committees as Appropriations, Ways and Means, Rules, Banking and Currency, Foreign Affairs, and others.[15] Although central cities are rapidly losing population, Congressional districts will not be reapportioned again until 1982, twelve years after the census on which the current districts are based. Not only will the big cities be overrepresented, but many of the city districts are safe seats where there is now no serious GOP opposition and seniority can easily be accumulated.

THE CHANGING ROLE OF THE HOUSE RULES COMMITTEE

Even as the political impact of seniority was changing, so too was the effect of the other major targets of Congressional reformers, the House Rules Committee and filibuster system. Since Speaker Sam Rayburn (D-Tex.) succeeded in expanding the Rules Committee in 1961, it has usually been reasonably responsive to the House Democratic leadership. While the filibuster system is still a formidable barrier to majority rule in the Senate, it is no longer an unassailable obstacle to civil rights legislation. Cloture has been achieved on a broad range of issues. On the other hand, liberals have had some success in turning the tables on conservatives by using filibusters to force delay and reconsideration of some popular conservative measures.

Close examination has shown that cri-

[11] *Congressional Directory*, 92d Cong., 1st Sess., 1971, pp. 235–37; 252–58.

[12] Ibid., pp. 268–76.

[13] *Congressional Directory*, 93d Cong., 1st Sess., 1973, pp. 286–306.

[14] Ibid.

[15] Ibid.

tics overestimated the power of the Rules Committee at its prime, and also that the 1961 enlargement of the committee made the group highly responsive to the House leadership in the great majority of cases. A relatively recent major study of the committee concluded that it was

by and large a body which cooperates relatively closely with the leadership and with the substantive committees which come before it requesting rules for their bills. Occasionally, perhaps two to five times a session, the Rules Committee acts in a fashion which others consider to be grossly unfair or arbitrary.[16]

One sign that the committee was not totally out of touch with the House majority was the rarity of efforts to force out legislation through discharge petitions. Even though the petitions are seen as threats to the established order of committee power, a legislative body with a truly disaffected majority should have produced more than one petition signed by most members in an average year. Between 1936 and 1960 the House passed only fourteen bills discharged from the Rules Committee, and only one major bill, the law setting minimum wages and maximum hours of work, finally became law.[17]

Sometimes when the Rules Committee takes the blame for killing a bill, it is actually responding to private urgings from the House leadership or House members who wish to avoid pressure to vote for a popular bill they privately think is bad. The Rules Committee can be a convenient scapegoat.

[16] Lewis A. Froman, Jr., *The Congressional Process* (Boston: Little, Brown, 1967), p. 53.

[17] James A. Robinson, *The House Rules Committee* (Indianapolis: Bobbs-Merrill, 1963), pp. 5–6.

During the 1950s the Rules Committee became a particularly serious obstacle to civil rights and education bills, issues near the top of the Democratic Party agenda. When President Kennedy came to office he succeeded in convincing Speaker Rayburn to exert his great influence in a hard but successful battle to expand the committee and break its conservative majority.

When the 1964 election produced a solid liberal majority impatient to enact legislation, a much more drastic limitation on the Rules Committee was rapidly adopted. The twenty-one-day rule gave any committee chairman the automatic right to bring a bill from his committee to the House floor after twenty-one days of Rules Committee delay, if the House majority approved. This rule forced six bills to the floor in 1965, including aid-to-education, job desegregation, and union organization measures.[18]

Although the twenty-one-day rule worked and did not interfere with orderly operation of the House, it was quickly repealed after the 1966 election destroyed the House's liberal majority. An effort to reinstate the rule in 1971 also failed. Apparently most House members favored more Rules Committee power.

The committee probably retained its power of taking arbitrary action on an occasional bill, because of its general skill in avoiding confrontations on issues where there was a strong majority for action. Even though the committee chairman passionately opposed the 1964 Civil Rights Act and the poverty program, for example, the committee allowed the House to act. On some rare occasions the committee supported a

[18] Froman, p. 98.

leadership strategy that resulted in action more progressive than most House members favored. When the committee sent the 1968 fair-housing bill to the floor, for example, the measure went with a rule to prevent weakening amendments that might well have been adopted on the House floor.

Contrary to the popular reform images of the Rules Committee as an omnipotent villain dictating to the House, the Rules Committee has great but limited power that is most effectively exercised on legislation of the second magnitude, or through tactical delay or procedural manipulation. Delay can be a very powerful tool. If a bill likely to provoke a subsequent Senate filibuster, for example, is held up for a good part of a year in the Rules panel, the chances of a successful filibuster increase. In the final days of a session, when there is a vast amount of work to do, timing becomes immensely important and the power to delay a measure is often the power to kill it.

The Rules Committee became more representative of the Democratic Party's majority faction when a Northern liberal finally became chairman in 1973. Neither of the two Southern members still on the committee was an old-school reactionary, and there were several liberal members. Southern spokesman Joe Waggonner (D-La.) was openly critical of the leadership's failure to consider any conservative Southerner for one of the three 1973 vacancies on the panel.[19]

The new membership of the committee dramatically changed its political function. After years of serving as a restraining influence on the House, the committee now sometimes found itself sending measures to the House floor

that the House was too conservative to enact. *Washington Post* writer Richard Lyons wrote in late 1973 that the committee "has now become such a liberal sieve it is regularly being overruled by a more conservative House."[20] During 1973 the committee was defeated on the House floor thirteen times, more than 1100 percent the average rate of defeats over the past four and a half decades. Among the issues on which the committee met defeat were an effort to roll back price levels, a major program of public service jobs for unemployed workers, an effort to require Congressional confirmation of the President's nominee for director of the powerful Office of Management and Budget, and several other initiatives.

The defeats and widespread criticism in the House helped produce a partial turnabout in early 1974, when the committee suddenly denied rules to major bills on land-use policy and urban mass transit. The actions were bitterly criticized. The *New York Times* attacked the committee as "subservient" and anti-city for holding up legislation badly needed by the New York City subway system. Representative Morris Udall (D-Ariz.), a leading supporter of the land-use measure, said that committee action on that bill reflected "immoral White House double-dealing."[21] Ironically, when the Rules Committee finally reversed itself and sent the land-use bill to the floor, House conservatives killed it, too.

In part, the actions resulted from the humiliations of the 1973 session. Repeated defeats were sapping the prestige of the committee and its ability to

[19] *Washington Post*, February 15, 1973.

[20] *Washington Post*, October 6, 1973.

[21] *Congressional Quarterly*, March 30, 1974, pp. 804–10; *New York Times*, March 7, 1974.

control the flow of House business. "Members made jokes about us," said Representative Spark Matsunaga (D-Hawaii). "The chairman got tired of hearing all those jokes. If there are going to be attempts to kill a bill by killing the rule, then we had better be more careful." Chairman Ray Madden (D-Ind.) said that now "when bills come along that look like they're going to be upset on the floor, we hold them up until some more work can be done on them."[22] Like the conservatives before them, the liberals on the Rules Committee were learning that successful exercise of the committee's power depended upon a skillful assessment of the temper of the House.

Table 1
Rules Defeated on House Floor

1961–62	0
1963–64	3
1965–66	1
1967–68	3
1969–70	1
1971–72	5
1973	13

Source: Congressional Quarterly, *March 30, 1974,* p. 808.

The Rules Committee did have somewhat greater success in its effort to initiate its own legislation. A 1973 Rules Committee resolution set in motion the most searching examination of the committee structure of the House since 1946, and the committee played a major role in the development of legislation to give Congress greater control over the budget and to limit the President's ability to impound money appropriated by

[22] *Congressional Quarterly,* March 30, 1974, p. 804.

Congress.[23] The much-maligned committee was actually showing reformist tendencies.

THE CHANGING IMPACT OF THE FILIBUSTER SYSTEM

Even if the seniority system and the Rules Committee no longer cast such a dismal conservative pall over the legislative process, reformers could still point to that classic antidemocratic device, the filibuster system. The Senate's self-congratulatory description of itself as the "world's greatest deliberative body" did little to obscure a record of decades of almost total paralysis in the face of open and brutal denial of basic rights to Southern blacks.

Until 1964 all twentieth-century attempts to enact significant civil rights legislation had been killed by filibusters. Decades of struggle to forbid even so intensely condemned an outrage as Southern lynchings proved futile, when Southerners repeatedly showed their willingness to bring the legislative process to a standstill.[24] Eleven times the Senate had voted on ending filibusters against measures to curb lynching, poll taxes, job discrimination, and unfair literacy tests for voter registration. Eleven times the two-thirds rule for ending debate had given the South a veto. Almost half of all filibusters had concerned racial issues, and Southerners were the leading defenders of the unlimited debate rule.[25]

[23] *Washington Post,* October 6, 1973.

[24] Franklin L. Burdette, *Filibustering in the Senate* (Princeton: Princeton University Press, 1940), pp. 133–37, 179–81, 191–99, 210.

[25] Congressional Quarterly, *Congress and the Nation,* Vol. 1, p. 1637.

It took an epic seventy-four-day battle for civil rights supporters to finally defeat Southern resistance, vote cloture, and enact the 1964 Civil Rights Act. Once the iron wall was broken and the basic framework of federal law had been established, filibusters were no longer so overpowering a barrier to legislation promoting racial change. The next year a sweeping federal Voting Rights Act passed the Senate after little more than a month of debate.[26] The change was even more evident in 1968, when the Senate surprised virtually all informed observers by breaking a filibuster against fair housing. In 1970 Southerners permitted extension of the controversial Voting Rights Act for another five years after only two weeks of debate, even though the President had called for weakening the law. Only when Senate Republicans joined the Southerners, as many did in the 1972 job discrimination filibuster, did the method of resistance still work.

During the Nixon years some surprising things began happening with regard to the filibuster system. Filibustering became a much more common tactic, even for issues of secondary importance, and liberals began to use the tool more frequently for their own ends. At the same time filibuster opponents succeeded far more frequently than in the past in cutting off debate, and fewer and fewer members had records of consistently supporting or opposing filibusters on philosophic grounds.

Faced with what they saw as a tidal wave of reactionary and ill-advised Presidential proposals during the Nixon Administration, liberals used both "extended debate" and full-fledged filibus-

ters on several occasions. Lengthy floor debate was very useful, for example, in building up national opposition to Mr. Nixon's controversial Supreme Court nominees, thus making possible their eventual defeat.[27]

In 1970 a brief filibuster led by Senator Proxmire (D-Wis.) played the key role in the environmentalists' battle to kill the supersonic transport. Proxmire's success in stopping a measure that would certainly have otherwise passed benefited from the fact that there were still a number of Senate conservatives opposed on principle to any limitation of debate. He picked up the votes of eleven Southern and Western members on this ground, even though they had earlier voted for the SST.[28] Increasing liberal use of the system soon eroded the number of its consistent supporters.

The filibuster is merely the ultimate extreme of a system of Senate procedure that gives great weight to strongly held views of any individual Senator. Since the Senate operates under an incredibly complex and inefficient set of formal rules, Senate leaders find it necessary to keep business moving by constantly negotiating unanimous consent agreements about the scheduling of proceedings and the limitation of debate. Any individual Senator who is prepared to incur the displeasure of his colleagues can make it extremely difficult for the Senate to operate effectively. When small groups of Senators feel strongly enough about anything to threaten a filibuster—particularly when

[26] Ibid., Vol. 2, pp. 360–61.

[27] Richard Harris's *Decision* (New York: Dutton, 1971) treats the Carswell nomination. The best coverage of the development of these historic struggles was by John McKenzie in the *Washington Post*.

[28] *New York Times*, December 20, 1970.

the Senate is under intense pressure for rapid handling of a wide variety of issues near the end of the session—their power is usually immense.

As the end of the 1970 session approached, Majority Leader Mike Mansfield (D-Mont.) noted that filibusters had been threatened on five major issues. "Senate rules," he said, "magnify the views strongly held by any single Member" and "project any one Senator into a position of particular predominance late in any Congressional session."[29] The leader could only appeal for restraint as tough-minded partisans, both liberals and conservatives, attempted to magnify their power over legislation through obstruction sufficient to kill a bill at this point in the session.

The 1970 logjam centered around the extremely important question of the President's power to wage war in Vietnam. One serious casualty of the stalemate was any chance for possible action on the President's welfare reform proposal, his most important domestic policy initiative. The measure had passed the House in April, but died without a vote on the Senate floor. Daniel Moynihan, a principal author of the welfare plan, describes its demise:

. . . a filibuster immediately broke out over a foreign aid supplemental authorization which was deemed by opponents of the Cambodian incursion to lend congressional sanction to it. Another filibuster was threatened by opponents of import quotas. Labor let it be known that . . . it would rather have no bill at all. In a terse statement . . . Mansfield told his colleagues they had made

a spectacle of themselves. There was nothing to do save wait until January and start again.[30]

When the new Congress came to Washington the next year, however, support for the reform was dissipated and the drive for enactment failed.

Although the filibuster system was reducing the Senate to helpless inaction on various occasions, there wasn't much interest in ending it. Shortly before he left office, Vice President Hubert Humphrey had tried to assist the chances for reform in early 1969 with a parliamentary ruling making it easier to change Senate rules. The Senate, however, reversed him. Two years later, in 1971, after a particularly bad year of filibustering, reformers waged a month-and-a-half fight over the rule but failed in four attempts to end the filibuster against closing debate on the change in the filibuster rule.[31]

An epic liberal filibuster against the draft law tied up the Senate for seven weeks in mid-1971 as antiwar Senators tried to force a rapid end to the Vietnam war. Debate was finally ended by a narrow margin of only three votes. This fight brought a major turning point in the filibuster system, as the philosophic positions of both its supporters and defenders were undermined by strong feelings about the issue. Nine Southern Senators who had consistently supported filibusters on the grounds of freedom of debate and protection of the rights of minorities in the Senate, now voted to "gag" the Senate. Suddenly

[29] *Congressional Record,* December 16, 1970 (perm. ed.), p. 41791.

[30] Daniel P. Moynihan, *The Politics of a Guaranteed Income* (New York: Vintage, 1973), p. 538.

[31] *Congressional Quarterly,* January 17, 1969, p. 138; *Congressional Record,* March 9, 1971, p. S2660.

the leaders of the anti-civil rights filibusters arrived at a new understanding of the system. On the other side, some traditional opponents of filibusters like Philip Hart (D-Mich.) now opposed cloture.[32] Yet another antiwar filibuster erupted after the conference committee deleted the Senate's end-the-war provision from the draft bill; as a result, the country was temporarily without a draft law as the war went on. After two months of debate the filibuster was broken by a single vote as the Southern Democrats voted two-to-one for cloture.[33]

One development lessening the political impact of the filibuster system in recent years has been the increasing success in obtaining the votes necessary to end debate. Since the cloture rule was first adopted in 1917, the Senate has shut off debate only seventeen times. Thirteen of these votes have come since 1960, and nine in the first four and a half years of the 1970s. During the 1970s, in other words, cloture votes have been coming thirteen times more frequenty than during the previous decades.

The dam burst with the breaking of major civil rights filibusters in 1964, 1965, 1968, and 1972. These successes permitted the enactment of the basic structure of civil rights law needed to dismantle the principal instruments of Southern discrimination, and to begin action against school and job discrimination in the North.

Liberals and moderates in the Senate have succeeded in cutting off debate on several less prominent issues. Cloture was voted for legislation providing public financing of Congressional campaigns and post-card voter registration across the country—measures intended to decrease the influence of wealthy contributors and increase the registration level of low-income voters. Debate was shut off on extending the controversial program of legal services lawyers to represent people otherwise unable to protect their rights through litigation. Conservative foreign policy filibusters against ratifying the 1972 arms limitation agreement with the Soviet Union, and against supporting the United Nations sanctions on trade with Rhodesia, were ended.

The changing perception of the system was strikingly evident in a Senate discussion of the filibuster system in late 1971. Senator Cranston (D-Calif.), a strong liberal, announced he had changed his position and would no longer vote for repeal of the filibuster rule.

I do not consider the filibuster horrendous; I think the draft and Vietnam are far worse. I look upon the filibuster as a means, not an end. When it can be used to good purpose, I support it and I shall use it as long as the rules of the Senate permit it.

Cranston now claimed that since 1969 "the procedure has since been used almost exclusively either in support of progressive measures or against legislation which was not in the best interests of the American people."[34]

Another liberal Vietnam War critic, Senator Frank Church (D-Idaho), agreed with Cranston's analysis. "Occa-

[32] *New York Times,* June 24, 1971; *Washington Post,* June 24, 1971.

[33] *Congressional Quarterly,* August 6, 1971, p. 1647; and September 25, 1971, p. 1973; *Washington Post,* July 19, 1971.

[34] *Congressional Record,* September 29, 1971, pp. S15266–67.

sionally," he said, "if the public interest is being too badly mauled, a determined minority in the Senate . . . can engage in a delaying action that often will force concessions and sometimes will even result in the rejection of the measure contested." Church thought that the success in killing the SST "boondoggle" and in substantially narrowing the Administration's proposed loan fund for bankrupt corporations, and the near success in ending the draft, made a "strong case" for keeping the rule.[35]

On several recent occasions liberal filibusters have also been defeated. In the 1960s a small band of liberals lost a battle for public ownership of the communications satellite business. Twice in the early 1970s they lost antidraft filibusters.[36]

While the impact of the filibuster system has changed, it has hardly become a great liberal tool. Most filibusters still succeed, and the filibuster system is still usually more useful to conservatives who want to prevent action than to liberals who want to force it. Between 1960 and early 1974, liberals and moderates failed to win cloture thirty times. Eight times the conservative filibusters defeated efforts supported by a majority of the Senate to end the filibuster rule. Filibusters weakened the civil rights legislation eventually enacted in 1960 and 1972, delayed action for several years against discriminatory literacy tests and housing, and prevented U.S. ratification of the United Nations genocide treaty. The tactic also frustrated the labor movement's intense drive against "right-to-work" laws, defeated a constitutional amendment for direct

election of the President, delayed the drive for federal financing of Congressional campaigns, and stalled the creation of a federal consumer protection agency.[37] Finally, in June 1974 it helped defeat a Senate drive for tax reform. Yet most of the time filibusters delayed rather than permanently defeated legislation enjoying broad liberal and moderate support.

Significant successful liberal filibusters were far less common. Filibusters did, however, help defend the Supreme Court's one-man, one-vote decision from a conservative attack, and helped kill the expensive SST project so hotly criticized by environmentalists. In 1972, civil rights supporters successfully employed a filibuster against a popular antibusing bill intended to drastically restrict the right of the courts to order urban school desegregation.[38] This filibuster frustrated a strong Presidential appeal for legislation that enjoyed majority support in the Senate, at the height of a national election campaign which had deeply stirred emotions on the issue.

Evaluating the full impact of the filibuster system involves, of course, much more than merely examining cloture votes. The fact that any measure may be filibustered is a constant constraint on policy-makers. It increases the disposition to compromise and greatly diminishes the likelihood of a hard battle to enact a measure that closely divides the Senate or deeply offends any significant group of Senators. In a number of cases informal filibusters or threats of filibusters succeed without any formal vote, and the matter is withdrawn. Extended debate, particularly

[35] Ibid., p. S15268.

[36] *Congressional Quarterly*, February 9, 1974, p. 317; March 9, 1974, p. 637.

[37] Ibid.

[38] Ibid.

when it is supported by the leadership who control legislative scheduling, can provide a great deal of time for developing an issue or changing national opinion. The tendency of the system toward compromise and deferral of tough divisive issues usually has a conservative impact on policy-making, while the ability to develop new issues and delay a vote until opinion changes has sometimes had a liberal or moderate impact in recent years.

Although the ideological impact of the filibuster system has become somewhat ambiguous in the early 1970s, the rule usually biases the legislative process against controversial liberal proposals requiring governmental action. Because President Nixon confronted liberals and moderates in the Senate with a variety of policy initiatives that they found worse than the status quo, this negative tool became a useful defensive measure. The system seems likely to reemerge as the leading target for critics of Congressional procedures, when a new liberal Administration next arrives in Washington.

The filibuster system is less important today chiefly because it no longer serves as the final invulnerable defense of Southern racism. Most of the old issues are gone, and most of the necessary legislation against legal segregation in the South is on the lawbooks. The filibuster rule stands, however, as a powerful barrier to the achievement of the next wave of basic social and economic reforms.

After encountering strong conservative filibusters against tax reform, public campaign financing, and consumer protection legislation, Senator Edward Kennedy (D-Mass.) concluded that this obstruction is already occurring. The Senate, he said, "is turning into rule by two-thirds." He claimed that "unless you have two-thirds, on an issue that really reaches at the important power bases of this country, you can't get a vote."[39]

ILLUSIONS ABOUT REFORM

Although critics of Congressional obstructionism continue to pour forth editorials, speeches, and columns that blame Congress's failure to solve the nation's problems on its arcane machinery and undemocratic rules, it is certainly not clear that the reforms they advocate would produce a more activist, progressive Congress. In some policy areas an end to the seniority system would replace a conservative committee chairman with a moderate, while in other cases an urban liberal might lose a position of strategic power. If the House Rules Committee was replaced by a newly constituted committee appointed by the Speaker and the GOP Leader, or newly elected by the party caucuses, the result would probably bring little change in the current policy decisions. Even the filibuster system is less of an unambiguous evil today in the view of progressives who have used it to block conservative measures. While the traditional obstacles often make Congress a tedious and stultifying place to work, particularly for young progressives on committees with very conservative chairmen, the belief that reform would free a progressive majority is an illusion fostered by those who believe in easy institutional solutions to basic political problems.

[39] *Washington Post*, July 1, 1974.

House of Ill Repute

Walter Pincus

Though it is over 190 years old, the House of Representatives today is suffering growing pains. A new House membership has forced a shift in staff structure, an increase in personnel and development of second echelon leadership that promise changes that go far beyond the highly publicized removal last month of two old committee chairmen. If organized properly, these reforms could help lead the House, lately in disrepute, back to a role in government coequal with the White House. That future however is far from certain. Blocking the way are the egos and personal ambitions of a few reformers, a handful of byzantine old-time Democratic chairmen and ranking Republican members, not to mention a Speaker, majority leader and minority leader who have trouble understanding and thus dealing rationally with change.

To understand the past House organization and what's now taking place, one must first know that unlike the Senate, where size of personal staffs is determined by state populations, each congressman has the same hiring allowance. It permits up to 16 employees at any one time so long as the total of annual salaries doesn't exceed $194,004. A quirk in the House rules apportions the money available in monthly installments, so if a member doesn't use up his allowance one month, he can't spend what's left over the next. Thus everyone in the House starts out even.

From *New Republic,* March 8, 1975, pp. 16–18. Reprinted by permission of *The New Republic,* © 1975, The New Republic, Inc.

Perhaps because there is this equality between congressional newcomer and veteran, it was almost inevitable that the committee staff system would be autocratic. Chairmen have ruled House committees jealously; power has almost never been shared; professional staffs have been kept small and subcommittees at a minimum. Thus the Education and Labor committee, with 122 employees, nine subcommittees and a one-year budget of $1.6 million, is a House giant. Yet it pales in comparison to the senate Judiciary Committee with its four million dollar budget, 17 subcommittees and 277 employees. At the other extreme was the powerful House Ways and Means Committee, which under Wilbur Mills had a $500,000 budget, a professional staff of 14 and clerical staff of 21—including two Mills chauffeurs—and responsibility for taxes, trade, health care and social security.

Aged tyrannical chairmen, entrenched by seniority, and small inevitably loyal staffs meant conservative, slow-moving committee operations prone to various sorts of corruption.

Last year, the administrative assistant in the office of Democratic Rep. Joe Evins of Tennessee, one William A. Keel, Jr., was paid a $36,000 salary by the House Select Committee on Small Business where he was listed as a "research analyst." Evins chairs the committee. In 1974, the House Public Works Committee carried James L. Oberstar as a $36,000 a year "administrator." In fact Oberstar ran the personal office of the

Editorial cartoon by Pat Oliphant; copyright, Washington Star. Reprinted with permission Los Angeles Times Syndicate.

The House examines the committee chairmen.

committee chairman, Minnesota Democrat John Blatnick. Oberstar ran it so well he succeeded his late boss in the last November's election and is now a congressman.

Two House rules were violated in these two cases. Standing committee staff members are not permitted to "engage in any work" or be "assigned any duties" outside the jurisdiction of the committee. Furthermore the maximum annual salary permitted a personal staff employee in 1974 was $33,710—less than that which could be paid a committee professional.

Abuses extend beyond individual staff members. The House Interstate and Foreign Commerce Committee in 1974 supported a $400,000-a-year investigative subcommittee that boasted a $36,000-a-year chief counsel, two

$32,750 staff assistants, two $31,000 staff attorneys, another $30,000 staff assistant, three more staff attorneys earning over $22,000 and four clerical assistants paid between $12,000 and $18,000 apiece. No subcommittee on Capitol Hill, House or Senate, boasted a pay scale approaching that special subcommittee on investigations chaired by Rep. Harley Staggers, who's also chairman of the Commerce Committee. Yet during the year, the Staggers investigative group turned out fewer than a dozen reports and held less than 30 days of hearings. The cost was so great and the performance so poor that the committee last month took the unprecedented step of replacing Staggers as leader of the investigations subcommittee.

The one man who has more to say than any other about House staffing is the redoubtable Rep. Wayne Hays of Ohio. As chairman of the House Administration Committee, Hays passes on the pay and expenses of all House committees. The story is often told of how Hays has used his power to satisfy his whims. When Rep. Donald Fraser ventured to oppose a Hays measure, for several weeks thereafter he couldn't get his pay vouchers approved.

A review of financial records of Hays' committee shows that the Ohioan is a bit looser with the pursestrings when he is the one doing the spending. In 1973–74, Hays' committee paid $2500 in consultant fees to E. Jean Walker. Mrs. Walker is the wife of John T. Walker, who at the time was Hays' chief counsel on the Administration Committee. Another Hays consultant over the past two years (at $1250 a month) is former Rep. Arnold Olsen—a Hays crony from the days when Olsen was chairman of the House Post Office and Civil Service Committee. A third Hays consultant during 1973, at $333.33 a month, was Ernest Petinaud, the former head waiter of the members' Capitol dining room. Also a pal of Hays, Petinaud gained some national recognition when it was discovered that Hays had taken him to Europe at government expense as part of a NATO parliamentarians' delegation.

Still another Hays consultant was writer Suzannah Lessard then also on the staff of the muckraking *Washington Monthly*. She was hired to rewrite, for $10,000, a history of the House, that originally had been compiled by the Library of Congress. According to Ms. Lessard, Hays said the research was brought up to date and redistributed every 10 years. He was not happy with the library version and wanted her to improve on it. She said she finished the work about two years ago, then found Hays' staff had lost one of her chapters and it had to be redone. For $1000 more she did that, and has not heard anything more since what became of the manuscript.

Hays is not the only chairman to call on consultants. The House Public Works Committee, among others, used them last year with apparent mixed results. One fellow, Max Taher, was an old friend of Chairman Blatnick and for his $1200 (or thereabouts) a month, did little for the committee outside helping redecorate its offices. Another consultant, Richard Royce, was a former staff member of the Senate Public Works Committee. Royce runs his own consulting firm in Miami. He commutes to Washington on committee assignments. One potential problem in the Royce relationship, however, is his interest in a corporation that does sewer work of the sort envisioned by legislation under study by the committee.

The ill repute in which the House has properly been held may have to be reconsidered if the new House takes advantage of its opportunities. As part of last year's House reforms, each committee was required to establish at least four subcommittees; the chairman and ranking member of each of them to get his own staff person. Once the bill had been approved, the House leadership should have started planning for the influx of new employees and the need to house them somewhere. There are 140 subcommittees so at least 280 new House staffers had to be expected. Where would they have their desks?

In typical House leadership fashion, the problem was treated with last-minute haste. In early February, the three members of the House Building Commission—Speaker Carl Albert, Majority Leader Thomas O'Neill and minority Leader John Rhodes—met with a House Appropriations subcommittee and asked urgent approval of $17 million to renovate and operate an office building several blocks from Capitol Hill. The building, being vacated by the FBI, had served as headquarters for its identification division and at one time housed 4000 employees. It was far too large for House needs, but it was, according to O'Neill, the only structure available. The $17 million was approved and eventually a passel of House offices including the House computer operation, party congressional campaign committees, and various other House services are expected to be moved out of the three House office buildings thereby releasing space for the new subcommittee staffs.

Lack of leadership planning in housekeeping and legislative matters may be the result of inadequate leadership staffs. Albert and O'Neill particularly have neglected to set up any substantive policy staffs of their own. Between them they have some $500,000 a year for hiring. Democratic House whip John McFall is allocated an additional $200,000 of which some $44,225 is spent by the chief deputy whip, Rep. John Brademas. Out of his funds, Albert pays for his Speaker's office, and O'Neill, while picking up the salaries of his own top assistants, also last year used part of his budget to pay key members of the Democratic Study Group.

A fourth leadership fund, $150,000 earmarked for the House Democratic Steering Committee (scheduled to go up to $227,520 next year) is more difficult to trace. There is a House Democratic Steering Committee that works for Speaker Albert, but it only has a staff of four and an outlay of some $92,000 a year.

The Republican leadership has funds comparable, though smaller than the Democratic majority. At the steering committee level, however, the House Republican Conference receives $148,710, plus an additional $212,115 for minority employees. With its funds, the Republicans have put together a staff that serves their House party caucus—a step the Democrats have yet to take. Since the caucuses are becoming more active, it's likely that Democratic Caucus leader Phil Burton will want funds for his operation.

Both parties, but particularly the Democratic leadership, ought to start planning and organizing the new House committee operations. They'll have some $20 million more in the coming year to pay salaries. Will the only change from the past be that more individual chairmen now can go off on their own—like a few did in the past? Or will action on the popular issues of energy and economy, be coordinated so the same witnesses are not asked the same questions before different committees. The House has to demonstrate that it will spend the new money for purposes other than self aggrandizement or featherbedding.

The Scandalous Senate

Walter Pincus

With winds of reform blowing over Capitol Hill, the Senate really ought to deal with one of Washington's biggest open secrets—the scandalous and hypocritical way in which it spends taxpayers' money on its own staff aides and committee operations. In the past five years, as the prestige and power of the Congress were on the decline, the cost and the size of Senate staffs nearly doubled. The bill was $10 million in fiscal 1971 and will be above $20 million in fiscal '76.

What do we get for the money? It's hard to say, since nobody investigates the Senate; and the Senate is incapable or unwilling to police itself. There are, however, some reports and payroll records from which to isolate abuses in the 15 standing committees and over 100 subcommittees.

Not too many people have ever heard of the subcommittee on improvements in judicial machinery of the Senate Judiciary Committee. It handles complex judicial branch legislation such as the current bill to create new judgeships. Under Chairman Quentin Burdick, the subcommittee in the past two years has undertaken a slow but careful review of the judicial system, starting with the local magistrates, proceeding to the district courts and ending with a soon-to-be completed study of the appeals courts. To do this job the subcommittee has on its payroll 12 persons

From *The New Republic*, February 22, 1975, pp. 16-19. Reprinted by permission of *The New Republic* © 1975, The New Republic, Inc.

and annually spends some $200,000. One listed staff member paid at an annual salary (in '73 and '74) of $20,000 was Roy M. Ogburn. While on the subcommittee staff Ogburn spent most of his time in Harrisburg, Pennsylvania as manager of Sen. Hugh Scott's office there. He evidently was available for consultation on subcommittee business, though most of Scott's committee work—he's the second-ranking Republican on the Judiciary subcommittee—was done by members of Scott's Washington office staff.

In April 1974 Obgurn left the Senate's employ to run unsuccessfully in a Pennsylvania Republican state primary race. He was replaced on the subcommittee staff by Edward K. Hamberger, who then and now goes to Georgetown Law School at night. Hamberger, who today works out of Scott's Capitol Hill office, is the brother of Scott's administrative assistant. Though not yet a lawyer, he gets the same $20,000 salary that previously went to Ogburn and he says he follows (for Scott) the actions of "the Judiciary committee as a whole rather than just the subcommittee."

Two other judiciary machinery minority staff members devote most if not all their time to matters other than subcommittee business. Lois J. Kovanda, ostensibly a $13,000-a-year minority clerk, works full-time in Scott's office, where she sometimes acts as the senator's appointments secretary. D. Eric Hultman, listed as a legislative counsel for the subcommittee, works primarily as a legislative assistant to Sen. Roman Hruska, ranking Republican member of the committee.

The use of subcommittee and committee employees to suplement a senator's personal staff is widespread. It goes on despite a Senate rule specifically stating that "professional staff members shall not engage in any work other than committee business and no other duties may be assigned to them." Some senators say that the rule applies only to staff members of the 15 standing *committees*—and not to *subcommittee* workers. In any case the practice is followed in both committees and subcommittees. Sen. James Eastland, chairman of the Judiciary Committee, has his own legislative assistant, William Simpson, on the committee payroll as the $34,770-per-year assistant chief clerk. Sen. Vance Hartke uses the Veterans Affairs Committee, which he chairs, to pay the $30,000 salary of his own special assistant, Dwight Jensen. The legislative assistant for Sen. Thomas Eagleton, who handled the back-up work on the Turkish military aid cutoff amendment, was J. Brian Atwood, who is paid $26,900 a year as a professional staff member of Eagleton's Committee on the District of Columbia.

What makes senators engage in such subterfuge? For some it is the simple desire to hand out patronage jobs that pay well but require little work. For the majority it seems to be a perceived need for personnel to deal with increasing constituent requests: senators and representatives have become ombudsmen over the federal bureaucracy. And for an ambitious few, more staff means publicity and the potential to be more active on a wide range of national issues.

It is in the proliferating subcommit-tees that the use of payrolls to support Senate office employees has been most flagrant. Sen. Eastland's Judiciary Committee has ballooned the most. Last year its total payroll, including 17 subcommittees, supported 227 persons at a cost of slightly more than four million dollars. It is no surprise that a good number of these people end up working primarily for individual senators. Sen. Edward Kennedy used in his own office seven of 22 staff members of the administrative practices and procedures subcommittee he chairs. At times the subcommittee jobs serve as a temporary way station until jobs became vacant on Kennedy's own payroll. In 1973, for example, Paul G. Kirk, Jr., Kennedy's top political aide, was on the subcommittee payroll as a $32,500 a year "research assistant." He then moved on to the Kennedy staff. Shortly thereafter Robert Edwards Hunter, Kennedy's newly recruited foreign policy specialist, went on the administrative practices payroll as a "special assistant" at $33,000 a year. He, too, later moved on.

Judiciary Chairman Eastland sometimes shifts his own aides from one subcommittee payroll to another. Clarence Pierce was listed as a $24,000-a-year investigator with the internal security subcommittee until June last year when he became an investigator for the subcommittee on immigration and naturalization. On the latter subcommittee payroll, Eastland already had another of his office staffers, Frank D. Barber, paid as a $24,000-a-year "legal assistant." The immigration subcommittee had, until last month, held no hearings for several years. Another of its subcommittee employees, Hermina Morita, listed as an $8400 a year clerk, has been Sen. Hiram Fong's office receptionist.

Even some of the smaller Judiciary subcommittees provide personnel. Vivian Ronca, the sole minority staff member of the tiny subcommittee on revision and codification at $12,000 a year, is a case worker in Sen. Scott's office.

The practice extends to both the upper and lower levels of the subcommittees. Sen. Jacob Javits last year used the payroll of a Government Operations subcommittee on reorganization to provide the $31,000 salary of his legislative aide, Charles Warren. A subcommittee on veterans' affairs supported three members of Sen. Clifford Hansen's staff: his $15,000 legislative aide, Mike Shoumaker; another $13,000 legislative aide, Sunny Nixon; and an $8500 clerk, Mary Keogh.

Along with payroll chicanery the Senate also must soon own up to its practices of keeping alive subcommittees whose functions have long since atrophied. A prime example is the $400,000-a-year Senate Judiciary internal security subcommittee. Established originally in the 1950s during the Joe McCarthy days, this relic of the Cold War has been plodding along with an aging staff and almost no visible output of work. Two years ago it held only eight hearings. Then, spurred by some criticism, it last year did a comprehensive study of marijuana—hardly relevant to internal security, its prime jurisdiction. When last spring the Senate Rules and Administration Committee, through Sen. Mark Hatfield, asked about the subcommittee, its 66-year-old, $36,000 a year chief counsel, Jay Sourwine, was called into an executive hearing. Sourwine, who has held his job for nearly 18 years, rambled on about the subcommittee's job and his own travels around the country to speak to unpaid informers and local police who aid in keeping up internal security's files. Many of the 23 individuals on the subcommittee have, like Sourwine, served for years—people such as Dorothy Baker, wife of former aide Bobby Baker (remember Bobby Baker?), and David Martin, who was the late Sen. Thomas Dodd's man handling the Communist menace. In recent years the internal security subcommittee has been moved to the Senate Office Building basement and the Rules Committee is expected shortly to deny it any funds to continue operation. Perhaps in a last ditch effort to stay alive, the subcommittee held a 10-minute hearing on February 10. Its chief investigator was the witness and he told Sourwine and subcommittee member J. Strom Thurmond, who presided, that "the Weatherman underground organization I feel is responsible for the bombing at the State Department." At that pitiful session the committee released a 136-page report on "The Weather Underground."

Internal security, however, is far from the only subcommittee whose moment has passed. The Judiciary Committee's juvenile delinquency subcommittee has hung on despite the current absence of interest in deliquency. A *Washington Post* survey of Senate expenditures found that 62 percent of the travel vouchers of that subcommittee went for trips to Indiana, the home state of its chairman, Sen. Birch Bayh, who was up for reelection in 1974.

Sen. Henry Jackson performed a neat but questionable trick in his subcommittee and staff shifting. Jackson for years used a Government Operations subcommittee as the base for his foreign policy expert, Dorothy Fosdick. When Jackson took over the permanent investigating subcommittee—historically the

Senate's principal investigative group—he merged his foreign policy staff into it. Thus, today, Fosdick, a specialist in international relations, and Richard Perle, Jackson's defense and arms control adviser, are both on the investigating subcommittee—Fosdick as the $35,000-a-year "professional staff director" and Perle as a $30,000-a-year staff member. The rest of the subcommittee continues its old investigative functions, looking into stolen securities, the Russian grain deal and energy matters.

The *Washington Post* survey found, furthermore, that senators make extensive use of their committee and subcommittee positions to run for reelection—and for the presidency. The *Post* found that 85.1 percent of all field hearings held in 1973 and 1974 were in the home states of members of those committees. Two of three hearings of Sen. George McGovern's Select Committee on Nutrition were held in South Dakota—where McGovern was facing a tough reelection campaign. Sen. Warren Magnuson's Commerce Committee showed a slightly different but equally advantageous use of committee funds. Magnuson was up for reelection in 1974. Frederick Lardan, staff director of the committee and a long-time political aide of Magnuson flew to Seattle on December 23, 1973 and remained in Washington state for 25 days, charging the committee $25 a day in expenses. In late January and early February, five more members of the Commerce staff, plus Magnuson himself, flew out to Seattle with the committee picking up the $2500 in round trip plane fares.

Not all committees have been expanded and used the way Judiciary has. Under Sen. J. W. Fulbright, the Foreign Relations Committee followed the prac-tice of keeping a relatively small staff serving both minority and majority members of the committee. Three years ago, Sen. Scott, joined by Sen. Robert Griffin and backed by the Nixon White House, began to press for a separate minority staff. Two years ago one staff member was designated for the minority and, after further pressure, Scott succeeded in getting another position opened up. His basic argument was that Republican committee members needed their own qualified staff representative to meet Republican needs.

Recently Scott selected his Foreign Relations Committee minority staff member. The man he chose, Robert Barton, turns out to have been Scott's next-door neighbor who was nearing the end of a not very illustrious career in the United States Information Agency. Despite his early demand that the minority needed a top-notch professional, Scott, when he got the opportunity, treated the opening as a simple patronage position.

Other Senate committees have taken different courses. For years Chairman Russell Long of the Senate Finance Committee kept a tight rein on his small committee staff and prohibitied other senators from bringing their own personal assistants to meetings when tax measures were being drafted and voted upon. In this way Long, having the only staff present, dominated the sessions.

Recently Long promised to change his ways. He has offered each committee member the chance to hire his own staff assistant who will be permitted to attend all committee meetings. Why the change of heart? The answer seems to be a Senate resolution introduced February 4 by Sen. Mike Gravel that would authorize additional funds for each senator in amounts directly related to committee and subcommittee memberships. Most senators could hire two or more additional employees for their own staffs, provided they handle only committee business. Despite the total cost of the Gravel proposal—it could run as high as $15 million—the Alaska senator already has 57 co-sponsors.

Not all senators want to increase staffs, but if that is what's to happen, at least the Gravel resolution guarantees it will be done openly. The Senate Rules Committee's public hearings this month on committee budgets, and sessions on the Gravel resolution, would be an opportunity for such openness. Perhaps Sen. Scott, a member of Rules, would like to talk about his own past staff practices. Like the old campaign statutes, the current Senate rules on staff are more loophole than law. Those rules should be enforced or changed.

Since I have twice worked on Senate Foreign Relations subcommittees, a personal note may be appropriate here. There is no practical way for Congress to keep up with the ever-expanding executive branch. Larger staff allocations might as easily make the Senate less, rather than more, effective as an equal branch of government. It already is difficult for active senators to stay in touch with their employees, and growth would only compound that problem. Committees should operate as committees—and not as personal vehicles for the chairmen. If that were to happen it would end the need for minority staffs, which frequently are just political leaf-raking. Fewer rather than more subcommittees—each with specific purposes and limited life spans—could help make the Senate a leaner but more effective branch of government.

QUESTIONS FOR DISCUSSION

1. What evidence has there been of congressional legislative initiative since Gerald Ford became president?
2. As "progressive" bodies, how do the Supreme Court and Congress compare since 1968?
3. Do we have good reason to fear anarchy in Congress?
4. Should members of Congress be required to file comprehensive annual reports on all their outside income?
5. Can the filibuster be defended "on principle"? How much of a breakthrough have Senate liberals achieved on the filibuster rule change?
6. Should the terms of representatives be extended to four years?
7. Compared to 1900, do current members of Congress possess higher or lower ability as legislators and more or less trustworthiness?
8. How do you evaluate the performances of the Senate Watergate Committee and House Judiciary Committee concerning the impeachment of Richard Nixon?
9. President Ford and Secretary of State Kissinger want Congress to stop interfering in foreign policy-making. Are there dangers here if the pendulum swings too far in the direction of Congress?
10. Should all members of Congress be prohibited from hiring close relatives to work on their staffs or for committees?

"Lately I've Been Getting This Sort-Of Double Image"

chapter five

The President and Vice President

THE NIXON IMPEACHMENT PROCEEDINGS—A LOSS OF TRUST

During the impeachment proceedings, Mr. Nixon's attorney, James St. Clair, argued that the only constitutional grounds for impeachment would be to find the president guilty of an indictable crime, that is, an act for which he could be prosecuted in a normal criminal proceeding. Certainly there was substantial evidence to suggest that Mr. Nixon participated in the same criminal activities for which his top aides later were indicted and convicted—ordering burglaries, obstructing justice, committing tax fraud, accepting bribes for choice ambassadorships. Yet, in large part, Richard Nixon was forced from office not because of specific criminal acts, but because the American people no longer trusted him.

The most damaging blows to Nixon were struck by conservative newspapers such as the *Chicago Tribune,* the *Omaha World-Herald*, and the Hearst papers and by conservative congressmen such as Senate Minority Leader Hugh Scott and House Minority Leader John Rhodes. They all concluded from the White House transcripts that the president's most basic goal had been the preservation of Richard Nixon. Senator Scott characterized the tapes as "deplorable, shabby, disgusting, immoral." The *Chicago Tribune* saw Nixon as having "a lack of concern for morality, a lack of concern for high principles." While the evidence at the time of the impeachment inquiry by the House Judiciary Committee was not conclusive to all members regarding "high crimes and misdemeanors," there was evidence of low morality and in the court of public opinion this was conclusive.

GERALD FORD AND THE "IMPERIAL PRESIDENCY"

For obvious reasons, much of what Gerald Ford has done as president has been an attempt to contrast himself with Mr. Nixon. Ford has made frequent references to engaging in "straight talk" with the American people. His relations with the press have been cordial, and he has attempted to work in a spirit of compromise and conciliation with a Democratic-controlled Congress. While Ford's unconditional pardon of Richard Nixon was widely criticized, it has allowed the nation's attention to be redirected to more pressing economic and social problems rather than continuing to focus on the latest Nixon countermoves in fighting the government's case against him.

President Ford has moved to combat the concept of the "imperial presidency" in a variety of ways. For example, he has yielded to Congress and withdrawn nominations that previous stronger presidents would have stood by. Ford moved rather slowly in changing the cabinet he inherited from Nixon. However, as holdovers were shifted to other positions outside the cabinet, Ford significantly upgraded the quality of individuals serving as cabinet secretaries. Regarding the White House staff, Ford has brought in many former congressional colleagues (in contrast to the advertising men without previous political experience who served in the Nixon Administration). No one person acts as "Chief of Staff," in the manner of H. R. Haldeman, and it is hard to tell which adviser is on top or who has the best access to the president on any particular issue. The Nixon "Palace Guard" has disappeared and the president is less isolated than in the past. Mr. Ford appears to be open to more diverse opinions than any president since John F. Kennedy.

Events since 1973 clearly have weakened the presidency. Ford and Rockefeller are in office only because an elected president and vice president were driven from power after committing criminal misconduct. Ford does not have a democratic mandate and his party was repudiated in the 1974 congressional elections.. Even within his own party, President Ford appears to lack a firm constituency on either the left or right. He is the first president to enter office without going through a national campaign and, unlike his predecessors, he did not have the usual two-and-one-half-month post-election period to organize his administration. However, Ford is not without significant resources since much of the president's power depends on his ability to articulate policy, to inspire public confidence, and to negotiate with Congress—all of which are closely related to the personality and energy of the individual in office.

In dealing with the Democratic-controlled Congress, President Ford has been surprisingly effective. Aided by the disarray of Democrats and the willingness of Republicans to stand together, the president has used the veto power to determine political events. For example, during the summer of 1975, the Democrats failed in 6 successive attempts to override crucial vetoes by Mr. Ford. One result was that Democrats began to trim their legislative goals in order to avoid vetoes. In his vetoes, Ford has acted very much in character. He does not hesitate to ask old colleagues in the House for favors—they like him and most often consent to his wishes.

SELECTION OF NELSON ROCKEFELLER AS VICE PRESIDENT

Ford's choice of Nelson Rockefeller as vice president was in keeping with the president's behavior when he was House minority leader. There Ford was willing to share authority and he did not fear the ambition of strong

Drawing by Wright; © 1975 The Miami News

associates. The Rockefeller nomination was most strongly opposed by conservative Republicans who remembered Rockefeller's challenge to Barry Goldwater in the 1964 presidential campaign. Confirmation of Mr. Rockefeller came only after substantial delay in Congress. Using the provisions of the 25th Amendment, Congress selected two vice presidents within a one-year period.

During the congressional confirmation hearings, much attention was directed to Rockefeller's generosity. For example, it was discovered that he had given former employee Henry Kissinger $50,000; he had canceled loans totaling $625,000 to William J. Ronan, who served in transportation posts when Rockefeller was governor of New York; and since 1968 he had contributed to the campaigns of at least 22 members of the House and Senate, including $28,750 to Senator Jacob Javits. Also damaging to Rockefeller was the disclosure that in 1970 his brother Laurance had put up $60,000 to finance a critical biography of Arthur Goldberg who was running for governor against Nelson Rockefeller at the time.

READINGS

A basic argument remains regarding the answer to why Watergate occurred. At the one extreme it is argued that we elected a president with moral myopia who surrounded himself with individuals who were morally blind. Thus Watergate was essentially the result of Mr. Nixon's character—it would not have occurred with someone else in office. At the other extreme is the argument that as power built up in the White House it was inevitable that Watergate or something similar would occur.[1] "The presidency," noted former presidential press secretary George Reedy, "was somehow out of hand. The White House has been building up to some kind of smash." The symposium participants struggle with this question and then move on to other considerations of institutional change and presidential character. As have other students of the presidency, they conclude that we need a strong presidency for leadership while also strengthening Congress, the cabinet, the parties, and the press as checks against abuse of executive power.

James Reston of the *New York Times* examines the Ford approach to the presidency in contrast to that of Mr. Nixon. Reston notes that in public Ford has been assertive, but in private he has reached out to his critics for help.

The article on the vice presidency presents an alternative means of selection. Such a proposal has as its goal up-grading the office of vice president as a source of policy advice to the president and avoiding the usual strained relationship between our two nationally elected officials.

[1] For examination of the inevitable buildup of corrupting power see Arthur M. Schlesinger, Jr., *The Imperial Presidency* (Boston: Houghton Mifflin, 1973). Professor Schlesinger is critical of most proposals for structural reform, such as a single six-year term or a plural executive. For an insightful examination of President Nixon's psychological stability see John Osborne, *The Last Nixon Watch* (New York: New Republic, 1975). In *Breach of Faith: The Fall of Richard Nixon* (New York: Atheneum-Reader's Digest, 1975), Theodore H. White concludes that our former president was an "unstable personality" whose conduct at the end had become "increasingly erratic."

The Presidency after Watergate: A Symposium

James David Barber, James MacGregor Burns, Thomas E. Cronin,
Alexander L. George, Fred I. Greenstein, Aaron Wildavsky,
David S. Broder (Moderator)

The Watergate crisis has forced almost all Americans to reexamine their views of the presidency. In no group has that responsibility been more clearly felt than in the political science profession.

From the time of Woodrow Wilson, a political scientist who became President, the structure of the presidency and its role in the American system has been at the center of political scientists' thought.

A week ago, during the American Political Science Association convention in New Orleans, six of the leading students of the presidency sat down for a 90-minute conversation on Watergate and the White House, with Washington Post political correspondent David S. Broder. They were:

• James David Barber, professor and chairman of the Department of Political Science, Duke University. Barber is the author of *The Presidential Character: Predicting Performance in the White House.*

• James MacGregor Burns, professor of political science at Williams College. His books include *Roosevelt: The Soldier of Freedom* and *Presidential Government.*

• Thomas E. Cronin, visting fellow at the Center for the Study of Democratic Institutions in Santa Barbara. He is the author of the forthcoming book, *The*

"The Presidency After Watergate." *The Washington Post* (September 16, 1973).

State of the Presidency, and co-editor of *The Presidential Advisory System* and *The Presidency Reappraised.*

• Alexander L. George, professor of political science at Stanford University. He is the author, with Juliette L. George, of *Woodrow Wilson and Colonel House: A Personality Study.*

• Fred I. Greenstein, Henry Luce professor of law, politics and society at Princeton University. His books include *Personality and Politics* and *The American Party System and the American People.*

• Aaron Wildavsky, dean of the Graduate School of Public Policy at the University of California, Berkeley. He is the author of *The Politics of the Budgetary Process* and co-author of *Presidential Election.*

BRODER: Let's begin with this question: When we talk about Watergate, are we talking about a problem of a specific President or about a problem that goes to the nature of the presidency and the way in which the office functions?

BURNS: I think the problem is obviously of both institution and individual, but I would say that it's essentially a problem of this particular President. It would be very hard for any democratic society to perfect an institution that could cope effectively with the kind of effort that was made last year to use the presidency to assault the opposition party and the opposition in general.

WILDAVSKY: We now have a President who has attempted to run foreign policy without the Senate, domestic and budgetary policy without the House and a political campaign without his party. He has adopted an essentially Gaullist view of the presidency. He says, "I'm the only one who counts to the people, and if anybody, including Congress, disagrees with me, so much the worse for them."

But I think that it is not really inherent in Nixon. I think that if he were able to get benefits and praise from the ordinary conduct of his job, he would have been less likely to do this. It's very difficult for any President now to achieve satisfaction, because the demands we make on him are essentially contradictory or so difficult that no one knows how to achieve them.

CRONIN: I would answer the question in two ways. First, I would call into question the schoolboy adage that all of us grew up learning, that the office uplifts the man. I have a feeling that if we look back over the past couple decades, that what actually may have happened is the reverse, namely, the weaknesses, the fragility and the smallness of character have frequently been accentuated by the office of the presidency.

One reason for this is the Cold War. The penchant for secrecy, the national security justifications, have made Presidents do things that, prior to the Cold War, were rarely done. So we ought to look much more critically at the institution.

My second response would be that the Nixon presidency is a different case. This is an unprecedented catalogue of breaking the rules, degrading the spirit of due process, degrading the institutions of the Internal Revenue Service, the FBI, the CIA and the competitive

two-party system. We cannot say that it is merely an accumulation of things that we have seen in recent Presidents; it's unprecedented.

GREENSTEIN: There is an extraordinarily intricate and inseparable mix of institution and individual in this case. To begin with, institutions vary in the degree to which they are what you might call resonators for the personalities of the people who are in them. Except during periods of weak Presidents, the White House has been a locus in American government where the particular quirks and manifestations of the individual could have very substantial consequences.

Now, we all know that the invisible presidency and the institutionalized presidency in an expanded White House have been a particular phenomenon of the period since the New Deal.

It's not just the way in which the presidency has taken over the Executive Office Building and the catacombs underneath, but the way in which it has successfully mined the entire federal government and the military establishment for its physical wherewithal.

His reluctance to take advice, his fugitive secretiveness, his readiness to sense persecution, I think, made Nixon the natural person to produce what he himself aptly described as highly motivated, overzealous subordinates.

BRODER: Let me restate the question: Are we talking about the problem of a particular President and his men or are we talking about a problem that has grown up in the presidential office?

BARBER: I think you can say at a minimum that the institution didn't require Watergate; it didn't impose the necessity for this kind of behavior in the presidential office. It's difficult in many ways to talk about the presidency as an institution, in the same way as we talk about Congress or the courts as institutions. The presidency is so highly personalized. It centers on one individual, to whom all the other actors in the presidential establishment look for their cues. And one way or the other, they'll find those cues. They'll discern from the President's apparent purposes what they ought to do.

The pathetic pleas of those who actually did the burgling in the Watergate case are that, if these powerful figures, the President or the Attorney General, wanted these things done, they must be all right.

Institutions, including the presidency, are largely in the participants' minds. They are not physical structures. They are a set of expectations that the actors have about what they should do and what is wanted from them. And we see that in Watergate in spades. There was a lapse of what I would call a sense of proportion, a monumental exaggeration of the importance of electing Richard Nixon and of supporting him, once in power.

The institution hasn't changed all that much from Kennedy to Johnson to Nixon, but the purposes the President has imposed on the people around him have.

The real question is, as Tom Cronin posed it, "What is the effect of this particular kind of office on the man?" The word I would use is "exaggeration." It tends to pull out temptations already in the character. Political power is like atomic energy, it can be used to create deserts or to make them bloom. The trouble Presidents have is keeping their balance, keeping their sanity in the midst of a tremendous storm of feeling that surrounds the office. So I would probably put considerably more stress

than anyone else here on the character of the President.

GEORGE: It isn't really possible, in my judgment, to separate the institution from the person filling it. It's the combination of the two, the interaction of the man in the presidency and the situations in which he finds himself.

Because of that, it is just terribly difficult to design a high confidence system for insuring that what we are calling Watergate would not happen again. Watergate is not one event; it's a cluster of events which are lumped together, because of the way in which we have come to know them.

CRONIN: I would like to throw two propositions out to my colleagues, to follow along with what Alex George was saying. The first is that the American people, and American political scientists as a profession, have been guilty of believing that whatever is advantageous for a President is necessarily good for the nation.

Now, after Vietnam and Watergate, we're beginning to realize that may not be the case. That's the first proposition. The second one is that in several of our recent Presidents, and Nixon in particular, we have seen an increasing tendency to separate partisan politics from the exercise of presidential leadership. Being a party leader, going out on the campaign trail and supporting people in your party, has become undignified, beneath the personal dignity of a President.

This separation of the presidency from politics is one which, in my judgment, is untenable. We can no more take politics out of the presidency than we can take the presidency out of politics.

WILDAVSKY: We'll come back, no doubt, to Tom Cronin's two points, but

I want to pick up on the challenge of Dave Barber that there was really no law that Watergate had to occur.

I would raise again the thought that if Watergate itself was not mandated, then some such presidential response is certainly in the cards, when you consider the tremendous pressure put on all Presidents and the fact that they can't get credit for domestic policy. You have an enormous push from the left to de-legitimize Presidents; not merely to say that Vietnam is wrong but to say that they don't have the right to make these decisions any more.

BRODER: Why do you say Presidents can't get credit for domestic policy any more?

WILDAVSKY: If you take a look at the record of the last Presidents, it just has become exceptionally difficult. If you provide more money for welfare, you add more people to the welfare rolls. If you provide less, you're making people suffer. And on and on like that.

GREENSTEIN: I'd like to bridge from Aaron Wildavsky's point to Tom Cronin's first point about the considerable celebration of the presidency that has gone on from time to time. It has not always and only been the case that Presidents have been celebrated. It's also been consistently the case that they've been demeaned. It's a matter of whose ox has been gored at each time in history.

BARBER: I don't think we're going to get very far by asking the public, as Tom Cronin suggests, to be skeptical about the President. The President is the focus of feelings that just aren't going to go away, no matter what we preach and teach.

It seems that in every Western industrialized society you have to have some focus for patriotic emotions and some way for public disillusionment to work itself out. What seems to me dangerous is the attitude we've heard expressed that Watergate is a kind of trivial and accidental set of happenings. That's the way liberty erodes.

It doesn't take too many bugging incidents or burglaries to have a pretty chilling effect throughout the society. So if you can't really control the President effectively by law, if you can't really control him effectively during his term of office by a skeptical attitude of public opinion, then basically what you're left with is the thought that you'd better control him at the time you're picking him.

BRODER: What kind of control are you talking about?

BARBER: I'm talking about picking someone, in the first place, who will control himself and who won't fall for these temptations of power. I think the controls have largely got to be internal.

We're just beginning to face up to the inevitable challenge of guessing before we select a President what kind of President he's going to be. After the fact, we always know that the character forces turn out to be the things that shape the presidency. We should learn from that experience and try to get some system for selection.

GEORGE: If I thought we knew how to carefully screen candidates for the presidency, with high confidence, fine. But I don't think we can do very much of a practical nature. So I think we have to take a multiple approach. Yes, let us improve our selection of candidates; let us do what we can to screen them with our inadequate tools.

But let us also monitor them after they get into office—monitor the health of men in high-stress office for severe mental illness or poor performance under stress.

BRODER: How would you do that?

GEORGE: Through the use of medical doctors. I wait for the day when a President will say. "I now have a personal physician who has had some psychiatric training." I think that would be a very wholesome precedent to set.

I think we may need a substitute for impeachment, something where the President could submit himself to an informal vote of confidence by Congress and consider voluntarily resigning if two-thirds of the Congress does not want him to continue.

The relationship between the press and the presidency needs very careful examination. Sometimes the press, in doing its job, severely exacerbates the problem for certain kinds of people in the presidency. Sometimes, on the other hand, it leans too far backwards, because members of the press are scared stiff that if they press too hard, they may create an even worse catastrophe.

BRODER: I'd like to ask Professor Burns, as a historian of the presidency, whether Watergate is simply part of an evolutionary process?

BURNS: I think in a sense President Nixon is scoring a final triumph over the presidency, when you hear the disillusionment reflected in the discussion here. It's as though there were something fated in Nixon, not only to seize the presidency, but to destroy it as an institution in the minds of those who have the greatest stake in a successful presidency.

We've been debating here whether or not the institution enhances the man. I think we should be very cautious about letting Nixon make our minds up on that score. I wish we would be more historical. After all, we have almost 200 years of experience with this office, and I will say rather flatly that the main thrust of this institution in the past century has been egalitarian and libertarian. It has been an institution for the redistribution of income, psychic as well as material, in this country.

The political scientists and the historians who were writing about this office over the decades weren't blind to some of the problems we're talking about now. One reason they were worried about a Nixon getting elected President is they realized what a threat he might be. Now, we're sitting here in the midst of a very unusual and unprecedented administration. We've never had a person remotely like Nixon in the presidency.

BARBER: I think we've had several who were essentially like Nixon in the presidency, though I do agree that Nixon has carried certain tendencies farther than any of the other 20th century Presidents that I've studied. But if you think of Presidents who have brought about many of their own difficulties by their characters—by a hard-driving, superambitious, rather rigid style of behavior—you can see that in Woodrow Wilson, you can see it in Herbert Hoover, you can see it in Lyndon Johnson.

In many ways, they were different from Richard Nixon. But in terms of their politics, the way their regimes resonated with their characters, there are a great many similarities. Now, whether you agree with that, at least we could agree that some kind of screening of presidential candidates is going to be done. It's done all the time by the politicians, by the press, by the primaries and the conventions.

It's a matter of improving the way we do it. Now, in Nixon's case, as Jim

Burns pointed out, we had all the evidence in the world, from his past behavior, about how he'd work as President. His history and his character, as we knew them, were in direct contradiction to his statements about how he'd work as President, that "open presidency" business. But his history and character were neglected, and his speeches were overemphasized, and this is what we got.

CRONIN: I want to side with Aaron Wildavsky, by quoting a previous writing of Jim Burns, one where he said that the crowning paradox of the American presidency is that we simultaneously ask our Presidents to be national unifiers and national dividers. This contradiction has been exaggerated as the swelling of the presidency, in the Cold War period, has taken place.

Let us not be too harsh on Nixon. It's the American people and the American mood and values which are forcing Nixon, consciously or unconsciously, to act according to a Hollywood script.

His challenge is how to look presidential without losing popularity. That's what's taking the politics out of the presidency. Nixon has run away time and again from critical, controversial domestic problems that need attention. He has also run away from his party. He is an apostate Republican; at least he was in 1972.

Why? Because, as Teddy White describes so beautifully in "The Making of the President 1972," we reward a President for being a supersecretary of state, a candidate for the Nobel Peace prize, an architect of a generation of peace. The rewards that we in the public give a President for getting into the critical issues of environment, energy, race, civil liberties and redistribution of income are increasingly diminished. This in large part explains the Nixon tragedy.

GEORGE: I want to pick up a theme that has been referred to several times and ask whether we have not, for very good historical reasons, overloaded the presidency in several different ways.

I don't disagree with Jim Burns on the need for a strong presidency, but these are not the 1930s, and I think we have to stop, as political scientists, and reexamine the premises that went into our concept of the presidency.

When FDR took over, everyone said, "Look to the presidency to save the system." Everyone said, "The President needs help; give him a lot of help." Now, we have a swollen White House, in which, step by step, we have miniaturized within the presidential office the rest of the executive branch. This was becoming very worrisome even prior to Watergate.

So I think we must develop a revisionist view of the presidency, and reexamine some of these assumptions. The central assumption in Richard Neustadt's famous and worthwhile book, "Presidential Power," is that if the President preserves his personal power stakes in every issue, if he is a successful political entrepreneur, that will be good for the country. That central assumption is now subject to reexamination. I'm not saying abandon the strong presidency, but we need to develop safeguards against the monster we've created.

WILDAVSKY: If I seem opposed to what Dave Barber says about being so careful about nominating Presidents, it's not because I wouldn't like to be as careful as he would, but because I think the tendency to failure in all institutions has to be accepted and compensated for. My understanding of whatever constitutional theory we have in this country is that we are supposed to have a political system, not single institutions, and that one component is supposed to be able to pick up, at least temporarily, the work of another.

The institution I think is performing worst now is not the presidency and not Congress but the parties. If there is any group of people that ought to hold the President to account, that should be telling him off when he oversteps his boundaries, it is the party leaders. Our problem is that we don't have significant corps of party leaders who have a stake in more than this President and this presidency, and who can, therefore, help set boundaries for acceptable political behavior.

Without suggesting panaceas, I think what we want is to have a variety of healthy and, to some degree, contentious political institutions. Part of our concern now is that we sense we're not entirely happy with the presidency and yet we're not sure that our other institutions are capable of taking over.

BARBER: I'd like to agree with that 1,000 percent, as has been said. There's too much tendency to blame all this on the people and on popular attitudes.

The original idea of the electoral college, which didn't work out in practice very well, was that you would have responsible leaders in the communities who would look over the range of leadership and recommend a President. That's been substituted for, to some degree, by the party leadership.

But where is the party leadership now in the Watergate incident? What are they saying? And, equally important, where are they in the nominating and electing process? We've developed a

system that encourages the superambitious early pursuit of the nomination, starting years before the election, with personal organizations separate from the parties. That reached its apex in the Committee to Re-elect the President.

If I had to say what kind of screening is most likely to be effective, it would be informed screening by party leaders, rather than a team of psychiatrists. The party leaders are familiar with the character and life histories of these contenders. But they have abdicated that screening role.

GEORGE: The party wants to win the election. Can you guarantee to me or to anyone else that the party leaders will choose a man who will govern well, rather than one who will win the election?

BARBER: There are no guarantees.

GEORGE: No. And I think you would not disagree with the assumption that they'd give much more weight to a man who will win the election, rather than one who will avoid Watergates—to which they attach very low probability, in any case. The real payoff is winning the election.

WILDAVSKY: I think there have not been enough public comments on the incredible composition of the Committee to Re-elect the President. Who the hell were they? What roots did they have in the American society? What connection with the party?

CRONIN: I think it's clear that it was a secretive, non-partisan, private sort of public relations firm. Essentially, Mr. Nixon chose in the wake of the 1970 elections to disband or abandon the Republican Party. He would run a private campaign, a clandestine, secretive, private affair.

BRODER: I think we have arrived at a

point in this discussion where there is general agreement that what we need is a healthy President, in mind and body, in a healthy political system. But I want to ask you where you think you reach into this situation for the leverage to change what we have?

GREENSTEIN: Well, Alex George has suggested in a number of his remarks that there simply may not be any easy leverage.

None of us here, for example, have suggested psychiatric screening of candidates, although we've all recognized the importance of the president's character.

We've said that the politicians in a party might decide that certain people whom they have seen close up are really going to have problems in the presidency. It would be nice to have a level of sensitivity and awareness about aspects of mental health, so that somebody with the interesting career that Nixon has had would be thought of in a much more suspect way.

BRODER: Do you really see a possibility that you're going to have a nominating system in which the results of the primaries are going to be weighed against the sensitive party leaders' views of the mental stability of the candidate?

GREENSTEIN: I think the fact that the nominating system is now becoming such a creature of the primaries, that it is being taken away from what used to be called "the bosses," is one of the serious problems here. While we might not have expected the bosses to become psychologically sophisticated, it's even more complex with the primaries playing the role they do now.

But we've said, "Let there be light," in the sense of understanding presiden-

tial character, even knowing the substantial problems, involved. We've also said, "Let there be light," with respect to the presidency itself. For many years, the phrase "the invisible presidency" has been used to describe the structure of the White House. And I think the time has come to make that entire institution more public and more accessible, whether this involves congressional scrutiny or something else.

BARBER: I think you're talking about the press when you talk about visibility, and also about the information that the party leaders can use in screening these candidates as they come along. There's a real problem here, in the pressure on the press for novelty. I think, for instance, of the continual rediscovery of "new Nixons," of Theodore White getting himself way out on a limb in this new book and then suddenly having to backpedal quite a bit in order to rediscover that the "old Nixon" was still there.

Another example would be the incident in which Sen. Muskie shed some tears in New Hampshire, which I think was much over interpreted as a single event supposedly revelatory of his character, when many newsmen knew much more about the ordinary Muskie way of acting and operating.

I'd put a lot of emphasis on the press materials that these king-makers are going to have to operate with being developed in a much more continuous way. I think there is room for some good initiatives from the press.

BURNS: The question Dave Broder has put, as I understand it, is, "Where do we go from here?" It seems to me that by the time of the Johnson administration, American political scientists had developed a number of ideas which were never tested because we didn't have enough sense of urgency about the problem of the presidency.

I would argue that if we have ordinary good-bad-mixed human being presidents in the future, the ideas that have come out of the political science profession should be tried out.

We ought to strengthen the role of the party, not to make it all-powerful, but to make the party a steadying and stabilizing matrix or context for the presidency. This relates to the whole question of screening. One of the geniuses of the British system is that party leaders have decades in which to scrutinize their colleagues, to watch them under pressure, before they become cabinet ministers.

Second, there is the whole question of making Congress an institution worthy to match the President. For decades, political scientists have been urging Congress to strengthen itself to serve as part of a balanced system of powers.

Third, there is the question of the electoral process. We have warned against moving into a system of presidential primaries which allows freebooters to come in from the outside and seize a nomination, a system where the party completely disappears.

And finally, there is the point I'm very glad Tom Cronin made about the problem of the bipartisan presidency and the whole doctrine of bipartisanship. Many of us have been conducting a campaign against that for years, but Nixon in many ways represents the epitome of this kind of bipartisanship gone wild.

So I would say that while we made mistakes and we all should be reassessing—as God knows we're busily doing these days, as we reel and stagger in the wake of these revelations—if we would go back and perfect some of these things that come out of the thinking of generations of political scientists, it might be useful.

We should use this crisis to project these ideas. If I reflected some worry earlier, it seemed to me a missed opportunity here, to seize on this crisis the way past crises have been seized on, to improve a governmental system and to perfect the ideas that have been coming out of generations of thought.

WILDAVSKY: Watergate has become like a litmus test, and the real question for us now is what, as a nation, will we learn. One thing I've learned—I've already touched on it, so I'll mention it only briefly—is that it's desirable to have a plurality of actors and institutions. You sleep better at night if you feel that you have a variety of capable actors on the scene.

The second lesson occurs when you ask not who behaved badly, but who were the few who behaved well? And what characterizes them? The single feature that I find most important is that they all had very powerful and important institutional loyalties.

Among people in public administration, it has been usually fashionable to denigrate bureaucratic loyalties as absolutely the worst kind of thing. You know: "They're parochial. They love their bureau. They don't care about anything else."

But in Watergate, the people who stood up best were those in the Justice Department, the FBI, the CIA who felt strongly about their agencies, who could think of themselves as surrounded by colleagues who had a code of professional behavior.

Those who did worst were the faceless, bright young men of the Nixon administration, who revered a presidential figure at some distance, but seemingly had no church, no family, no sense of values. So they had to be taught and the senators gave them little sermons: "young man, don't you understand that what you did was terrible?" And obviously they did not so understand, or they would not have done it.

So, to put the two answers together and to put the burden where I really think it belongs—on the people collectively—unless we are willing to build a plurality of institutions, including strong political ones, we'll be faced again with situations where atomized individuals, without a sense of loyalty to others than the leader, will behave badly.

BURNS: Even though the plurality of institutions may thwart the realization of the kinds of goals that we might all share here?

WILDAVSKY: My understanding is that the very nature of our system is that the parts are supposed to check and oppose and, indeed, thwart one another. My favorite motto these days is "There is no such thing as a free lunch," so, of course, there is a price to pay. Maybe one advantage of Watergate is that we have a little more sense of sin now. That may be all to the good.

GEORGE: I would like to ask Jim Burns how he weighs the utility of a single presidential term. Surely, it would have saved us from Watergate, but is that a sufficient reason for going in that direction? President Nixon has said he would favor a single 6-year term.

BURNS: The idea of having perpetual lame duck Presidents would bother me. I would say, on the contrary, I would favor abolition of the 22d Amendment (the two-term limit).

CRONIN: I would like to second Jim Burns. I'm irrevocably opposed to a single-term limit and to the 6-year term. In fact, in my weaker moments, I favor a 2-year presidential term.

If I could, however, attempt a summary, I would say that it is typical of our profession to think that major progress comes after catastrophes. I would like to raise some skepticism about this. I would nominate Watergate and all its sordid siblings as a test case of whether catastrophe is necessarily followed by progress.

What we have done here this afternoon has been to pull out of our desk drawers, if you will, some of our old articles and some of our old panaceas, which all of us have favored.

BURNS: But they've not been tried.

CRONIN: That's right. Some of them have not been appropriately tried, as Professor Burns suggests. We've talked about party reform, a dismissal of mindless bipartisanship, other things. But I think we've got to come back to the multiple approach that Professor George mentioned earlier.

We need a stronger President, but a stronger presidency is going to have to be a lean and clean one, an open one, and one subject to numerous checks. We need a stronger Congress. We need a press that has more guts.

Why didn't the press get the Watergate story earlier? Why didn't Congress? Congress is in a very ebullient mood right now, a feeling that it's being resuscitated and getting a new lease on life. I am suspicious of that. I don't think Pennsylvania Avenue is a seesaw, with one branch going up as the other goes down.

We need a strong cabinet, strong parties, a strong press. We need strong institutions across the board.

My final comment would be that the doctrine of self-restraint, which is subtle and implicit in the U.S. Constitution, has got to be made more explicit by the attentive public in America. Our system cannot work and function smoothly if we do not insist that each branch abide by the doctrine of self-restraint which is implicit in the Constitution.

I would argue that all three of our branches and, on occasion, the press and the bureaucracy, too, have egregiously shattered the doctrine of self-restraint. In the past decade or so, the presidency may have shattered it more badly than the other branches. But who gave Congress the right to muck around in administrative politics and bureaucratic politics, as it does in the Department of Agriculture and so many other places? Who gave the Supreme Court the right to be the chief legislature of the land?

My point is that the territorial imperative, which the pop sociologists and anthropologists write about, is very relevant here. The doctrine of self-restraint is one which can only work if we as a country talk about values and talk about ends-and-means relationships.

We are not going to be able to pass a statute or have an Ervin Committee report or a court decision that is going to remedy the excesses the presidency has been involved in during the past decade.

We are going to have to change our attitudes, our beliefs and the way in which we look at ourselves, our system and our institutions.

WILDAVSKY: Which is to say, we are not going to change.

Nobody's Mad at Jerry

James Reston

Funny thing about President Ford: Almost everybody is grumbling these days about something he has done or hasn't done, but nobody's really sore at *him*. The opposition around here to Rockefeller, Kissinger, and Simon is savage and personal, but unlike Nixon, who was blamed for everything, Ford somehow manages to avoid personal blame for anything.

From *The New York Times*, March 9, 1975, p. 17E. © 1975 by the New York Times Company. Reprinted by permission.

He flies around the country condemning the Congress for loafing on the job, but comes back and plays golf with Tip O'Neill, the Democratic Majority Leader in the House, and compromises on the side with Speaker Albert and Mike Mansfield on the energy problem.

He accepts spectacular budget deficits, which in another day he used to condemn, and appoints liberals to his Cabinet at the Justice, Transportation, Labor, and Housing Department, but when the Republican conservatives condemn him for his deficits and appointments, he defends his decision but invites his critics to the White House to have a drink and talk it over.

He avoids personal attack because he never attacks his opposition personally. In many ways, his record of dealing with the economy is appalling. First, he was for austerity, more taxes, and whopping big import fees on gas and oil, but second, when even his own party began to feel this was inflationary and almost ridiculous, he switched to tax cuts and accepted spectacular budget deficits.

In short, President Ford may have been wrong, but unlike Nixon, he didn't pretend he was always right, and he didn't personalize the struggle, but dealt with the facts, and again unlike Nixon, kept in touch with his opponents.

There is a serious issue here about President Ford, for on the record, it is not clear whether he has mastered the substance of the economic problem, or whether he is simply relying on the judgment of a staff that differs on whether inflation or recession is the central question. So he swings from one extreme to the other. One day he is the old conservative, budget-balancing Jerry Ford out of Grand Rapids, Mich., and the next he is a Keynesian, supporting budget deficits, struggling to hold together the liberal Democratic majority in the Congress and the aggrieved conservative Republican minority, which used to be his main political support.

He has dealt with things, and on the whole fairly effectively, in human terms. His strategic concept of the economic problem may be defective, but his tactical handling of the political and human problem has been very effective.

Unlike Nixon, he has not pretended that he knew all the answers or that it was important to be consistent. In public, he has been bold and assertive, but in private, he has used the "dumb-boy" technique, admitting that he was in trouble and was reaching out to his critics for help.

Paradoxically, the President's weaknesses are his strength. His personality and character are more important than his intelligence. He has been around here just long enough and is just shrewd enough to know that nobody else has the answers either.

So he does not shut himself off in the White House, but brings everybody in—the Republican and Democratic leaders, old buddies from his days on Capitol Hill, friends and critics from the newspapers, radio, and television.

He has no "enemies list." When his new liberal Cabinet appointees were sworn in at the White House the other day, the place was full of prominent Democrats, including Joe Rauh, a Washington lawyer who led the fight against Ford's nomination as Vice President.

This sort of thing doesn't bother Ford. He doesn't choose up sides, or worry about the press. John Hersey, the novelist, who wrote a brilliant account of one week in the life of Harry Truman long ago, asked the President the other day whether he could do the same thing with Ford for The New York Times Magazine.

Sure, the President said. Sit in on anything you like, have dinner with the family, follow me around if you can stand it for a whole week except—and this is interesting—during my private conversations on foreign policy with Henry Kissinger.

He seems to see himself accurately as an accidental President, with problems beyond his or anybody else's control, but while he's around, he is making it clear that he will act as best he can, listen to anybody who differs, and at least avoid unnecessary conflict.

It is an appealing approach to an intimidating job. He is just modest enough to know his limitations, but experienced and confident enough to know that probably nobody else around here is equal to it either.

Often he may be wrong, but his strength is that he is honest, and after the last few years in Washington this is a big change.

There's Still Hope for the Vice Presidency

David C. Saffell

Because of recent problems involving Thomas Eagleton and Spiro Agnew, a new urgency has been given to seeking ways to improve the selection of the vice president and attention has been directed to the nature and function of the office. Moreover, as a nation we have become increasingly concerned about the possibility of an incumbent president's death, disability, or assassination. Underscoring this concern is the fact that three of the past six presidents have moved up from the vice presidency upon the death or resignation of the president.

The vice presidency has been a failure from the time of its first incumbent, John Adams. Since Adams and his successor, Thomas Jefferson, the office has been occupied by only a few individuals whom a majority of the people would have wished to be a candidate for president. The vice presidency has been powerless, leading political figures have avoided it, and political parties typically have chosen unknown men who have left office equally unrecognized by their contemporaries. It is a mark of the office that it has been vacant on numerous occasions and Americans have scarcely noticed the absence of the vice president.

From the time of President Truman there has been an upgrading of the job of vice president, but the selection process and job description have remained largely unchanged. The basic pattern of on-the-job activities for contemporary vice presidents was established by Richard Nixon. As vice president, Mr. Nixon presided over the Cabinet and the National Security Council in Eisenhower's absence, worked with Congress, was the chairman of an interdepartmental committee, and undertook good will missions abroad. Although ignored on many occasions, Vice Presidents Humphrey and Johnson performed similar duties. Still, like Nixon, their chief utility continued to be to relieve the president of ceremonial functions and to visit foreign countries. As vice president, Spiro Agnew's main responsibilities (other than serving as a

White House mouthpiece) were working with state governors and supporting the administration's revenue sharing plan.

Political columnist Hugh Sidey points out that for the past 23 years the office of vice president has been cast in the image of two men—Richard M. Nixon and Lyndon B. Johnson. For eight years as vice president, Nixon was not trusted by President Eisenhower. Even as vice president, Nixon was remote and isolated. When Nixon left office, Johnson took over. As vice president, the more restless Johnson became, the more suspicious the Kennedy people became of him. As president, Johnson was totally unwilling to share power with Hubert Humphrey. Thus the contemporary role of the vice president has been warped by the unique personalities of Nixon and Johnson.

Under truly unique circumstances, Rockefeller and Ford have operated in an atmosphere of harmony and cooperation. The fact that Ford selected someone of Rockefeller's stature indicated that, unlike many of his predecessors, Mr. Ford was secure enough to coexist with a prestigious associate. As a result of this unusual situation, Rockefeller has been given substantial authority as vice chairman of the Domestic Council and charged with directly supervising its activities. Additionally, two of Rockefeller's top aides were named by Ford to head the Council's day-to-day operations. The Domestic Council, which helps shape all domestic legislation and programs, was itself strengthened when President Ford added the heads of the Economic Policy Board and the Energy Resources Council to its membership.

Although Rockefeller as vice president has not made decisions or given significant policy announcements (no vice president ever has), he has been effective by counseling the president on a variety of issues and by recruiting talent for the Ford administration.

While the Ford–Rockefeller experiment has worked well, the very uniqueness of their coming to office does not offer much hope that this administration will mark the beginning of a new era in vice presidential–presidential relations. Indeed, it is likely that when the next president and vice president are selected at a national party convention, their relationship and the job of the vice president will slip back into the traditional pattern of distrust and inactivity.

It is unrealistic to think that under our present system a president would make the vice president a top assistant in the manner of Nixon aides H. R. Haldeman or Alexander Haig. Presidents will not delegate significant power to an individual they cannot remove from office. In the absence of a constitutional amendment, the best hope for improvement of the vice president's job seems to rest in improving the selection process. If both parties would nominate for vice president only those persons well qualified by experience and character for the presidency, then we could rest more easily about succession. Also, the presence of top-flight persons as vice president (here Rockefeller is a good example) would at least put some additional pressure on the president to involve the vice president in important governmental decision-making and thus upgrade the existing role of the office.

Under the current system, the presidential nominee has virtually a free hand in selecting his running mate. Not since Adlai Stevenson in 1956 has the presidential nominee opened the selec-

"In this great land of ours, *anyone* can grow up to be Vice-President."

tion of a vice president to the delegates at a national convention. In each instance since 1956, the convention has acted quickly to ratify the choice of vice president on the first ballot. Thus in seeking to "balance the ticket" (the traditional strategy in choosing the vice presidential nominee) the party's standardbearer could do as Richard Nixon in 1968 and tap the then unknown Spiro Agnew as a representative of borderstate suburbia to help the ticket in the South and gain support among conservative "law and order" voters in the North. The existing system allows only twelve hours between the presidential nomination and the selection of the running mate. Such pressure of time in part helps explain the choice of Thomas Eagleton by George McGovern in 1972.

Since the resignation of Spiro Agnew, there has been a flood of proposals concerning how to pick the vice president. However, as columnist David Broder notes, "The easiest proposition in the world to prove is that the way we pick our vice presidents is crazy. The hardest may be to find the right way to remedy the system."

To date, the most serious effort to reform the selection process for the vice president has come from the Democratic party's Commission for Vice Presidential Reform, headed by Senator Hubert Humphrey and political scientist Jeane Kirkpatrick. Of the many proposals heard by the commission, the more widely supported are listed below:

1. To ease the pressure of time, at least a thirty-six hour interval could be provided between the time of the nomination of a presidential candidate and the recommendation of a running mate. In addition, a screening committee would be established to check the background of vice presidential possibilities.
2. To ensure even more deliberation, the selection of a vice president could be put off until a few weeks after the convention. A name could then be submitted by the presidential nominee to a group of party leaders for approval in a way similar to the manner in which R. Sargent Shriver was selected to replace Thomas Eagleton in 1972.
3. To democratize the convention selection, the presidential nominee could be required to submit several names for vice president to the delegates.
4. To allow for greater public and press scrutiny, all presidential contenders could be required to disclose their vice presidential choices a week before the convention convened.
5. Vice presidential hopefuls could be required to run in separate primaries or the runner-up in the presidential

primaries could be designated as the party's vice presidential nominee.
6. Candidates for vice president and president could be elected separately, not on the same ticket. This would be in keeping with the intentions of the Founding Fathers when they wrote the Constitution.

Each of these proposals has its weaknesses.[1] Even with a thirty-six hour delay, there would be only a short time for deliberation and by then most of the convention delegates are exhausted. In all cases where the presidential nominee would submit a person or persons to the convention or to a special mini-convention of party leaders, there would be overwhelming pressure to accept his choice. If several names were presented, the first choice of the presidential nominee would be clear to those making the final selection. Proposals calling for vice presidential candidates to run in primaries could produce an even weaker vice president who was not well liked or trusted by the president. Since the job of vice president will continue to be what the president wants it to be, it is imperative that a good relationship exist between the two persons heading our government. Having separate elections raises the obvious possibility of the voters' selecting the vice president from one party and the president from the other. This is analogous to the situation which exists in many states in which the lieutenant governor runs independently of the

[1] Senator Robert Griffin (R., Mich.) has sponsored a proposed constitutional amendment which would allow a president to wait until after his election to nominate a vice president, who would take office after confirmation by Congress, as did Gerald Ford.

governor. If there is one political office in the United States weaker than the vice presidency it is the state lieutenant governor.

An extreme proposal, supported by such persons as historian Henry Steele Commager, would simply abolish the office of vice president. The constitutional duties of the vice president could easily be distributed to a few persons in the Senate and in the executive branch. Curiously, as historian-political scientist Clinton Rossiter tells us, "Some of the more astute members of the Convention of 1787 doubted there was any need for a vice president."[2] Were the office abolished, we would have to rely on the Presidential Succession Act of 1947[3] or on a special election to fill a vacancy in the presidency.

[2] Clinton Rossiter, *The American Presidency*, rev. ed. (New York: Harcourt Brace Jovanovich, 1960), p. 135.

[3] The 1947 act provides that if the president and vice president both are unable to serve as president, succession passes to the Speaker of the House, the president pro tempore of the Senate, and then to the cabinet beginning with the secretary of state.

As noted previously, the office of vice president often has been vacant. This is beacuse the Constitution did not provide a way to select a new vice president upon the death of the president or the death of the vice president. When John Kennedy was assassinated in 1963, Lyndon Johnson became president, the office of vice president was vacant, and House Speaker John McCormack stood next in line to become president. The manner of Kennedy's death and the prospect of Mr. McCormack's serving as president spurred Congress to approve the 25th Amendment. This amendment deals with presidential disability and it also provides that the former vice president upon becoming president will nominate a new vice president subject to congressional approval. In part, the effect of the 25th Amendment is to make resort to the Succession Act of 1947 highly unlikely as a means of filling a vacancy in the presidency.

Former Franklin Roosevelt presidential adviser Rexford Guy Tugwell has recommended a nine-year presidential term, with a vote of confidence after three years.[4] His new constitution would provide for two vice presidents—one for internal affairs and the other responsible for foreign, financial, military, and legal affairs. The vice presidents would be elected with the president and the president would designate which of the two would be first in line for succession.

There is, however, serious doubt that presidents would utilize these vice presidents as intended. Moreover, the inevitable development of vice presidential aides and assistants might simply add to the already top-heavy federal bureaucracy and put an ever greater distance between the president and cabinet secretaries.

Even if the vice president's sole function is to be available to succeed the president, this is a significant role. Were the office of president filled by the Speaker of the House, we would find ourselves in the undesirable position of elevating a person who was elected by only 1/435th of the national electorate and selected for House leadership on the basis of much different criteria than would be considered for a presidential nominee. Indeed, many people would like to rewrite the Succession Act to assure that the Speaker would not become president. Were a special election held soon after a vacancy occurred in the presidency, we would still need an interim president.

The proposal favored in this paper is to retain the office of vice president but

[4] Rexford Guy Tugwell, *Model for a New Constitution* (Palo Alto, Calif.: James E. Freel, 1970), pp. 56–60.

on a basis that would make the incumbent ineligible to run for president. Under such a plan the parties could be encouraged to nominate an admired elder statesman who might well be accepted as a close presidential adviser because he would not present a threat to the chief executive's power or public standing. The elder statesman (vice president) would be available to serve as interim president until a special election was held to fill out the president's term. This plan would avoid placing younger ambitious individuals in a job which invariably frustrates them, leads to conflict with the president, and creates a powerless office.

Such a system seems to be a logical alternative to our present system which has produced such forgettable vice presidents as Thomas Hendricks, Levi Morton, Garret Hobart, Hannibal Hamlin, and George Dallas. Yet as David Broder states in *The Washington Post*, " . . . this being a country that prefers politics to logic, we will probably keep the system we have—and discover to our continual amazement, that presidents and vice presidents just don't seem to get along."

QUESTIONS FOR DISCUSSION

1. Given the developments since 1932 in the office of the presidency, was Watergate inevitable?
2. As president, how unique was Richard M. Nixon among 20th century chief executives? With whom might we draw comparisons?
3. What is your reaction to such proposed institutional changes as a single six-year presidential term or a six-person directorate to replace the president?
4. How practical is it to suggest monitoring the physical and mental health of the president?
5. Would you favor the abolition of the vice presidency?
6. Would it be possible to operate under a system in which there were three vice presidents, each responsible for a functional area such as international affairs, economic and judicial affairs, and social-welfare affairs?
7. How do you react to the explanation given by several Republican members of Congress that they voted against confirmation of Nelson Rockefeller because he could never receive substantial support among the Republican voters in their district?
8. Among the symposium participants, whose views did you find most convincing?
9. How would you rank Gerald Ford among 20th century presidents?
10. How do you interpret the phrase "high crimes and misdemeanors" in regard to presidential impeachment?

Ed Gamble cartoon reprinted courtesy The Register and Tribune Syndicate, Inc.

"... and you assure me, Colby, that the CIA has stopped all of its domestic spying ...?"

chapter six

The Presidential Staff and the Federal Bureaucracy

THE WHITE HOUSE STAFF

During the first four years of the Nixon administration the presidential establishment grew by 20 percent. As discussed by political scientist Thomas E. Cronin, this "swelling of the presidency" has had a variety of disturbing effects. Most significant is the fact that unelected, anonymous aides, isolated from the traditional checks and balances, help negotiate international commitments and control the spending of billions of dollars in funds appropriated by Congress. In turn, the cabinet has suffered a loss in prestige and authority and the president has become increasingly isolated from political realities. Watergate revealed the irresponsible use of power by arrogant presidential aides who turned the executive branch into a closed society of faceless managers.[1] Reformers stress that future Watergates can only be prevented by reducing the size of the Executive Office and restoring power to the cabinet and other governmental institutions.

As president, Mr. Ford has reorganized the White House staff in an obvious move to contrast with the Nixon administration. Under the direction of Donald Rumsfield, the goal has been to find a middle way between the Nixon system of concentration of power and the genial chaos of Ford's first months in office. There are nine staff members who see the president on a regular basis. In addition to Mr. Rumsfield, they include the head of congressional relations, the chief speechwriter, the press secretary, the adviser for economic affairs, the director of the Domestic Council, and the assistant for national security affairs.

While Mr. Rumsfield has tried to stick to organizational matters and avoid policy-making, he does present some policy ideas to the president and he has had an influence on major executive appointments. Power clashes are inevitable among ambitious and energetic staff members. Indeed conflict, rather than managed group consensus, would be an encouraging development.

Another sign of post-Watergate effects is that it takes the Ford administration considerably longer than past administrations to fill top administration posts. Because Congress and the public are more sensitive to conflict

---

[1] See Dan Rather and Gary P. Gates, *The Palace Guard* (New York: Harper & Row, 1974).

of interest or wrongdoing than in the past, some persons hesitate to accept nominations and the administration is more careful to investigate the backgrounds of its nominees.

MISUSE OF FEDERAL AGENCIES

The Justice Department

The federal agencies most seriously affected by Watergate were the Justice Department, the CIA, and the FBI. Among departments, Justice probably was more deeply wounded than any other. Nixon appointed four attorneys general. John Mitchell was convicted of five felonies, Richard Kliendienst pleaded guilty to a misdemeanor, Elliot Richardson resigned in protest at the firing of Special Prosecutor Archibald Cox, and William Saxbe was hardly a legal giant. As attorney general, Edward Levi in the Ford administration has been faced with the task of redirecting a department which in recent years has authorized mass arrests without cause, planted *agents provocateurs*, and used illegal wiretaps.

Under such circumstances, it is natural that reformers have called for the Justice Department to be taken out of politics. *New York Times* columnist Anthony Lewis suggests that in a partisan sense the attorney general must guard against politicization of law enforcement, especially the use of the Justic Department to harrass political enemies. However, Lewis cautions that the department can be strong only if it gets leadership from an attorney general who has the confidence of the president. Thus to detach the department from politics in the broad sense would be a disastrous reaction to Watergate. (Other more specific reforms for the Justice Department as well as the FBI and CIA are discussed in the next chapter.)

The CIA

When the CIA was created in 1947 the House added to the bill the statement that "the agency shall have no police, subpoena, law enforcement powers, or internal-security functions." Despite this language, charges have long existed that the CIA has engaged in widespread domestic spying. In fact, the CIA has secretly provided funds to academic centers; it has subsidized student, labor, business, and church groups through foundation fronts; in the early 1960s it established a Domestic Operations Division one block from the White House; all but one of those involved in the Watergate break-in had been career or contact CIA operators at one time or another; top CIA officials, at the request of the White House, provided the "plumbers" group with technical assistance; the agency prepared psychological profiles on Daniel Ellsberg; and the CIA cooperated for a time in President Nixon's attempt to use it to divert the FBI from its investigation of the Watergate break-in and cover-up conspiracy.

Ed Gamble cartoon reprinted courtesy The Register and Tribune Syndicate, Inc.

In late 1974, *New York Times* reporter Seymour Hersh charged that the CIA had engaged in illegal domestic spying on political dissidents in the late 1960s and early 1970s and that the agency had dossiers on nearly 10,000 Americans. CBS newsman Daniel Schorr followed the charge in the *Times* by suggesting that one of the reasons for the resistance of the Ford administration to an investigation of the CIA is the belief that the agency might have been involved in the assassination of at least three foreign officials in the late 1950s and early 1960s. In early 1975 it became known that the CIA had spent $350 million in an effort to raise a Soviet submarine from the bottom of the Pacific Ocean.

In response to charges against the CIA, Director William Colby acknowledged the existence of the dossiers, but denied that this amounted to a "massive, illegal domestic intelligence operation," as defined in the *New York Times*. Agency officials contend that the law is written broadly enough to allow them to collect foreign intelligence within the United States. They note that the 1947 law makes the director of the CIA responsible for protecting "intelligence sources and methods from unauthorized disclosure" and that it gives the CIA the authority to perform "other functions and duties related to intelligence" as directed by the National Security Council.

The CIA also admitted that it had opened mail addressed to Congresswoman Bella Abzug and kept a file on her since 1953. For some persons, however, this "true confession" by the CIA was viewed as a predictable, devious bureaucratic response. When warned that an embarrassing story is about to break, the bureaucrat bravely comes forward and gives his usually limited version of what is going on. The confession creates the impression of candor and then the bureaucrat stonewalls further inquiry. In picking the controversial Ms. Abzug, the CIA found a good way seemingly to tell all while offending the fewest average Americans.

In response to allegations of illegal CIA activities, President Ford appointed an eight-member investigation commission headed by Nelson Rockefeller. Its task was to find out what the CIA has done, determine if there are adequate safeguards to prevent its happening again, and, if not, to recommend reform. Both houses of Congress have also moved ahead with investigations.

The report of the Rockefeller Commission confirmed that the CIA was involved in a variety of break-ins, wiretaps, and buggings. Moreover, new evidence was uncovered indicating that the CIA administered LSD to persons without their knowledge, infiltrated the campaign of a congressional candidate, monitored telephone calls to Latin America, and contributed money from its budget to support a White House project. Among its recommendations, the Rockefeller Commission suggested the creation of a joint congressional committee to oversee CIA operations and the creation of a similar executive agency; limitations on the tenure of CIA directors; and requirements for public disclosures of parts of the CIA budget.

The Rockefeller Commission did not report on allegations of CIA involvement in assassination plots against leaders of foreign governments. This task, plus a general review of the CIA, was turned over to special House and Senate investigating committees. However, it was learned that the CIA had enlisted the help of Mafia personnel in an attempt to assassinate Cuban Premier Fidel Castro and several of his close associates.

Most CIA activities, as well as figures on personnel and budget, remain unknown. While investigation of the agency needs to be thorough enough to reveal the truth about its domestic activities, concern has been voiced regarding interference with legitimate CIA activities in foreign countries. However, the foreign adventures of the CIA (for example, spending $8 million to "destabilize" the Allende government in Chile) also have created controversy. Difficult questions remain regarding the continuation of secret government operations in a democratic nation. The balance between liberty at home and protection of legitimate national security interests has been precariously maintained at best. Columnist James Reston has suggested that the main hope for survival of an effective CIA is a clean sweep of present leadership and the creation of a powerful new joint committee of Congress to oversee future activities.

The FBI

Following allegations of illegal CIA activities, there has been evidence that the FBI maintains files concerning the personal life of many public figures, including congressmen. In addition, the FBI was seriously involved in

Watergate. Acting Director L. Patrick Gray resigned when it became known that he had destroyed material taken from Watergate burglar E. Howard Hunt's safe. In general, the FBI was criticized for its lackluster investigation of the Watergate burglary and cover-up. Upset by CIA and FBI activities, Senator Adlai E. Stevenson III (D., Ill.) stated that "the danger of the police state is no longer unreal." In response to both Democratic and Republican concern, the Senate set up a select committee to investigate "the extent, if any, to which illegal, improper or unethical activities were engaged in by any agency" of the United States government from the days of the Cold War until the present.

It is encouraging to those supporting an expansion of civil liberties that Congress has abolished the House Internal Security Committee, which from 1938 until 1974 (for the most part under the name of the House Un-American Activities Committee) focused on investigating individuals whose criticism of the government allegedly threatened national security. More recently, congressional investigation has centered on public agencies such as the CIA, FBI, and IRS whose activities clearly have violated citizen rights and privacy.

READINGS

In this chapter psychologist Irving Janis discusses the phenomenon of Groupthink, which, he believes, helps explain why government decision-makers have lapses in judgment which result in fiascoes such as

Editorial cartoon by Pat Oliphant; copyright, Washington Star. Reprinted with permission Los Angeles Times Syndicate

"Of course I brought them with me—how do you think I got in here?"

the Bay of Pigs invasion and Vietnam. Groupthink—the psychological drive for consensus at any cost that suppresses dissent and appraisal of alternatives in cohesive decision-making groups—appears to be an accurate way to describe why Watergate occurred. Although written in 1972, Janis' description of the major symptoms of Groupthink provides an uncanny insight into the Nixon White House.

The other two articles offer contrasting views of the bureaucracy. To Woll and Jones, bureaucrats emerged from Watergate as a basic safeguard of the democratic system by holding to established rules and refusing to be misused by Nixon aides. With his attention directed to bureaucrats in local government, sociologist William Chambliss believes that bureaucrats generally follow the line of least resistance. Chambliss states that because bureaucrats have a high degree of discretion in applying rules, they often adopt a "tolerance policy" toward vice, and thus "the crime cabal" becomes a part of the governmental structure.

Generalizations: Who Succumbs, When, and Why?

Irving L. Janis

A WORKING ASSUMPTION ABOUT WHO IS SUSCEPTIBLE

Who is susceptible to groupthink pertains not only to the nationality of the policy-makers but also to their personality predispositions. Some chief executives, for example, probably become more dependent than others on an inner circle of advisers and set up group norms that encourage unanimity. Psychological studies have shown marked individual differences in responsiveness to social pressure. Some individuals consistently yield to the views of the majority, and others consistently adhere to their own independent judgments. Recent research suggests that conformity tendencies may be strongest in persons who are most fearful of disapproval and rejection. People with strong affiliative needs prefer their work colleagues to be good friends, even if those friends are not very competent. Such people give priority to preserving friendly relationships, at the expense of achieving success in the group's work tasks.

Most of the systematic research from which these findings are derived, however, has dealt with superficial conformity in groups made up of strangers who meet together once and do not expect to see one another again. To understand the predispositions conducive to groupthink, we need studies of groups that meet together for many weeks and work on decisions to which each member will be committed. Such studies are also essential to find out whether other characteristics of group members in addition to personality factors give rise to individual differences in susceptibility to groupthink—for example, social class, ethnic origin, occupational training, prior experience in group decision-making. Richard Barnet, in *The Economy of Death*, emphasizes the homogeneous social and educational backgrounds of the officials who man the top posts in Washington. This type of homogeneity may also be an important factor that increases the chances of groupthink.

Groups of individuals showing a preponderance of certain personality and social attributes may prove to be the ones that succumb most readily to groupthink. But persons with the most detrimental of these attributes would seldom survive the career struggles required to reach high executive positions. Nevertheless, my own observations of the way successful as well as unsuccessful executives react when they become involved in two-week workshops in group relations training suggest that none is immune to groupthink. Even individuals who are generally high in self-esteem and low in dependency and submissiveness are quite capable of being caught up from time to time in the group madness that produces the symptoms of groupthink. In certain powerful circumstances that make for groupthink, probably every member of every policy-making group, no matter whether strongly or mildly predisposed, is susceptible. I propose to adopt the general working assumption that all policy-makers are vulnerable whenever circumstances promote concurrence-seeking.

HOW WIDESPREAD IS GROUPTHINK?

At present we do not know what percentage of all national fiascoes are attributable to groupthink. Some decisions of poor quality that turn out to be fiascoes might be ascribed primarily to mistakes made by just one man, the chief executive. Others arise because of a faulty policy formulated by a group of executives whose decision-making procedures were impaired by errors having little or nothing to do with groupthink. For example, a noncohesive committee may be made up of bickering factions so intent on fighting for political power within the government bureaucracy that the participants have little interest in examining the real issues posed by the foreign policy question they are debating; they may settle for a compromise that fails to take account of adverse effects on people outside their own political arena.

All that can be said from the historical case studies I have analyzed so far is that groupthink tendencies sometimes play a major role in producing large-scale fiascoes. In order to estimate how large the percentage might be for various types of decision-making groups, we need investigations of a variety of

policy decisions made by groups of executives who have grossly miscalculated the unfavorable consequences of their chosen course of action. The "only-in-America" question posed at the beginning of this chapter could be pursued further in an examination of a substantial number of ill-considered decisions made by various European and other foreign governments, including some from earlier centuries. Among the most recent fiascoes to be considered would be the Nasser government's provocations in 1967 that led to the outbreak of the 6-day Israeli-Arab war and the Pakistan government's provocations in 1971 that led to the outbreak of the 13-day Indian-Pakistani war.

A selection of United States government decisions to be used in further research on the incidence of groupthink-dominated deliberations should include some made during Republican administrations that might be comparable to the ones made during the Roosevelt, Truman, Kennedy, and Johnson administrations. The sample might also contain representative instances of governmental decisions made by executive groups below the top level—comparable to the decisions of Admiral Kimmel's naval group in Hawaii in 1941—including some having nothing to do with war and peace. One example would be the decision made by United States Department of Justice attorneys who spent several years preparing a case against Dr. Andrew Ivy, an American scientist who was distributing a worthless drug known as Krebiozen and claiming that it was a cure for cancer. The group of government lawyers, with the concurrence of administrators in the Food and Drug Administration, made the mistake of bringing a massive indictment charging conspiracy, fraud, and a variety of related crimes that could have put Dr. Ivy in jail for more than a hundred years. When the trial took place in 1966, they failed to convince the jury of the truth of these extreme charges; they undoubtedly would have had a solid case on lesser charges. The archives of other nations might also provide evidence of groupthink among comparable groups of bureaucrats, as in the case of the decision by Britain's National Coal Board to ignore warnings about a coal tip slide in Aberfan, Wales, in order to save the money and time that would have been required for taking proper precautions. When the predicted slide disaster occurred in October 1966, the local school was completely buried and all the town's school children were killed.

Unwise and disastrous policy decisions made by industrial firms might also be examined in order to investigate groupthink tendencies in organizations outside of governmental bureaucracies. Here are some likely candidates:

A lethal decision was made in 1961 by a group of nine directors and scientists of Grünenthal Chemie, the German firm that was making huge profits from marketing Thalidomide as a tranquilizer, to ignore alarming reports from physicians all over the world about dangerous side effects and to advertise that their cherished money-making drug was safe enough to be used by pregnant women, even though the firm had not run a single test to find out its effects on the unborn. Within less than a year after the advertising, approximately seven thousand deformed children were born. The German government brought criminal charges against the directors and, as a result of civil suits by parents of "Thalidomide babies," the firm had to pay millions of dollars in damages.

During the 1950s a clique of general managers and vice presidents of General Electric, Westinghouse, Allis-Chalmers, McGraw-Edison, and other electric companies met together informally at golf clubs and hotels to make illegal price-fixing arrangements, confident that their firms would support them in the unlikely event they were caught. But caught they were—then convicted of conspiracy, fired, fined, and imprisoned.

In 1956, the directors of Ford Motor Company decided to proceed with their plans to introduce the Edsel, a medium-priced car loaded with costly extra ornamentation designed to appeal to status-aspiring consumers, despite mounting evidence that the market was rapidly shifting to low-priced cars. An analysis of this marketing misadventure, which cost the company a net loss of more than $300 million, indicates that "among several sources of failure, stereotypes of their market blinded the company to accelerating sales of foreign cars, which Detroit contemptuously dismissed as 'the teacher trade.' "

From 1957 to 1963, the top executives of American Express Field Warehousing gave warehouse receipts of 1.9 billion pounds of salad oil to Anthony De Angelis, a shady businessman who had been repeatedly indicted for cheating on contracts. The executives ignored widespread rumors of trickery and never took the elementary precaution of ordering a careful inspection of De Angelis' storage tanks, which in fact were empty or filled with water. Their failure enabled De Angelis to use the good-as-gold warehouse receipts to obtain huge loans from the American Express Company and from fifty banks, brokerage houses, and export firms, which collectively sustained losses of $175 million when "the great salad oil swindle" finally came to light in 1963.

Before looking into such decisions for symptoms of groupthink, we first must check the facts in detail to make sure that each decision in the sample was a group product and not simply based on the judgment of one powerful leader who induced the others to go along with him regardless of whether they thought his decision was good, bad, or indifferent. This consideration has kept me from nominating as candidates a number of fiascoes caused by totalitarian governments—Mussolini's decision to enter the war in 1940 when Italy was completely unprepared, Stalin's failure to anticipate a German invasion while implementing the Nazi-Soviet pact in 1941, Hitler's fatal decision to invade Russian in 1941—although it is conceivable that in some of these decisions the dictator's advisers participated as genuine policy-makers, not merely as sycophants.

THE LEADER'S ROLE: FACT VERSUS MYTH

Even in nontotalitarian countries, a powerful leader's advisers may conform with his wishes, thinking "it is not up to me to make this decision." This type of surface conformity, as noted earlier, is not the same as groupthink, which involves genuine judgments made by all members of the advisory or planning group. Consequently, in each instance of an apparent group decision, we must try to find out if the members concur on a misconceived policy because of internalized group norms, rather than because of motivations such as fear or respect for the leader's power, which could make them insincerely converge on what they think the leader wants.

In attempting to make these discriminations, we must try to separate facts from myths. In America, according to traditional political doctrine, the President has sole responsibility for every decision authorized by the executive branch. Thus President Eisenhower was responsible for the erroneous decision to send U-2 spy planes over the Soviet Union even though he was not even informed about them by the Pentagon until after he had publicly denied that the United States had launched any such flights. President Truman, according to the doctrine, had sole responsibility for the Korean War decisions even though he was highly responsive to his advisers' recommendations and on at least one important decision was induced to change his mind completely. (It will be recalled that Truman had wanted to accept Chiang Kai-shek's offer to send Chinese Nationalist troops to Korea but was talked out of it by members of his inner circle.) John F. Kennedy reinforced the traditional myth by publicly assuming full responsibility for the Bay of Pigs fiasco. Nevertheless, his advisers knew that they shared the responsibility, and some of them acknowledged feeling personally humiliated. The known facts about how these decisions were arrived at certainly do not correspond to the myth.

The problem of discerning whether advisers participated as policy-makers arises in connection with the major decisions made by business firms, educational institutions, and other large organizations, whenever a leader has nominal responsibility for the organization's policies. Only decisions in which the consensus of a stable in-group plays a crucial role in determining the chosen policy are relevant to investigations of the groupthink hypothesis. Thus the list of potential candidates needs to be cut by eliminating those that cannot be classified as group decisions.

I expect that investigations of a wide variety of group decisions will probably show that clear symptoms of groupthink are present in at least a substantial minority of all miscalculated executive decisions—governmental and non-governmental, American and foreign. Furthermore, I expect that if the series of decisions made by any single policy-making group (in the government, industry, medicine, law, education, or any field) is examined carefully over a period of several years, a sizable percentage of that group's decision errors probably will prove to be attributable to groupthink tendencies, if the group is moderately or highly cohesive. This is what I mean in tentatively suggesting that every executive who participates in group decisions is potentially susceptible to groupthink.

HYPOTHESES ABOUT WHEN GROUPTHINK OCCURS

When groupthink is most likely to occur pertains to situational circumstances and structural features of the group that make it easy for the symptoms to become dominant. The prime condition repeatedly encountered in the case studies of fiascoes is group cohesiveness. A second major condition suggested by the case studies is insulation of the decision-making group from the judgments of qualified associates who, as outsiders, are not permitted to know about the new policies under discussion until after a final decision has been made. Hence a second hypothesis is that the more insulated a cohesive group of executives becomes, the

greater are the chances that its policy decisions will be products of groupthink. A third hypothesis suggested by the case studies is that the more actively the leader of a cohesive policy-making group promotes his own preferred solution, the greater are the chances of a consensus based on groupthink, even when the leader does not want the members to be yes-men and the individual members try to resist conforming. To test these hypotheses we would have to compare large samples of high-quality and low-quality decisions made by equivalent executive groups.[1]

THE GROUPTHINK SYNDROME: REVIEW OF THE MAJOR SYMPTOMS

In order to test generalizations about the conditions that increase the chances of groupthink, we must operationalize the concept of groupthink by describing the symptoms to which it refers. Eight main symptoms run through the case studies of historic fiascoes. Each symptom can be identified by a variety of indicators,

[1] Comparative studies should provide us with fairly dependable evidence on situational and structural factors that make a difference. This type of research ought to enable investigators not only to test hypotheses concerning the effects of situational factors we already know something about but also to discover the circumstances present when the quality of a group's decision-making is adversely affected by groupthink and absent when the same group (or a comparable group) functions effectively as a decision-making body. Comparative investigations might also provide evidence concerning the interactions of predispositional factors (personality, social background, training) and situational or structural factors (nature of the crisis, type of risks, role assignments), so that we could gradually build up our knowledge of the sorts of persons most vulnerable to each type of circumstance that promotes groupthink.

derived from historical records, observer's accounts of conversations, and participants' memoirs. The eight symptoms of groupthink are:

1. an illusion of invulnerability, shared by most or all of the members, which creates excessive optimism and encourages taking extreme risks;
2. collective efforts to rationalize in order to discount warnings which might lead the members to reconsider their assumptions before they recommit themselves to their past policy decisions;
3. an unquestioned belief in the group's inherent morality, inclining the members to ignore the ethical or moral consequences of their decisions;
4. stereotyped views of enemy leaders as too evil to warrant genuine attempts to negotiate, or as too weak and stupid to counter whatever risky attempts are made to defeat their purposes;
5. direct pressure on any member who expresses strong arguments against any of the group's stereotypes, illusions, or commitments, making clear that this type of dissent is contrary to what is expected of all loyal members;
6. self-censorship of deviations from the apparent group consensus, reflecting each member's inclination to minimize to himself the importance of his doubts and counterarguments;
7. a shared illusion of unanimity concerning judgments conforming to the majority view (partly resulting from self-censorship of deviations, augmented by the false assumption that silence means consent);

8. the emergence of self-appointed mindguards—members who protect the group from adverse information that might shatter their shared complacency about the effectiveness and morality of their decisions.

When a policy-making group displays most or all of these symptoms, the members perform their collective tasks ineffectively and are likely to fail to attain their collective objectives. Although concurrence-seeking may contribute to maintaining morale after a defeat and to muddling through a crisis when prospects for a successful outcome look bleak, these positive effects are generally outweighed by the poor quality of the group's decision-making. My assumption is that the more frequently a group displays the symptoms, the worse will be the quality of its decisions. Even when some symptoms are absent, the others may be so pronounced that we can predict all the unfortunate consequences of groupthink.

ARE COHESIVE GROUPS DOOMED TO BE VICTIMS?

The major condition that promotes groupthink has been emphasized as the main theme of this book: The more amiability and esprit de corps among the members of an in-group of policymakers, the greater is the danger that independent critical thinking will be replaced by groupthink, which is likely to result in irrational and dehumanizing actions directed at outgroups. Yet when we recall the case studies of the Cuban missile crisis and the Marshall Plan, we surmise that some caveats about applying this generalization are in order. A high degree of "amiability and esprit de corps among the members"—that is, group cohesiveness—does not invariably lead to symptoms of groupthink. It may be a necessary condition, but it is not a sufficient condition. Taking this into account, I have introduced an explicit proviso in the wording of the generalization, asserting that the greater the cohesiveness of the group, "the greater is the danger" of a groupthink type of decision. Dangers do not always materialize and can sometimes be prevented by precautionary measures. In effect, then, the hypothesis asserts a positive relationship, which may be far from perfect, among three variables that can be assessed independently: A high degree of *group cohesiveness* is conducive to a high frequency of *symptoms of groupthink*, which, in turn, are conducive to a high frequency of *defects in decision-making*. Two conditions that may play an important role in determining whether or not group cohesiveness will lead to groupthink have been mentioned—insulation of the policy-making group and promotional leadership practices.

Obviously, the main generalization about the relationship of group cohesiveness and groupthink is not an iron law of executive behavior that dooms the members of every cohesive group to become victims of groupthink every time they make a collective decision. Rather, we can expect high cohesiveness to be conducive to groupthink except when certain conditions are present or special precautions are taken that counteract concurrence-seeking tendencies.

When appropriate precautions are taken, a group that has become moderately or highly cohesive probably will do a much better job on its decision-making tasks than if it had remained noncohesive. Compliance out of fear of recrimination is likely to be strongest when there is little or no sense of solidarity among the group members. In order to overcome this fear, a person needs to have a great deal of confidence that he is a member in good standing and that the others will continue to value his role in the group, whether or not he argues with them about the issue under discussion. Social psychological studies indicate that as a member of a group is made to feel more accepted by the others—a central feature of increased group cohesiveness—he acquires greater freedom to say what he really thinks. Dittes and Kelley, for example, discovered in a social psychological experiment that when individuals in a group were given information indicating that they were highly accepted by their fellow members, they became more willing to express opinions that deviated from the group consensus. Members who were made to feel that they were not accepted by their colleagues became subdued. After being informed about the low acceptance ratings, they participated in the group discussions only half as often as they had before. When they did speak, they showed much more conformity with the group consensus than any of the other members did. However, these conformists had developed an attitude of inner detachment from the group. This was revealed in their answers to questions that elicited their private views, which showed little conformity to the group's norms and low valuation of membership in the group. Their superficial conformity appears to have been motivated by a fear of being humilated by being expelled from the group altogether.

The unaccepted members in the Dittes and Kelley study probably reacted the way most people do in a group of high-status people who are strangers, before cohesiveness and feelings of security have developed. The highly accepted members probably reacted like members of cohesive groups. In the Dittes and Kelley study, the accepted members were more responsive than unaccepted members to new information that contradicted the group's earlier assumptions and more freely expressed opinions differing from the group consensus. This pattern of relatively independent thinking is probably characteristic of group members who have developed a relationship of mutual acceptance in which each person assumes that the others in the group want to know what he really thinks and will want him to continue as a member regardless of what he says.

When a group has a low degree of cohesiveness, there are, of course, sources of error in decision-making in addition to deliberate conformity out of fear of recrimination. One that is especially likely to plague a noncohesive group of politicians or administrators is a win-lose fighting stance, which inclines each participant to fight hard for his own point of view (or the point of view of his organization), without much regard for the real issues at stake. When unlike-minded people who are political opponents are forced to meet together in a group, they can be expected to behave like couples in olden times who were forced to live together by a shotgun marriage. The incompatible members of a shotgun committee often indulge in painfully repetitive debates, frequently punctuated with invective,

mutual ridicule, and maneuvers of one-upmanship in a continuous struggle for power that is not at all conducive to decisions of high quality. This is another reason for expecting that policy-making groups lacking amiability and esprit de corps, even though spared the unfavorable symptoms of groupthink, will sometimes show more symptoms of defective decision-making and produce worse fiascoes than groups that are moderately or highly cohesive. When we consider the two major sources of error that beset noncohesive groups—deliberate conformity out of fear of recrimination and a win-lose fighting stance—we see that cohesive groups can have great advantages if groupthink tendencies can be kept from becoming dominant.

As the members of a decision-making group develop bonds of friendship and esprit de corps, they become less competitive and begin to trust each other to tolerate disagreements. They are less likely to use deceitful arguments or to play safe by dancing around the issues with vapid or conventional comments. We expect that the more cohesive a group becomes, the less the members will deliberately censor what they say because of fear of being socially punished for antagonizing the leader of any of their fellow members. But the outcome is complicated because the more cohesive a group becomes, the more the members will unwittingly censor what they think because of their newly acquired motivation to preserve the unity of the group and to adhere to its norms. Thus, although the members of a highly cohesive group feel much freer to deviate from the majority, their desire for genuine concurrence on all important issues—to match their opinions with each other and to conduct themselves in accordance with each other's wishes—often inclines them not to use this freedom. In a cohesive group of policy-makers the danger is not that each individual will fail to reveal his strong objections to a proposal favored by the majority but that he will think the proposal is a good one, without attempting to carry out a critical scrutiny that could lead him to see that there are grounds for strong objections. When groupthink dominates, suppression of deviant thoughts takes the form of each person's deciding that his misgivings are not relevant, that the benefit of any doubt should be given to the group consensus. A member of a cohesive group will rarely be subjected to direct group pressures from the majority because he will rarely take a position that threatens the unity of the group.

Prior research on group dynamics indicates that at least three different types of social rewards tend to increase group cohesiveness—friendship, prestige, and enhanced competence. Concurrence-seeking tendencies probably are stronger when high cohesiveness is based primarily on the rewards of being in a pleasant "clubby" atmosphere or of gaining prestige from being a member of an elite group than when it is based primarily on the opportunity to function competently on work tasks with effective co-workers. In a cohesive policy-making group of the latter type, careful appraisal of policy alternatives is likely to become a group norm to which the members conscientiously adhere; this helps to counteract groupthink. But even when the basis of high cohesiveness is enhancement of task-oriented values in a well-functioning group whose members trust each other sufficiently to tolerate disagreements, there is still the danger that groupthink

will become a dominant tendency. Each member develops a strong motivation to preserve the rewards of group solidarity, an inner compulsion to avoid creating disunity, which inclines him to believe in the soundness of the proposals promoted by the leader or by the majority of the group's members.

A cohesive group that on one occasion suffers from groupthink is capable on other occasions of gaining the advantages of high morale and free expression of dissent, depending on whether special conditions that promote groupthink are present. The duality of cohesiveness may explain some of the inconsistencies in research results on group effectiveness. For example, Marvin Shaw in a recent book, *Group Dynamics*, presents as a plausible hypothesis the proposition, "High-cohesive groups are more effective than low-cohesive groups in achieving their respective goals," but he acknowledges that the evidence "is not altogether consistent." A major source of inconsistency may be variation in the strength of concurrence-seeking tendencies, which counter the goals of a work group on any task requiring planning or decision-making. This is how I interpret the difference between the ineffective Bay of Pigs decision and the effective Cuban missile crisis decision made by nearly identical cohesive groups of policy-makers headed by the same leader.

For most groups, optimal functioning in decision-making tasks may prove to be at a moderate level of cohesiveness, avoiding the disadvantages of conformity out of fear of recimination when cohesiveness is low and the disadvantages of strong concurrence-seeking tendencies when cohesiveness is high. If, however, the latter disadvantages can be held to a minimum by administrative practices that prevent group-think tendencies from becoming dominant, then the optimal level of cohesiveness for effective decision-making could prove to be much higher.[2]

RUDIMENTS OF AN EXPLANATORY THEORY

The problem of *why* groupthink occurs is more difficult to investigate than the problem of *who* is vulnerable and *when*. But *why* is the heart of the matter if we want to explain the observed phenomena of groupthink. An adequate explanation would account for the

known conditions that encourage or discourage concurrence-seeking tendencies and would enable us to predict the effects of conditions that we do not yet know about.

The search for an explanation forces us to tread through a quagmire of complicated theoretical issues in still largely uncharted areas of human motivation. For many years, psychologists have been trying to formulate general psychological principles that would apply to all the observed phenomena of group dynamics, but no well-established theory is generally accepted by behavioral scientists. However, promising leads extracted from recent

[2] Some of the implications of the distinction between deliberate conformity based on fear of recrimination and nondeliberate conformity based on concurrence-seeking tendencies are illustrated in the diagram below.

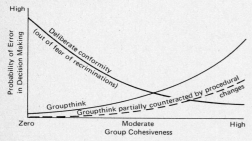

Hypothetical curves showing expected relationships between cohesiveness of the group and errors from deliberate conformity and from groupthink tendencies.

The inverse relation between cohesiveness and deliberate conformity out of fear of recrimination is represented by the descending curve in the diagram. In contrast, a positive relation between groupthink tendencies and cohesiveness is represented by the ascending (solid-line) curve. The assumption that groupthink tendencies can be partially counteracted is represented by the dashed line, which shows the expected decrease in groupthink tendencies from various administrative changes that meet the conditions for preventing or counteracting concurrence-seeking tendencies. (The dashed line could also represent

the lower degree of concurrence-seeking expected when cohesiveness is based on enhancement of competence and other task-oriented values rather than on purely social rewards of friendship and prestige.) When none of the conditions that counteract groupthink are present, the combination of the two conformity curves (deliberate conformity out of fear of recrimination and concurrence-seeking) will produce a U-shaped curve, with the optimal level falling somewhere in the middle range of cohesiveness, where deliberate conformity is substantially lower than at zero cohesiveness but where concurrence-seeking tendencies have not yet become very strong. By optimal level, I mean the degree of cohesiveness that gives rise to the fewest errors in decision-making. The optimal level corresponds to the lowest point on the combined U-shaped curve, which, for two combinable curves like those shown in the diagram, occurs near the point where they intersect. When groupthink is partially counteracted, the combination of the curve for groupthink tendencies (the dashed line) with the curve for deliberate conformity results in a U-shaped curve whose lowest point is much farther to the right; that is, the optimal level is at a higher level of cohesiveness. Theoretically speaking, if groupthink could be eliminated, there would be nothing to add to the curve for deliberate conformity, and the optimal level would be at the highest possible degree of cohesiveness. The main point is that the more effectively groupthink is counteracted, the higher will be the optimal level of cohesiveness.

social psychological research may point the way to an adequate explanation of the groupthink syndrome. The evidence needed to test hypotheses about the causes of groupthink must ultimately come from field experiments and other systematic investigations specifically designed to pin down causal sequences, rather than from historical case studies, which are useful mainly for suggesting hypotheses.

The central explanatory concept involves viewing concurrence-seeking as a form of striving for mutual support based on a powerful motivation in all group members to cope with the stresses of decision-making that cannot be alleviated by standard operating procedures. Anxieties aroused by salient risks of material losses for themselves and for their organization or their nation will generally impel members to become vigilant, to set in motion the administrative machinery for obtaining objective information, and to institute other standard operating procedures for working out careful plans in order to eliminate the threat. However, other sources of stress in decision-making cannot be coped with so easily. For example, few, if any, operating procedures enable a policy-maker to cope with the threat of losing self-esteem from violating ethical standards of conduct. Often the group's deliberations about policy issues generate within each participant an intense conflict between humanitarian values on the one hand and the utilitarian demands of national or organizational goals, practical politics, and economics on the other. The participant may try to reassure himself with the platitudinous thought that "you can't make an omelet without breaking some eggs." Nevertheless, each time he realizes that he is sacrificing moral values in order to arrive at a viable policy, he will be burdened with anticipatory feelings of shame, guilt, and related feelings of self-depreciation, which lower his self-esteem. Similar feelings are generated whenever a decision-maker is faced with a perplexing choice that he considers beyond his level of competence or that forces him to become keenly aware of his personal inadequacies. For all such sources of stress, participating in a unanimous consensus along with the respected fellow members of a congenial group will bolster the decision-maker's self-esteem.

Some individuals are extraordinarily self-confident and may not need the support of a cohesive group when their decisions are subject to social criticism. For example, the spirited symphony orchestra conductor Sir Thomas Beecham once said, "I have made just one mistake in my entire life and that was one time when I thought I was wrong but actually I was right." Not everybody who is accustomed to putting it on the line as a decision-maker is able to maintain such an unassailable sense of self-assurance.

PSYCHOLOGICAL FUNCTIONS OF THE EIGHT SYMPTOMS

Concurrence-seeking and the various symptoms of groupthink to which it gives rise can be best understood as a mutual effort among the members of a group to maintain self-esteem, especially when they share responsibility for making vital decisions that pose threats of social disapproval and self-disapproval. The eight symptoms of groupthink form a coherent pattern if viewed in the context of this explanatory hypothesis. The symptoms may function in somewhat different ways to produce the same result.

A shared illusion of invulnerability and shared rationalizations can counteract unnerving feelings of personal inadequacy and pessimism about finding an adequate solution during a crisis. Even during noncrisis periods, whenever the members foresee great gains from taking a socially disapproved or unethical course of action, they seek some way of disregarding the threat of being found out and welcome the optimistic views of the members who argue for the attractive but risky course of action.[3] At such times, as well as during distressing crises, if the threat of failure is salient, the members are likely to convey to each other the attitude that "we needn't worry, everything will go our way." By pooling their intellectual resources to develop rationalizations, the members build up each other's confidence and feel reassured about unfamiliar risks, which, if taken seriously, would be dealt with by applying standard operating procedures to obtain additional information and to carry out careful planning.

The members' firm belief in the inherent morality of their group and their use of undifferentiated negative stereotypes of opponents enable them to minimize decision conflicts between ethical values and expediency, especially when they are inclined to resort to violence. The shared belief that "we are a wise and good group" inclines them to use group concurrence as a major criterion to judge the morality as well as the efficacy of any policy under discussion. "Since our group's objectives are good," the members feel, "any means we decide to use must be good." This shared assumption helps the members avoid feelings of shame or guilt about decisions that may violate their personal code of ethical behavior. Negative stereotypes of the enemy enhance their sense of moral righteousness as well as their pride in the lofty mission of the ingroup.

Every cohesive group that is required to make policy decisions tends to develop a set of policy doctrines, derived from the members' subculture, that provides the members with a cognitive map for conceptualizing the intentions and reactions of opponents, allies, and neutrals. But to be effective decisionmakers, the members need to exercise a certain flexibility in the use of those doctrines in order to take account of new information and their own feelings of empathy. They can then evolve sophisticated concepts that enable them to weigh the prospects for negotiations in the light of fresh evidence about their opponents' current objectives and strategies. During a confrontation involving the threat of open hostilities, the loss of flexibility is the price a cohesive group pays to gain the greater sense of moral righteousness from sharing an image of the enemy as intractable and deserving of punishment. Stereotypes that dehumanize outgroups alleviate guilt by legitimizing destructive and inhumane acts against

[3] Roger Brown (1965) has suggested a similar influence process in his discussion of social psychological experiments on the "risky-shift" phenomenon, which show that individuals are frequently led to favor risky decisions after they have participated in a group dicussion:

the risky members would seem to be influential only because they have happened to hold views or values to which the group is already disposed. They seem to influence because they are representative of what the group in any case wishes to do. They are in the vanguard only because they are going the way the herd is already headed (Brown, pp. 687–88).

them. As Donald Campbell says, "The out-group's opprobrious characteristics seem [to the in-grouper] to fully justify the hostility and rejection he shows toward it." Focusing hostility on out-groups probably also serves the psychological function of displacing aggression away from the in-group, thereby reducing stress arising from latent jealousies and antagonisms within the group.

When most members fall back upon the familiar forms of social pressure directed against a member who questions the group's wisdom or morality, they are in effect protecting a prop that helps them to keep anxiety and guilt to a minimum. If subtle pressures fail, stronger efforts are made to limit the extent of his deviation, to make him a domesticated dissenter. We have seen this clearly in the case of President Johnson's in-group when one or two of the members disagreed with the majority's position that air attacks against North Vietnam should be increased. A doubter who accepts the role is no longer a problem because his objections are confined to issues that do not threaten to shake the confidence of the group members in the reasonableness and righteousness of their collective judgments. At the same time, the doubter's tamed presentation of an opposing viewpoint permits the others to think that their group is strong-minded enough to tolerate dissent. If the domestication efforts do not succeed, the dissenter is ultimately ostracized, so that the relatively tranquil emotional atmosphere of a homogeneous group is restored.

When a member is dependent on the group for bolstering his feelings of self-confidence, he tends to exercise self-censorship over his misgivings. The greater the dependence, the stronger will be the motivation to ahdere to the group's norms. One of the norms that is likely to become dominant during a crisis involves living up to a mutual nonaggression pact. Each individual in the group feels himself to be under an injunction to avoid making penetrating criticisms that might bring on a clash with fellow members and destroy the unity of the group. Adhering to this norm promotes a sense of collective strength and also eliminates the threat of damage to each participant's self-esteem from hearing his own judgments on vital issues criticized by respected associates. We have seen how much painful emotion was generated in Kennan's group of critical thinkers working on the Marshall Plan and in Kennedy's Executive Committee debating alternative ways to get rid of the Soviet missiles in Cuba. In contrast, the emotional state of those who participated in the groupthink-dominated deliberations that led to fiascoes was relatively placid. When the mutual nonaggression pact and other related norms for preserving the unity of the group are internalized, each member avoids interfering with an emerging consensus by assuring himself that the opposing arguments he had in mind must be erroneous or that his misgivings are too unimportant to be worth mentioning.

The various devices to enhance self-esteem require an illusion of unanimity about all important judgments. Without it, the sense of group unity would be lost, gnawing doubts would start to grow, confidence in the group's problem-solving capacity would shrink and soon the full emotional impact of all the stresses generated by making a difficult decision would be aroused. Preserving the sense of unity can do more than keep anxiety and guilt to a minimum; it can induce pleasant feelings of elation. Members of a group sometimes enjoy an exhilarating sense of omnipotence from participating in a crisis decision with a group that displays solidarity against an evil enemy and complete unanimity about everything that needs to be done.[4]

Self-appointed mindguards help to preserve the shared sense of complacency by making sure that the leader and other members are not exposed to information that might challenge their self-confidence. If the mindguard were to transmit the potentially distressing information, he and the others might become discouraged by the apparent defects in their cherished policy and find themselves impelled to initiate a painful reevaluation.

CONCLUSION

The greater the threats to the self-esteem of the members of a cohesive decision-making body, the greater will be their inclination to resort to concurrence-seeking at the expense of critical thinking. If this explanatory hypothesis is correct, symptoms of groupthink will be found most often when a decision poses a moral dilemma, especially if the most advantageous course of action requires the policy-makers to violate their own standards to humanitarian behavior. Under these conditions, each member is likely to become more dependent than ever on the in-group for maintaining his self-image as a decent human being and accordingly will be more strongly motivated than ever to maintain a sense of group unity by striving for concurrence.[5]

Until the explanation of groupthink in terms of mutual support to cope with threats to self-esteem is verified by sys-

[4] One implication of the speculative notions about elation and the sense of omnipotence is that members of a cohesive policy-making group would actually enjoy undergoing an external crisis requiring drastic action against an enemy. But obtaining evidence of such reactions among government policy-makers is difficult because no responsible government official would be likely to admit publicly that he enjoys having his country plunged into a crisis that brings it to the brink of war. However, positive reactions of elation have occasionally been reported by leading participants in nonmilitary battles over social issues. Romain Rolland, for example, has described his elation in response to the upsurge of protest among French liberals who displayed a remarkable degree of unity in attacking the French military establishment at the time of the Dreyfus affair. In February 1898, when the Dreyfusards were mobilized by the opening of the sensational trial of Emile Zola, who had accused the French military authorities of a frame-up, Romain wrote in his diary: "I would rather have this life of combat than the mortal calm and mournful stupor of these last years. God give me struggle, enemies, howling crowds, all the combat of which I am capable." Senator Ranc, another supporter of Dreyfus, recalled that during that period, "It was exciting; one felt alive; nothing is so good as a time of action, in combat in the consciousness of the cause" (Quoted in Tuchman, 1966, pp. 204–205).

[5] Some predictions about personality predispositions also follow from an explanation of groupthink in terms of self-esteem enhancement. We would expect the symptoms of groupthink to occur with the highest frequency in small groups made up of persons who are disposed to seek for social support whenever they are required to assume responsibility for controversial policy decisions likely to be criticized by friends as well as by opponents. On the basis of recent studies of personality and social conformity, we would expect that this disposition would be strongest in persons who are characterized by relatively low-esteem, relatively high responsiveness to social disapproval, and unusually acute conflict in situations where there is an opportunity to indulge in rewarding but unethical actions or to exercise power in a way that could gratify unacceptable self-aggrandizing needs.

tematic research, it is risky to make huge inferential leaps from theory to the practical sphere of prevention. Ultimately, a well-substantiated theory should have valuable practical applications to the formulation of effective prescriptions. As Kurt Lewin pointed out, "Nothing is so practical as a good theory." But until we know we have a good theory—one that is well supported by controlled experiments and systematic correlational research, as well as by case studies—we must recognize that

any prescriptions we draw up are speculative inferences based on what little we know, or think we know, about when and why groupthink occurs. Still, we should not be inhibited from drawing tentative inferences—so long as we label them as such—in order to call attention to potentially useful means of prevention. Perhaps the worst consequences can be prevented if we take steps to avoid the circumstances in which groupthink is most likely to flourish.

Bureaucratic Defense in Depth

Peter Woll and Rochelle Jones

The Watergate hearings have intensified the debate over the growth—and proper limits—of Presidential power. Among many concerned people in and out of government the feeling is that Richard Nixon was making an unprecedented attempt to concentrate political power in the White House. For evidence the critics point to Nixon's attempt to dismantle the Office of Economic Opportunity, an office created by Congress, his impoundment of funds appropriated by Congress for water pollution, highways and other programs, and his repeated disregard of Congressional resolutions on the war in Southeast Asia. Only after he was pushed to the wall by Congres-

Peter Woll and Rochelle Jones, "Bureaucratic Defense in Depth." *The Nation*, September 17, 1973. Reprinted with permission.

sional action that threatened to cut off funds for the entire federal government if he did not stop the bombing of Cambodia, did he agree to an August 15th deadline for a bombing halt. In a recent series of articles in *The New York Times* Henry Steele Commager said that the United States is closer to one-man rule than at any time in its history.

While there is no doubt that Nixon frequently thwarts the will and intent of Congress, it does not necessarily mean we are on the verge of one-man rule. Nixon apparently would like to retitle the federal government "U.S. Government, Inc.; President: Richard M. Nixon," but the federal bureaucracy, composed of the Cabinet, independent regulatory commissions and administrative agencies, puts important limits on the power of the President. Under the

Nixon Administration the bureaucracy is turning into a vital although little noticed safeguard of the democratic system.

The bureaucracy, sometimes with Congress but often by itself, has frequently been able to resist and ignore Presidential commands. Whether the President is FDR or Richard M. Nixon, bureaucratic frustration of White House policies is a fact of life. Furthermore, the bureaucracy often carries out its own policies which are at times the exact opposite of White House directives. A classic case occurred during the India-Pakistan war in 1971 when the State Department supported India while the White House backed Pakistan. The State Department's behind-the-scenes maneuvering in support of India prompted Henry Kissinger's famous enraged order "to tilt" toward Pakistan.

In a system marked by a weak Congress and a Supreme Court that is increasingly taking its direction from Nixon appointees, the bureaucracy is turning into a crucial check on Presidential power. Under the Constitution Nixon is chief executive, but this does not mean he has legal authority or politcal power to control the bureaucracy. On the contrary, the bureaucracy has become a fourth branch of government, separate and independent of the President, Congress and the courts. There are limits to bureaucratic discretion, but these are set as much by Congress and the courts as by the President. Decisions of independent regulatory commissions may be overturned under certain circumstances by the courts. And while the administrative agencies created by Congress are delegated considerable discretionary authority, this authority must be exercised within broad

guidelines that are set by the legislature. It is precisely this accountability of the bureaucracy to the courts and Congress that helps it to be a powerful constraint on Presidential power. For example, in *State Highway Commission of Missouri* v. *Volpe* (1973) the Eighth Circuit Court of Appeals ruled that the Secretary of Transportation could not legally follow Nixon's directives and impound highway funds. The court held that Congress had clearly specified in the Federal Highway Act that appropriated funds were to be apportioned among the states. In effect, the court was saying that the Department of Transportation, a Cabinet department presumably under Presidential control, must comply with the intent of Congress, as it is interpreted by the court, instead of following the orders of the President.

Ultimately the bureaucracy curbs the President because it has independent sources of political power. Nixon's attempt to cut back governmental programs and reduce spending conflicts with the vested interests of powerful groups in and out of government. Like Congress and the President, administrative agencies and regulatory commissions have constituencies that are relied on for political support. The Defense Department needs the armaments industry, Agriculture the farmers, Labor the AFL-CIO, and ICC the railroads and truckers, and the Food and Drug Administration the giant pharmaceutical companies.

Because the bureaucracy depends on the political support of these allies for its continued existence, and because this alliance survives the four or eight years a President is in office, the bureaucracy is apt to prefer its interests over the wishes of the President. This is not new. On numerous occasions, for instance, the independent regulatory agencies have adopted policies that directly opposed the programs of the President. In the early 1960s both the Interstate Commerce Commission and Civil Aeronautics Board ignored White House directives in approving railroad and airline mergers that reduced competition.

Outside political support enables agencies to act independently. The regulatory agencies have been able to resist, for the most part, attempts by Presidents from Franklin D. Roosevelt to Richard Nixon to organize and bring them under Presidential supervision. A number of Presidents on a number of occasions have tried to transfer the regulatory functions of the Interstate Commerce Commission to a Cabinet department like the Department of Transportation, which is more capable of being controlled by the White House. But the railroads' support for the ICC has been felt in and reflected by Congress, and the ICC has retained its separate identity. With the help of equally strong support from their allies, other agencies have defeated attempts, most recently by Nixon, to reorganize them. In 1971 Nixon proposed a major reorganization of the executive branch that would have meant a major shift of authority. The Department of Agriculture, for example, would have lost control over a variety of programs to a proposed super Department of Natural Resources. But the Department of Agriculture rallied its constituency behind it, and the reorganization plan languished in Congress.

Agencies that lack independent political support in Congress and are not supported by private pressure groups are apt to be swayed by the President. There is a big difference between the Department of Transportation and the Department of State. The former is supported by a wide range of groups, from proponents of federal airport subsidies to groups connected with aviation safety, urban transit, highway safety, and the Coast Guard. The latter is without Congressional and interest group backing. When Nixon tried to create a "super-Cabinet" at the start of his second term, Secretary of Transportation Claude S. Brinegar announced loudly and repeatedly that he was not going to be subordinate to the super-Cabinet Secretary James Lynn, Secretary of the Department of Housing and Urban Development, who had been named his superior by Nixon. But Secretary of State William Rogers was upstaged from the very start of the Nixon Administration by Henry Kissinger. Kissinger has usurped the major foreign policy-making responsibilities of the State Department while serving as an unofficial ambassador at large and roving emissary to foreign governments, a pleasant duty that is traditionally the prerogative of the Secretary of State. Secretary of State John Foster Dulles played such a role in the Eisenhower administration. But this is possible only if the Secretary of State enjoys the confidence of the President as Dulles did. If he doesn't, the Secretary of State will be a mere figurehead in the foreign policy field because the State Department is exceedingly vulnerable to domination by the White House. Its lack of domestic allies enables it to win very little support from Congress. When Sen. Joseph McCarthy launched his witch hunt after subversives in government, he wisely tackled the State Department first. As long as he was battling the State Department, he was safe. When he turned on the Department of the Army with its close links to a powerful domestic constituency and hence to key Congressional committees, his downfall was imminent.

In addition to its political support the bureaucracy contains the President in other ways. The President has minimal influence within the bureaucracy because of its size, complexity, wide-ranging responsibilities, and continuity. More than one-half of the 3 million civilian employees of the federal government work for the Defense Department, for one good example. Tens of thousands of them are in key policy-making positions. All recent Secretaries of Defense, with the possible exception of McNamara, have had difficulty keeping up with day-to-day shifts in policy that are the result of decisions made by subordinates. Obviously Nixon cannot keep up with the operations of this mammoth department. And this is true in every large department of government. The President must delegate authority, and by doing so tends to lose control. Admittedly Nixon has made a strong attempt to change this. Before Watergate heightened the debate over the limits of Presidential power, Washington civil servants were operating in an atmosphere that was permeated with fear. Since the Watergate hearings started, however, bureaucrats have resumed their traditional independent stance.

Moreover, since Nixon can't know what is going on in every nook of the federal bureaucracy, he must rely on the information that is provided by it for his decision making. By carefully controlling the information that reaches the President, the bureaucracy can control his decision making. This is not necessarily Machiavellian. Very often administrators, even subordinate administrators, are the only ones who possess the background and arcane knowledge to fill in the details of vague Congressional legislation. The strength of the bureaucracy is magnified when the President and Congress must come to it for the necessary information and technical skills to formulate and implement public policy. In a highly technical and increasingly specialized society the power of bureaucracy grows because the bureaucracy is the domain of the specialist, while the Congress and President are necessarily generalists.

The use of bureaucratic expertise in Congressional policy making will be facilitated through the Office of Technological Assessment (OTA), being formed under the sponsorship of Sen. Edward Kennedy (D., Mass.). The OTA, created by legislation in 1972, is a way of challenging the present power of the Office of Management and Budget to prevent agencies from going directly to Congress with policy-making proposals. Such administrative inputs to the legislative process must first be cleared by the OMB. But the OTA is authorized to use the technical resources of the bureaucracy to draft policies that reflect the priorities of Congress. With these outside sources of information Congress will be able to challenge the President in a way previously impossible. Because Congress will be relying on information that comes from the bureaucracy, the bureaucracy will have vastly increased influence in the policy-making process. And since agency personnel assigned to the OTA will be working for Congress, not the President, they can give substantial help in developing programs that may directly contradict the programs of the President. A new bureaucratic check on the President is emerging.

Presidents come and go; the bureaucracy stays. Even if the President's only concern were the control of the bureaucracy, he would find this extremely difficult to accomplish in eight years. Obviously the President has many other pressing concerns besides the bureaucracy. At the beginning of his first term he is concerned with making a good impression. With the election mandate behind him and the Congressional honeymoon ahead of him, the President wants to charge ahead, to do great things which, if they don't win him a place in the history books, may at least win him a second term in office. But such great plans can be abruptly halted by the bureaucracy. The newly elected President can find that many top bureaucrats who were appointed by the previous President are entrenched in power, protected by civil service regulations or terms of office that are set by statutes. The President is reduced to watching helplessly as the bureaucracy stymies his key programs. By the start of his second term the President may decide to make a determined effort to control the bureaucracy in a final, valiant attempt to push through his program.

And in fact, Nixon tried exactly that, finding that it is easy to try to curb the bureaucracy but exceedingly difficult to succeed. Nixon created a super-Cabinet last January in an attempt to centralize power in the White House; it was a dismal failure. It never functioned as it was supposed to. Agencies ignored it and did as they pleased or by-passed it and went directly to the President. Nixon finally junked the super-Cabinet four months after it was established.

In opposing Presidential programs, the bureaucracy relies heavily on informal contacts with Congress. The White House may, and often does, try to muzzle administrators, but the bureaucracy has ways of getting necessary information to key Congressmen. Information flows back and forth among bureaucrats and Congressmen over the phone, at casual meetings and cocktail parties. Pressure groups also channel information from the agencies to Congressional committees.

For example, the President can order the Department of Agriculture to eliminate or reduce various agriculture programs, but these orders are likely to fail eventually because of the strong support for the department in Congress and among various agricultural interest groups. The department might have to go along with the President temporarily, but it would not have to wait long for Congressional support to back up its policy favoring maintenance of such programs. This happened in 1972 when the Department of Agriculture abolished several key programs at the request of Nixon. An angry Congress overwhelmingly voted to restore the programs.

Many agencies are closer to Congress than to the President. The Securities and Exchange Commission (SEC) is a good example of an agency that has stronger ties to the House and Senate than to the White House. Rep. John Moss (D., Calif.), chairman of the House Subcommittee on Commerce and Finance, and Sen. Harrison Williams (D., N.J.), chairman of the Securities Subcommittee of the Senate Banking Committee, deal directly with the SEC on a continuous basis. The SEC supplies these legislators with information, and they, in turn, prod the agency to implement the policy positions that they favor. With the help of a strong professional staff, these men are directly involved in the regulation of the securities industry. Of course, the White House can wield a certain amount of power, as it did when it influenced the SEC staff to withhold important information on the financial dealings of financier Robert Vesco because the information might embarrass the Committee for the Re-election of the President. But this influence is sporadic and limited to specific issues, while Congress deals with the SEC and other agencies on an almost daily basis.

Nixon can exert some control over the bureaucracy through his power of appointment. The President directly controls the appointment of more than 2,000 top-level bureaucrats. These positions were filled during Nixon's first term with people considered "reliable." After the 1972 election all of these appointees were required to submit their resignations. Many have been fired, producing great disillusionment throughout the ranks. As a result of the insensitive behavior of Nixon's staff, the White House faced enormous difficulty in recruiting new people, and many positions remain vacant in the top echelons of departments and agencies.

Nixon has been appointing former White House aides and CREEP employees as an elite corps of "agents," numbering more than 100, to departments, independent regulatory commissions and agencies to find out what is going on and to carry out the Nixon philosophy. Such agents have been installed at the Under Secretary level in Treasury, Interior, Transportation and HEW. At lower levels agents were placed in Commerce (25), Interior (13), Agriculture (17), Treasury (11), the Environmental Protection Agency (20), Veterans Administration (11), FAA (5),

and FTC (9). Nixon has filled twenty-eight of the thirty-eight positions on six major regulatory commissions and named the chairmen of all six. White House clearance has been required of many staff appointments. This attempt to control the independent regulatory commissions prompted the House Interstate and Foreign Commerce Committee to begin an investigation of what its chairman, Harley O. Staggers (D., W. Va.), considers inappropriate White House pressure.

For a short time Nixon's appointees can undoubtedly influence administrative policy making. But Nixon has failed more often than he has succeeded in changing the direction of the bureaucracy through the appointment process. He has created anxiety, frustration and disillusionment, and impeded independent policy making by the bureaucrats in those limited number of agencies where he has placed his agents.

In the case of the independent regulatory commissions the President may be able to stack them in his favor, but this is only a temporary impediment to the commissions' inherent ability to limit Presidential power. Nixon's appointees will constitute a major limitation on the next President. From the standpoint of the Presidency, the influence of one President on regulatory agencies through appointments can lay the groundwork for future agency resistance to a new President. Similarly, the expansion of the bureaucracy in line with the philosophy of a President who believes in an activist government, such as FDR, limits future Presidents who believe in a concept of limited governmental intervention. Thus the appointment process is a two-edged sword, working against Presidential power in the long run while giving short-term advantage.

Many of Nixon's appointees, even in his elite corps, were given jobs as a political payoff for their loyalty to him and their work in his campaigns. These strictly political types have been put in showcase jobs in many cases, often as assistants to top-echelon people, consultants, and in public affairs jobs. Even "deputy administrators" are often phony jobs with an impressive title but little clout. Moreover, most political types know little or nothing about the agencies they are appointed to. They cannot rival the top-grade permanent civil servants in policy making. And while the political appointees often have short stays in their jobs, the civil servants tend to be permanent employees. In the final analysis the expertise, continuity and political ties of the permanent civil service severely limit the ability of any President to alter bureaucratic practices through his appointments.

The courts can help the bureaucracy in imposing limits on the President. In recent years, an active judiciary has forced administrative agencies to adhere closely to Congressional intent, as defined by the courts, reinforcing the ability of the bureaucracy to resist Presidential control. Within the last few months the courts declared *ultra vires* Nixon's actions to impound funds that would be appropriated to administrative agencies under normal circumstances. The courts also preserved, at least temporarily, the Office of Economic Opportunity which was in the process of being dismantled under orders from Nixon.

The Watergate affair clearly reveals the value of a semi-autonomous bureaucracy. A President who could direct the activities of all administrative agencies would threaten our constitutional system. If the White House had been able to use the FBI and CIA as it had planned, a far-flung political intelligence operation would now be operating in a way that would undermine basic guarantees of our constitutional system, such as the Fourth Amendment guarantees against unreasonable searches and seizures. It was because J. Edgar Hoover and the FBI resisted that the efforts of the White House to set up a secret police operation with the approval of Nixon were stymied. Asst. Atty. Gen. Henry Petersen, a career attorney, refused to go along with Ehrlichman's improper requests. Richard Helms and General Walters of the CIA likewise maintained their independence under pressure by Haldeman and Ehrlichman. And it seems evident that a number of career professionals at the FBI leaked information to the press in order to frustrate what they saw as a move to corrupt the bureau.

At the same time, however, bureaucrats need to be imbued with the values of our constitutional democracy because, for the most part, the limits on them are those they impose upon themselves. It is ironic that the independence of the FBI and J. Edgar Hoover, so often criticized as a potential threat to responsible government, turned out under the Nixon Administration to be a bulwark of freedom. Perhaps, in the final analysis, we are saved from tyranny by the pluralism of our system and even its inefficiency. The pluralistic and independent bureaucracy, although often inefficient and yielding to special-interest group pressure, helps to preserve the balance of powers among the branches of government that is necessary for the preservation of our system of constitutional democracy.

Vice, Corruption, Bureaucracy, and Power

William J. Chambliss

At the turn of the century Lincoln Steffens made a career and helped make a president by exposing corruption in American cities.[1] In more recent years the task of exposure has fallen into the generally less daring hands of social scientists who, unlike their journalistic predecessors, have gathered their information from police departments, attorney generals' offices, and grand jury records.[2] This difference in the source of the information has probably distorted the descriptions of organized crime. It may well have led to a premature acceptance of the justice department's long-espoused view that there is a national criminal organization.[3] It most certainly has led to an overemphasis on the *criminal* in organized crime and a de-emphasis on *corruption* as an institutionalized part of America's legal-political system.[4] Concomitantly it has led to a failure to see the degree to which the structure of America's law and politics creates and perpetuates syndicates that supply the vices in our major cities.

Getting into the bowels of the city rather than the records and IBM cards of the bureaucracies brings the role of corruption into sharp relief. It also makes it clear that "organized crime" is not something that exists outside the law and government, but is instead a creation of them or perhaps more accurately, a hidden but nonetheless integral part of the governmental structure. The people who are most likely to be exposed by public inquiries (whether conducted by the FBI, a grand jury, or the Internal Revenue Service) may be of-

William J. Chambliss, "Vice, Corruption, Bureaucracy, and Power," from *Sociological Readings in the Conflict Perspective*, Chambliss (ed.), 1973, Addison-Wesley, Reading, Mass.

I am grateful to W. G. O. Carson, Terence Morris, Paul Rock, Charles Michener, Patrick Douglas, Donald Cressey, and Robert Seidman for helpful comments on earlier versions of this paper.

[1] J. Steffens, *The Shame of the Cities* (1904). See *The Autobiography of Lincoln Steffens* (1931).

[2] D. Cressey, *Theft of the Nation* (1969); Gardiner, "Wincanton: The Politics of Corruption," Appendix B of *The President's Commission on Law Enforcement and Administration of Justice, Task Force Report: Organized Crime* (1967); in W. Chambliss, *Crime and the Legal Process* 103 (1969).

[3] The view of organized crime as controlled by a national syndicate appears in D. Cressey, *supra* note 2. For a criticism of this view see H. Morris and G. Hawkins, *The Honest Politicians Guide to Crime Control* (1970).

[4] Most recent examples of this are D. Cressey, *supra* note 2; H. Morris and G. Hawkins, *supra* note 3; King, "Wild Shots in the War on Crime," 20 *J. Pub. Law* 85 (1971); Lynch & Phillips, "Organized Crime—Violence and Corruption, 20 *J. Pub. Law* 59 (1971); McKeon, "The Incursion By Organized Crime Into Legitimate Business," 20 *J. Pub. Law* 117 (1971); Schelling, "What is the Business of Organized Crime?," 20 *J. Pub. Law* 71 (1971); Thrower, "Symposium: Organized Crime, Introduction," 20 *J. Pub. Law* 33 (1971); Tyler, "Sociodynamics of Organized Crime," 20 *J. Pub. Law* 41 (1971). For a discussion of the importance of studying corruption see W. Chambliss, *supra* note 2, at 89; W. Chambliss and R. Seidman, *Law, Order and Power* (1971); McKitvick, "The Study of Corruption," 72 *Pol. Sci. Q.* 502 (1957).

ficially outside of government, but the cabal of which they are a part is organized around, run by, and created in the interests of economic, legal, and political elites.

The study of Rainfall West (a pseudonymn), which is the basis of the analysis of the relationship between vice and the political and economic system which follows, makes it quite clear that the business of vice in the city is an integral part of the political and economic structure of the community. The cabal that manages the vices is composed of leading businessmen, law-enforcement officers, political leaders, and a member of a leading local trade union. Working for, and with, this cabal of "respectable" community members is a staff who coordinate the daily activities of prostitution, gambling, bookmaking, the sale and distribution of drugs, and other vices. Representatives from each of these groups, which comprise the political and economic power centers of the community, meet regularly to distribute the profits, discuss problems, and make the necessary organizational and policy decisions which maintain a profitable, trouble-free business.

DATA COLLECTION

The data reported in this paper were gathered over a period of seven years, from 1962–1969. Most of the data came from interviews with persons who were members of either the vice syndicate, law-enforcement agencies, or both. The interviews ranged in intensity from casual conversations to extended interviews (complete with tape recording) at frequent intervals over the full seven years of the study. In addition, I partici-

pated in many, though not all, of the vices that comprise the cornerstone upon which the corruption of the law-enforcement agencies is laid.

There is of course considerable latitude for discretion on my part as to what, ultimately, I believe to characterize the situation. Obviously not everyone told the same story, nor did I give equal credibility to everyone who gave me information. The story that emerges is one that fits most closely with my own observations and with otherwise inexplicable facts. I am confident that the data are accurate, valid, and reliable. But this cannot be demonstrated by pointing to unbiased sampling, objective measures, and the like for alas, in this type of research such procedures are impossible.

THE SETTING: RAINFALL WEST

Rainfall West is practically indistinguishable from any other city of a million inhabitants. The conspicuous bulk of the population that is the middle class shares with its contemporaries everywhere a smug complacency and a firm belief in the intrinsic worth of the area and the city. The smugness may be exaggerated here due to the relative freedom from "urban blight" that is the fate of larger cities. This, plus the fact that Rainfall West's natural surroundings attract tourists thereby provide the citizenry with confirmation of their faith that is indeed a "chosen land!"[5]

[5] Thinking of one's own residence as a "chosen land" need not of course be connected with any objectively verifiable evidence. A small Indian farm town where the standard of living is scarcely ever above the poverty level has painted signs on sidewalks which read "Isn't God good to In-

There is of course an invisible, although fairly large, minority of the population that does not think they live in the promised land. These are the inhabitants of the slums and ghettos that make up the invisible center of the city. The invisible center is kept so by urban renewal programs which ring the slums with brick buildings and skyscrapers. Yet it requires only a very slight effort to get past the brick and mortar and into the not-so-enthusiastic city center (as contrasted with the wildly bubbling "civic center" which is located less than a mile away). Despite the ease of access, few of the residents who live in the suburbs and work in the area surrounding the slums take the time to go "where the action is." Those who do go for specific reasons: to bet on a football game, to find a prostitute, to see a "dirty movie," or to obtain a personal loan that would be unavailable from conventional financial institutions.

BUREAUCRATIC CORRUPTION AND ORGANIZED CRIME: A STUDY IN SYMBIOSIS

Laws prohibiting gambling, prostitution, pornography, drug use, and high interest rates on personal loans are laws about which there is a conspicuous lack of consensus. Even among persons who agree that such things are improper and should be controlled by law, there is considerable disagreement as to what the proper legal action should be. Should persons found guilty of committing such acts be imprisoned or coun-

seled? Reflecting this dissension is the fact that there are large groups of people, some with considerable political power, who insist on their right to enjoy the pleasures of vice without interference from the law.

In Rainfall West those involved in providing gambling and other vices enjoyed pointing out that such services were profitable because of the demand for them by members of the "respectable" community. Prostitutes work in apartments which are on the fringes of the lower-class area of the city precisely because they must have an appearance of ecological respectability to avoid "contaminating" their clients. Although the prostitutes may exaggerate somewhat out of professional pride, their verbal reports are always to the effect that "all" of their clients are "very important people." My own observations of the comings and goings in several apartment houses where prostitutes work generally verified the girls' claims. Of some fifty persons seen going to prostitutes' rooms in apartment houses, only one was dressed in anything less casual than a suit.

Observations of "panorama," i.e., pornographic films shown in the back rooms of restaurants and "game rooms," confirmed the impression that the principal users of vice are middle- and upper-class clientele. During several weeks of observations over seventy percent of the consumers of these pornographic vignettes were well-dressed, single-minded visitors to the slums who came for fifteen or twenty minutes of viewing and left as inconspicuously as possible. The remaining thirty percent of those who viewed the panoramas were poorly-dressed, older men who lived in the area.

Information on gambling and book-

---

dians?" Any outside observer knowing something of the hardships and disadvantages that derive from living in this town might well answer an unequivocal "no." Most members of this community nevertheless answer affirmatively.

making in the permanently established or floating games is a little less readily available. Bookmakers reported that the bulk of their "real business" came from "doctors, lawyers, and dentists" in the city:

It's the big boys—your professionals—who do the betting down here. Of course, they don't come down themselves; they either send someone or they call up. Most of them call up, cause I know them or they know Mr. [one of the key figures in the gambling operation].

Q. How 'bout the guys who walk in off the street and bet?

A. Yeh; well, they're important. They do place bets and they sit around here and wait for the results. But that's mostly small stuff. I'd be out of business if I had to depend on them guys.

The poker and card games that are held throughout the city are of two types: the small, daily game that caters almost exclusively to local residents of the area or working-class men who drop in for a hand or two while they are driving their delivery route or on their lunch hour; and the "action game," which takes place twenty-four hours a day in the city and is located in more obscure places such as a downtown hotel suite. (The hotel and these games are, like the prostitutes, located on the fringes of the lower-class areas.) The "action games" were the playground of well-dressed men who were by manner, finances, and dress clearly well-to-do businessmen.

Then of course there are the games, movies, and gambling nights at the private clubs—country clubs, Elks, Lions, and Masons clubs—where gambling is a mainstay. Gambling nights at the different clubs varied in frequency. The largest and most exclusive country club in Rainfall West has a "funtime" once a month at which one can find every conceivable variety of gambling and a limited, but fairly sophisticated, selection of pornography. The admission is presumably limited to members of the club, but it is relatively easy to gain entrance simply by "joining" with a temporary membership and paying a two-dollar fee at the door. Other clubs, such as the local fraternal organizations, have pinball machines present at all times, and in some there are also slot machines. Many of these clubs have on-going poker and other gambling card games which are run by people who work for the crime cabal. In all of these cases, the vices are of course catering exclusively to middle- and upper-class clients.

Not all the business and professional men in Rainfall West partake of the vices. Some of the leading citizens sincerely oppose the presence of vice in their city. Even larger numbers of the middle and working classes are adamant in their opposition to vice of all kinds. On occasion, they make their views forcefully known to the politicans and law-enforcement officers, thus making it necessary for these public officials to express their own opposition. The law enforcers must appear to be snuffing out vice by enforcing the law.

Into this situation must be added the fact that there are very large, tax-free profits to be had by those willing to supply the vices under these circumstances, that is, where a demand by people with money exists; where the profits from supplying the demand are high and the risks of punishment minimal, then it is a certainty that there will be people willing to provide the services demanded.

The law-enforcement system is thus placed squarely in the middle of two essentially conflicting demands—on the one hand it is their job to "enforce the law," albeit with discretion. At the same time there is considerable disagreement as to whether or not some acts should really be against the law. The conflict is heightened by the fact that there are some persons of influence in the community who insist that all laws be rigorously enforced while other influential persons demand that some laws not be enforced, at least not against themselves.

Faced with such a dilemma and such an ambivalent situation, the law enforcers do what any well-managed bureaucracy would do under similar circumstances—they follow the line of least resistance. They use the discretion that is inherent in their positions to resolve the problem by establishing procedures which minimize organizational strains and which provide the greatest promise of rewards for the organization and the individuals involved. Typically, this means that the law enforcers adopt a "tolerance policy" toward the vices and selectively enforce these laws only when it is to their advantage to do so. Since the persons demanding enforcement are generally middle-class persons who rarely go into the less prosperous sections of the city, the enforcers by controlling the ecological location of the vices, can control their visibility and minimize complaints. The law enforcers can, then, control the visibility of such things as sexual deviance, gambling, and prostitution and thereby appease those persons who demand the enforcement of the applicable laws. At the same time, since controlling visibility does not eliminate access for persons sufficiently interested to ferret out the tolerated vice areas, those who demand these services are also appeased.

Another advantage deriving from such a policy is that the legal system is in a position to exercise considerable control over potential sources of "real trouble." Violence which may accompany gambling can be controlled by having the cooperation of the gamblers. Since gambling and prostitution are profitable, there will be competition among persons who want to provide these services. This competition is likely to become violent, for if the legal system is not in control of who is running the vices, competing groups may well go to war to obtain dominance over the rackets. If, however, the legal system cooperates with one group, there is sufficient concentration of power to avoid these uprisings. Prostitution can be kept "clean" if the law enforcers cooperate with the prostitutes; the law can minimize the chance, for example, that a prostitute will steal money from a customer. In these and many other ways, then, the law-enforcement system maximizes its visible effectiveness by creating and supporting a shadow government that manages the vices.

Initially this may necessitate bringing in people from other cities to help set up the necessary organization. Or it may mean recruiting and training local talent or simply co-opting, coercing, and purchasing the knowledge and skills of entrepreneurs who are at the moment engaged in vice operations. When this move is made it often involves considerable strain, since some of those being brought in may not initially cooperate. Whatever the particulars, the ultimate result is the same: there emerges a syndicate composed of politicians, law enforcers, and citizens capable of supplying and controlling the vices in the city.

The most efficient cabal is one that has representatives of all the leading centers of power. Businessmen must be involved because of their political influence and their ability to control the mass media. The latter note for business was illustrated when a fledgling magazine published an article intimating that some leading politicians were corrupt. Immediately the major advertisers cancelled their advertisements in the magazine. One large chain store refused to sell that issue of the magazine in any of its stores. And when one of the leading cabal members was accused of accepting bribes, a number of the community's most prominent businessmen sponsored a large advertisement declaring their unfailing support for and confidence in the integrity of this "outstanding public servant."

The cabal must also have the cooperation of businessmen in procuring loans, loans which enable them individually and collectively to purchase legitimate businesses as well as to expand the vice enterprises. For this a member of the banking community is a considerable asset. In Rainfall West the vice-president of one of the local banks (who was an investigator for a federal law-enforcement agency before he entered banking) is a willing and knowing member of the relationships necessary. Not only does he serve on the board of directors of a loan agency controlled by the cabal, he also advises cabal members on how to keep their earnings a secret. He sometimes serves as a go-between, passing investment tips from the cabal on to other businessmen in the community. In this way the cabal serves the economic interests of businessmen indirectly as well as directly.

The political influence of the cabal is obtained more directly. The huge, tax-free profits make it possible for the cabal to generously support political candidates of its choice. Often the cabal supports both candidates in a race, thus assuring influence regardless of who wins. Usually there is a favorite, ultracooperative candidate who receives the greater proportion of the contributions, but everyone is likely to receive something.

THE BUREAUCRACY

Contrary to the prevailing myths that universal rules govern bureaucracies, the fact is that in day-to-day operations the rules can and must be applied selectively. As a consequence, the possibility and in the end the certainty, of some degree of corruption is built into the structure of bureaucratic organizations.

The starting point for understanding this structural invitation to corruption in bureaucracies is the observation that there is inevitably a high degree of discretion possible in the application of all the rules and procedures which are the foundation of the organization. Rules can specify what should be done only when the actions being considered fall clearly into unambiguously specifiable categories. But "unambiguously specifiable categories" about which there can be no reasonable grounds for disagreement or conflicting interpretation are a virtual impossibility given the inherently ambiguous nature of language. Most events therefore fall in the penumbra of the bureaucratic rules where the discretion of office-holders must hold sway.

Furthermore, since discretion must be applied for most decisions this means that it may be applied for any decision the office-holder chooses. If one has a reason to look for it, vagueness and ambiguity can be found in any rule, no matter how carefully it has been stipulated. In addition, if ambiguity and vagueness are not sufficient to justify particularistic criteria being applied, contradictory rules or implications of rules can be readily located which have the same effect of justifying the decisions which, for whatever reason the office-holder wishes, he can use his position to enforce.

Finally, since it is characteristic of organizations to develop their own set of common practices which take on the status of rules (whether written or unwritten), the entire process of applying rules becomes totally dependent on the discretion of the office-holder. The bureaucracy thus has a set of "precedents" which can be invoked whenever the articulated rules do not match up very well with the decision desired by the office-holder.

This amounts, then, to a situation in which the office-holder in effect has a license to apply "rules" from a practically limitless set of choices, thus forcing persons to depend on their ability to ingratiate themselves to office-holders at all levels in order to see that the rules most useful to them get applied. It is not, as prevailing myths would have it, a rational system with universal standards. It is instead, irrational and particularistic. The bureaucracy is a type of organization in which the organization's reason for being is displaced by a set of goals that often create effects which are exactly opposite of the organization's presumed purpose. This is precisely the consequence of the organizational response to the dilemma created by laws prohibiting the vices. It is the bureaucratic nature of law enforcement and political organization which makes possible the corruption of the legal-political bureaucracy.

In Rainfall West and most other American cities, the goal of maintaining a smoothly functioning organization takes precedence over all other goals of law as an institution. Where conflict arises between the long-range goals of "the law" and the short-range goal of sustaining the organization, the long-range goals lose out even at the expense of undermining the socially agreed-upon purposes for which the organization presumably exists.

But note that the law-enforcement agencies' tendency to follow "the line of least resistance" of maintaining organizational goals in the face of conflicting demands is in fact a choice of whose demands will be granted. The bureaucracies are not equally susceptible to all "interests" in the society. They do not fear castigation, interference, and disruption from the alcoholics on skid row or the cafe-owners in the slums. Although some residents of the black ghetto in Rainfall West and of other lower-class areas of the city have been campaigning for years to rid their communities of the gambling casinos, whore houses, pornography stalls, and bookmaking operations, their pleas continue to fall on deaf ears. Their pleas are literally limited to the letters they write and the committees they form which receive no publicity and create no stir in the smoothly functioning organizations that occupy the political and legal offices of the city. On the other hand, when the president of a large corporation in the city objected to the "slanderous lies" being spread about one of the leading members of the crime cabal in Rainfall West, the magazine carrying these "lies" was removed from newsstand sale, and the editors lost many of their most profitable advertisers. Similarly, when any question of the honesty or integrity of the policemen, prosecuting attorneys, or judges involved in the cabal is raised publicly, it is either squelched before it can be aired (the editor of the leading daily newspaper in Rainfall West is a long-time "friend" of one of the cabal's leading members), or it arouses the denial of influential members of the banking community (especially those banks which loan money to cabal members) as well as leading politicians, law-enforcement officers, and the like.

In short, the bureaucracies are susceptible to differential influence according to the economic and political power of the groups trying to influence them. Cabal links with the most powerful economic groups in the city make it virtually impossible to expose the ongoing relationships, since every facet of politics and the mass media is subject to reprisals by cabal members and their friends.

The fact that the bureaucrats must listen to the economic elites of the city and not the have-nots is, then, one important element that stimulates the growth and maintenance of a crime cabal. But the links between the elites and the cabal are more than merely spiritual. It is not simply that the economic elite of the city plays golf with the political and legal elite. There are in fact important economic ties between the two groups.

Most obvious is the fact that the political and legal elites are strongly influenced by campaign contributions from the economic elite. We need not dwell on this here; it is well documented in innumerable other studies. What is not well recognized is that the crime cabal is itself an important source of revenue for the economic elite. In at least one instance the leading bankers and industrialists of the city were a part of a multi-million dollar stock swindle which was engineered and manipulated by the crime cabal with the assistance of confidence-men from another state. This entire case was surrounded with such secrecy that the eastern newspapers were calling people at the University of Rainfall West to find out why news about the scandal was not forthcoming from local wire services. When the scandal was exposed the fact that industrialists and cabal members were heavily financing the operation (and taking the profits) was conveniently ignored in the newspapers and the courts; the "evil-doers" were limited to the "outsiders" who were in reality the front men for the entire confidence operation.

In a broader sense, key members of the economic elite in the community are also members of the cabal. The day-to-day, week-to-week operations of the cabal are determined by the criminal-political-legal elite, but the economic elite benefits mightily from the cabal. Not surprisingly, any threat to the cabal is quickly squelched by the economic elite under the name of "concerned citizens"; indeed they are.

The crime cabal is thus an inevitable outgrowth of the political economy of American cities. The ruling elites from every sphere benefit economically and socially from the presence of a smooth-running cabal. The bureaucracies that are the law-enforcement agencies and government function best when a cabal is part of the governmental structure. And the general public is satisfied when the control of the vices gives an appearance of respectability, but a reality of availability.

QUESTIONS FOR DISCUSSION

1. How can the role of cabinet members as advisers in presidential decision-making be improved? Should the president, as well as cabinet secretaries, be subjected to a regular "question hour" before a forum of Congress?
2. Do you believe that President Nixon was a victim of an overzealous staff or was he, in fact, in complete charge of their activities?
3. Under J. Edgar Hoover the FBI was criticized for its independence. In Watergate, some have praised the agency for its independence from the president. Can we strike a happy balance between independence and presidential direction? If bureaucracies are permitted to operate as Woll and Jones suggest, then can we hold top leadership responsible for policy implementation?
4. How much, if any, is the role of the CIA in foreign intrigue overstated by its left-wing critics?
5. Should the office of a permanent, independent government prosecutor be established outside the Justice Department?
6. Should the Justice Department be made an independent agency, separate from both the legislative and executive branches?
7. Should all presidential assistants who are in policy-making positions (such as the special assistant for national security affairs) be subject to senatorial confirmation?
8. How correct was Nixon's view of federal bureaucrats as "enemies"? How would you suggest that future presidents deal with this problem?
9. When confronted with political and ethical choices between loyalty to the "team" and loyalty to conscience, most public officials in American history have retreated rather than embarrass the team and endanger their public careers. Would a higher rate of protest resignation (as in Great Britain) be an effective way of improving the moral sensibilities of government decision-making? See Edward Weisband and Thomas M. Franck, *Resignation in Protest* (New York: Grossman, 1975).
10. Chambliss states that ". . . the people who run the organizations which supply the vices in American cities are members of the 'criminal' society. Furthermore, it is also clear from this study that corruption of political-legal-organizations is a critical part of the life-blood of the crime cabal. The study of 'organized crime' is thus a misnomer: the study should be of corruption, bureaucracy and power." From your knowledge of any large cities, how do you evaluate the Chambliss position?

chapter seven

Civil Liberties, Constitutional Issues, and the Courts

ASSAULT ON CIVIL LIBERTIES BY THE FBI, THE CIA, AND THE IRS

As discussed in the previous chapter, the activities of the Justice Department, the FBI, and the CIA have raised serious questions regarding individuals' rights to privacy, association, free speech, and freedom from illegal searches. In general, of course, Watergate was a massive assault on individual rights as carried out by the White House plumbers and, in particular, agents of the CIA and FBI. While widespread government abuse has been uncovered and there has been congressional outrage, few concrete actions have followed in this area.

During his brief tenure as attorney general, William Saxbe released the most complete information ever regarding the counterintelligence program (COINTELPRO) that the FBI carried out against activists on the left and right during the period 1956 to 1971. The aim of COINTELPRO was to disrupt the activities of target groups, not just to gather data to be used in future prosecutions. Saxbe noted that such operations are "not something we in a free society should condone." In contrast, FBI Director Clarence Kelley felt that FBI agents would have abdicated their responsibilities had they not conducted counteractions against "violence-prone groups whose publicly announced goal was to bring America to its knees."

When it was disclosed in 1974 that the CIA had helped to "destabilize" the Allende government, President Ford confirmed certain intelligence field work and added that "The Forty Committee . . . reviews every covert operation undertaken by our Government." The little known Forty Committee has consisted of the assistant to the president for national security affairs, the chairman of the Joint Chiefs of Staff, the deputy secretary of defense, the undersecretary of state for political affairs, and the director of the CIA. There is no evidence that the Forty Committee reviews any domestic covert operations of the CIA nor is it known for certain that its major decisions are checked with the president. During the Nixon administration, Attorney General John Mitchell sat as a member of the Forty Committee.

Major questions regarding the CIA's domestic spying remain. They include: Why was it begun? Who knew of the operation? and What will happen in the future? For the past 20 years Congress has responded with predictable outrage to a series of intelligence scandals. David Rosenbaum, in the *New York Times*, notes that over the years more than 200 separate measures to make the CIA more responsive to Congress have been introduced. None has been enacted. Congressional oversight of the CIA continues to be minimal. Money for the agency is hidden in the budgets of various other agencies and appropriations are masked in several different funding bills. Four small congressional subcommittees review the CIA. All hold their meetings in secret, no minutes are kept, and reports are seldom published. The intelligence subcommittee of the Senate Armed Services Committee met twice in 1974.

Such congressional weaknesses, as just noted, suggests that in practice it is the president who must be responsible for controlling domestic covert activities. While the federal courts have most often acted as safeguards in protecting individual liberties, they cannot act until presented with a legal controversy; thus, their policy-making role is limited. Of course, the courts cannot monitor such activities, nor can they enforce their decisions.

The Internal Revenue Service (IRS) has also been involved in collecting vast amounts of information on American citizens. In the post-Watergate period the IRS has not been criticized for corruption, but for overzealous snooping and political harassment. In "Operation Leprechaun" an IRS informant allegedly was assigned to gather details of the sex lives and drinking habits of 30 Florida politicians.

CONSTITUTIONAL ISSUES: IMPEACHMENT AND EXECUTIVE PRIVILEGE

The Nixon impeachment proceedings raised several constitutional issues. The most fundamental concerned the grounds for impeachment. As noted in Chapter Five, Mr. Nixon's attorneys argued that a president could be impeached only for indictable crimes. Others, including constitutional scholar Raoul Berger, have argued that impeachment is as much a political as a legal weapon and that the test of an impeachable offense in England was not an indictable common law crime.[1]

In supporting three articles of impeachment, members of the House Judiciary Committee appeared to agree with the indictable crime interpretation. However, the impeachment process was short-circuited by the Supreme Court in its decision in *United States* v. *Richard M. Nixon, President* (1974). The Court ruled that Mr. Nixon could not continue to withhold tapes sought in a pending federal criminal trial. Shortly thereafter the president resigned. The information contained in the tapes clearly was damaging to Mr. Nixon and was a major factor in increasing the pressure for his resignation. Thus, further congressional inquiry into the legal nature of impeachment was precluded. In its decision, the Court found for the first time that *executive privilege* was "intrinsically rooted" in the con-

---

[1] Raoul Berger, *Impeachment: The Constitutional Problems* (Cambridge, Mass.: Harvard University Press, 1973), pp. 80–82.

stitutional separation of powers. The justices suggested that a presidential claim to privilege based on national security might prevent even judges from reviewing the material. This interpretation also conflicts with the position of Mr. Berger who maintains that executive privilege is totally without a constitutional basis.[2]

CONSTITUTIONAL ISSUES: FAIR TRIAL VS. FREE PRESS

By 1975, twenty-four individuals had been indicted or convicted for their roles in the Watergate cover-up, the burglary of Daniel Ellsberg's psychiatrist's office, assorted "dirty tricks," and the original Watergate burglary. Most significant were the convictions of H. R. Haldeman, John Mitchell, John Erlichman, and Robert Mardian on several counts of conspiracy in the Watergate cover-up trial.

Before the trial, Mr. Nixon's complicity was firmly established by the tapes which recorded him ordering that the CIA block the FBI investigation of Watergate. At the trial another tape indicated that Nixon had discussed with aide Charles Colson clemency for burglar E. Howard Hunt more than three months before the president had claimed he was first informed of the Watergate cover-up by John W. Dean.

Yet even after the trial and with all the tape evidence, many questions remain unanswered. No one knows why the sabotage operation was first established or what evidence they hoped to gain by tapping Lawrence O'Brien's office in the Watergate building. Also unknown is who created the famous 18½ minute gap in a crucial Nixon–Haldeman conversation on June 20, 1973. Several money questions remain. Did Nixon knowingly falsify tax documents? Why did H. R. Haldeman order $350,000 in campaign cash kept in the White House? For what purpose did Bebe Rebozo collect $100,000 from Howard Hughes? Also left unresolved is the *second* obstruction of justice which was designed to hide Nixon's participation in the first cover-up. Again, evidence was destroyed, false statements made, and secret offers of cash payments and pardons were made.

The Watergate experience also raises questions about fair trials and the free press. Former Watergate prosecutor Leon Jaworski has said that the unprecedented news coverage of Nixon's resignation could have precluded him from receiving a constitutionally guaranteed fair trial. Had Nixon not been pardoned, Mr. Jaworski would have faced a classic dilemma in deciding whether or not to prosecute the former president. The same question of fairness applies to the Watergate conspiracy trial. The defendants argued that the massive publicity before the case was brought to trial meant that no impartial jury could be found to decide their guilt or innocence. While the rights of defendants must be protected, this does not

---

[2] Raoul Berger, *Executive Privilege: A Constitutional Myth* (Cambridge, Mass.: Harvard University Press, 1974).

Parade of the Watergate defendants

© 1974 The Courier-Journal

mean that in all such cases the charges should be dismissed. As Columbia Law School Professor Abraham Sofaer notes, "No one has the right to get away with a crime that is so notorious everybody knows about it."

Senator Gaylord Nelson (D., Wis.) discusses the dangers to our right to privacy that are presented by government wiretaps. Senator Nelson reviews legislation he has introduced which would require *all* wiretaps (including those for so-called "national security" reasons) to have prior approval by a neutral court.

The article by Alan Wolfe, a political scientist and sociologist, discusses the "dual state" (one part open and generally powerless; the other covert and ready to operate wherever necessary) and the creation of the CIA in 1947. Mr. Wolfe suggests that the CIA will weather the current storm of controversy, but perhaps in a less effective form.

As chief Justice, Warren Burger has been a strong and persistent advocate of major court reform. In this interview, he discusses some of his major proposals. They include increasing the number of federal judges; easing the workload of the Supreme Court; creating closer consultation among the courts, Congress, and the White House; and producing better qualified attorneys and judges.

"National Security" and Electronic Surveillance: The Need for Corrective Legislation

Senator Gaylord Nelson (D., Wisconsin)

During the summer of 1974, the Senate and the House, by overwhelming votes, repealed the "no knock" provisions of the Federal drug law and the District of Columbia Criminal Code. In so doing, the Congress signaled its intention to correct a past mistake and to insure that individual liberties are not sacrificed on the altar of political expediency.

That same sensitivity to individual liberty should move the Congress to end the wiretapping abuses perpetrated in the name of "national security." Congress should enact legislation which requires all wiretaps to have the prior approval of a neutral court.

The need for such legislation is beyond doubt. Because the need is so clear, I have proposed legislation to prohibit the use of wiretaps and electronic bugs which do not have the prior authorization of a judicial warrant. The effect of this legislation would be the establishment of a law prohibiting the Federal government's use of warrantless wiretaps for so-called "national security" reasons or for any other purpose. This assurance would merely be a reaffirmation of the rights guaranteed to every individual by the Fourth Amendment to the Constitution.

One need not be an historian or a

From *Intellect*, January 1975. Reprinted by permission.

lawyer to understand the basic purpose of this amendment. It is designed to protect an individual's privacy against unreasonable intrusions by the government. To provide this protection, the amendment contemplates that a neutral court—not the government—shall first determine whether any planned search is reasonable enough to justify the issuance of an approving warrant based on probable cause.

It is noteworthy, moreover, that the Fourth Amendment's protection applies to all government searches. No exception is made for "national security" cases.

In 1967, the Supreme Court ruled that, as a matter of constitutional law, telephone wiretaps constitute government searches which are subject to Fourth Amendment limitations. This ruling means that government wiretaps must have the prior authorization of a judicial warrant based on probable cause. The Court has upheld this position in every subsequent wiretap case.

Despite the clear meaning of the Fourth Amendment and interpretive decisions by the Supreme Court, the government continues to authorize warrantless wiretaps in so-called national security cases. A Justice Department spokesman testified at a recent Congressional hearing that approximately 100 warrantless wiretaps are operative at any given point of time. It was argued that such wiretaps are necessary to protect the nation's security.

Such wiretaps pose a grave danger to the individual's right to privacy and other fundamental constitutional liberties. Often, they reflect nothing more than a desire to pry into an individual's private affairs. Generally, they are not supported by concrete evidence to justify the invasion of an individual's privacy. Moreover, they always escape the scrutiny of the courts, the Congress, and the public at large because the government is not required to disclose their existence unless it prosecutes the individual involved—a rare occurrence in the history of national security wiretaps.

In a word, warrantless wiretaps are dangerous because they confer unlimited and unreviewed power in the executive branch. There is virtually no way for either the Congress or the courts to check the exercise of that power. Warrantless wiretaps thus violate the basic premise underlying our Constitution that all power is "fenced about."

The dangers of warrantless wiretaps are not confined to the criminal and truly subversive elements within our society. Those wiretapped in recent years include Joseph Kraft, the syndicated newspaper columnist; 17 newspapermen and government officials who were suspected of leaking or reporting sensitive information in 1969—despite the fact that some of those tapped did not even have access to such information; Congressional aides who knew reporters involved in the publication of the Pentagon Papers; and friends of a White House official suspected of pasing information to the Chairman of the Joint Chiefs of Staff of the U.S. Armed Forces.

These and other incidents show that national security wiretaps often have been used to protect an administration from adverse publicity, rather than to protect the nation against foreign attack or subversion.

The abuses of warrantless wiretaps have rightly aroused concern among the public. In a recent opinion poll, Louis Harris found that 75% of the public now favors legislation to curb the government's power to wiretap.

These opinion polls are not difficult to understand. The vast majority of the public instinctively recognizes that lack of control breeds an official state of mind that condones the government's invasion of a citizen's privacy. This official attitude is a dangerous threat to freedom. It led to Watergate and other illegal acts of political espionage.

THE SCOPE OF THE FOURTH AMENDMENT'S PROTECTION

To appreciate the need to prohibit the use of warrantless wiretaps, it is first necessary to understand the scope of the Fourth Amendment's protection. This amendment restricts the government's power over the individual. It protects each citizen's privacy from unreasonable invasion by the government.

The Fourth Amendment was born from the American Colonies' bitter experience with their British rulers. The English king's officers—armed with nothing more than a general warrant and a desire to suppress political dissent—frequently entered an individual's home and rummaged through his personal effects. Those warrants, and the indiscriminate searches which they sanctioned, quickly became a subject of dread among the American Colonies.

In drafting a constitution to govern their new nation, the American citizens were concerned that there be no resurrection of those indiscriminate searches by the government. The Fourth Amendment was adopted to meet that justified concern.

The Fourth Amendment's protection is twofold. On the one hand, it precludes unreasonable invasions of an individual's privacy by the government. On the other hand, the Fourth Amendment guarantees that that privacy can be invaded only when there is a judicial warrant based on probable cause.

It is quite clear, moreover, that the Fourth Amendment's protections were not to be suspended in cases of national security. When the Fourth Amendment was adopted, our nation was only 11 years old. Foreign threats to the nation's newly won independence remained ever present. Yet, the Fourth Amendment provides for no exception to its application. The compelling conclusion is that the amendment should be applicable to all situations, including cases involving national security crimes.

Our Founding Fathers, of course, did not contemplate the advent of telecommunications. Consequently, the amendment does not expressly include wiretaps of telephones within the ambit of its protection. However, there is no question that the constitutional right to privacy is no less important in cases where the government listens to a telephone conversation than when it physically enters an individual's home.

In the 1967 decisions of *Berger v. New York* and *Katz v. U.S.*, the Supreme Court held that the Fourth Amendment generally requires the government to obtain a judicial warrant before it can wiretap a citizen's phone. The soundness of the Berger and Katz decisions has been reaffirmed repeatedly by the Supreme Court. See, for example, *Alderman v. U.S.*, 394 U.S. 165 (1969). Most recently, in *U.S. v. U.S. District Court*, 407 U.S. 297 (1972), the Court held that the government could not wiretap American citizens without a judicial warrant—even when the citizens' activities threatened the "domestic security" of the nation. Again, the Court made it clear that wiretaps must adhere to the safeguards delineated by the Fourth Amendment: "Though physical entry of the home is the chief evil against which the wording of the Fourth Amendment is directed, its broader spirit now shields private speech from unreasonable surveillance."

The Supreme Court has not yet decided whether the Fourth Amendment's protections apply to cases involving foreign powers and their agents. Because the Court has not ruled on these national security wiretaps, the government maintains that it may install warrantless wiretaps in certain situations. In a September, 1973, letter to Sen. William Fulbright, Attorney General Elliot Richardson stated that the administration would continue to install warrantless wiretaps against American citizens and domestic organizations if the administration believed that their activities affected national security matters.

Mr. Richardson's comments apparently reflect current administration policy as well. A representative of the Justice Department testified at a recent Congressional hearing that, at any point in time, approximately 100 warrantless wiretaps are operative. The representative stated, furthermore, that these wiretaps often include surveillances of American citizens.

The discretion to determine when such warrantless wiretaps are justified and properly executed has been the sole province of the executive branch. There has been virtually no opportunity for the Congress, a court, or any other public body to examine the exercise of that discretion in order to prevent abuses. The results are not suprising. Warrantless wiretaps have produced, and continue to produce, the very evils which the Fourth Amendment was designed to eliminate.

THE HISTORY OF WARRANTLESS WIRETAPS

Warrantless wiretaps were first employed early in the 20th century. Almost from the very beginning, constitutional scholars and law enforcement officials recognized the serious dangers of warrantless wiretaps. By 1939, pervasive reservations about wiretapping had inspired enactment of a law by Congress. In 1934, Congress passed the Communications Act. Section 605 of that act prohibits the "interception and divulgence" or "use" of the contents of a wire communication. From the moment of enactment, the provision seemed to erect a total prohibition to wiretapping and the use of information obtained from wiretapping. See *Nardone v. U.S.*, 308 U.S. 338 (1939), and *Nardone v. U.S.*, 302 U.S. 379 (1937). As the Supreme Court stated: "[The] plain words of the statute created a prohibition against any persons violating the integrity of a system of telephone communication and that evidence obtained in violation of this prohibition may not be used to secure a federal conviction" *Benanti v. U.S.*, 355 U.S. 96, 100 (1957).

This interpretation was shared by civil libertarians acquainted with the legislative history. Indeed, subsequent efforts in the 1940s and 1950s to legalize certain kinds of wiretapping were repeatedly rebuffed by those in Congress who feared the consequences which wiretapping would have for civil liberties.

On the eve of World War II, however, Pres. Franklin D. Roosevelt became convinced that use of warrantless wiretaps would be necessary to protect the nation against the "fifth column" and other subversive elements. Yet, Pres. Roosevelt was not insensitive to the risks which wiretapping could have for constitutional rights and liberties. In a memorandum to Attorney General Robert Jackson dated May 21, 1940, he indicated that he was aware of section 605 and had read the Supreme Court's interpretive decisions. Pres. Roosevelt basically agreed with the restrictions against wiretapping, indicating that "Under ordinary and normal circumstances wiretapping by Government agents should not be carried on for the excellent reason that it is almost bound to lead to abuse of civil rights." Accordingly, he subsequently instructed Attorney General Jackson "to limit these investigations so conducted to a minimum and to limit them insofar as possible to aliens."

Pres. Roosevelt's sensitivity to the dangers of warrantless wiretaps did not necessarily rescue their legality. Many legal scholars have suggested that, until enactment of Title III of the Omnibus Crime Control and Safe Streets Act of 1968, all wiretapping was illegal.

The questionable legality of wiretapping did not deter its use after World War II. In the 1950s and 1960s, the government's reliance on warrantless wiretaps mushroomed. No precautions were taken, though, to minimize the dangers to civil liberties. Concern for "national security" consequently led to the use of warrantless wiretaps against political dissidents—including Dr. Martin Luther King, Jr., who was wrongly suspected of being an unwitting dupe of the communists.

The use of warrantless wiretaps has become a monster with its own momentum. Even the President did not always know the full extent to which such taps were used. Thus, upon learning of the taps on Dr. King and others, Pres. Lyndon B. Johnson became irate and, on June 30, 1965, issued a directive placing severe restrictions on the use of warrantless wiretaps.

Nonetheless, Pres. Johnson ordered that wiretaps be permitted for national security cases—but only with the specific authorization of the Attorney General. The President apparently believed, in good faith, that authorization of warrantless wiretaps by the Attorney General would prove to be an adequate safeguard for the individual's constitutional right to privacy and other constitutional liberties.

Sadly, but not unexpectedly, this belief proved to be illusory. Recent events have demonstrated that warrantless wiretaps—no matter how benign the government's motives—can not insure the sanctity of the individual's right to privacy.

On December 5, 1973, Eugene La-Rocque, a retired rear admiral in the U.S. Navy, revealed that the Pentagon currently has a unit which is authorized to engage in the same kind of surveillance activities conducted by the "Plumbers Unit" in the Nixon White House. The purported basis of these activities is a need to protect "national security." Rear Adm. LaRocque emphasized that there is currently no procedure for Congress, the courts, or the public to determine the scope—or lawfulness—of the Pentagon unit's surveillance activities.

In 1973, it was disclosed that, in 1969, the administration installed warrantless taps on 13 government officials and four newsmen for the purported reason that these individuals were leaking or publishing sensitive foreign intelligence information. In virtually all the cases, there was little or no concrete evidence to justify the taps. In many cases, the evidence shows that the individual tapped did not even have access to such information. In none of the cases were the individuals breaking the law. Indeed, in at least two cases, the taps were continued after the individual had left government service and had joined the Presidential campaign staff of Sen. Edmund Muskie.

In 1969, the White House authorized the burglary of the home of newspaper columnist Joseph Kraft so that a warrantless tap could be installed. The alleged basis for this action was again national security. Again, there was, and is, no concrete evidence to establish that Mr. Kraft was acquiring or reporting any information which compromised national security, nor was there any evidence to even suggest that he was violating the law.

Testimony before the Senate Watergate Committee revealed that the White House authorized warrantless wiretaps "from time to time" when it was conducting an independent investigation of the publication of the "Pentagon Papers" in 1971. The taps were placed on numerous citizens, including aides of members of Congress, whose only connection with the "Pentagon Papers" was a personal relationship with some of the reporters involved. Again, the taps were justified on "national security" grounds, and, again, there was, and is, no concrete evidence to support the need for the taps.

In 1970, the White House conceived and drafted a broad plan which proposed warrantless wiretapping, burglary, and other insidious surveillance practices. The staff assistant responsible for the plan stated in a memorandum to Pres. Richard M. Nixon that certain aspects were "clearly illegal." Nonetheless, the plan was approved on the basis of "national security," only to be scrapped shortly afterward when FBI Director J. Edgar Hoover objected.

In addition to these abuses, the *Washington Post* disclosed in January, 1974, that four more warrantless wiretaps were conducted by the White House "plumbers" in 1972 against American citizens. The presumed basis of these taps was again "national security," but no foreign powers or their agents were involved. Nor were the taps in any way necessary to protect our nation from foreign attack or subversion. Instead, the taps were justified on the grounds that a White House official was distributing certain information to the Chairman of the Joint Chiefs of Staff of the U.S. Armed Forces. To stop this distribution, the plumbers believed it necessary to wiretap the official's friends.

The abuses of warrantless wiretaps underscore the wisdom of the Fourth Amendment's protections. It would be naive to assume that the government can make a disinterested judgment as to whether a planned search by government agents is reasonable.

Our Founding Fathers recognized this problem, and adopted the Fourth Amendment. That amendment contemplates that a disinterested court will decide whether searches desired by the government are reasonable. The need for this disinterested judgment is no less necessary in cases involving the national security than it is in other cases. This essential point was advanced eloquently by Justice William O. Douglas in the Katz case:

Neither the President nor the Attorney General is a magistrate. In matters where they believe national security may be involved, they are not detached, disinterested, and neutral as a court or magistrate must be. . . . Since spies and saboteurs are as entitled to the protection of the Fourth Amendment as suspected gamblers like petitioner, I cannot agree that where spies and saboteurs are involved adequate protection of Fourth Amendment rights is assured when the President and Attorney General assume both the positions of adversary-and-prosecutor and disinterested, neutral magistrate. (Concurring opinion, 389 U.S. at 359–60).

In short, regardless of how beneficent the government's intentions, warrantless wiretaps—whether in national security cases or in any other kind of case—pose serious dangers to the right to privacy, as well as to other constitutional rights and liberties.

LEGISLATION TO PROTECT AGAINST WIRETAP ABUSES IN NATIONAL SECURITY CASES

The legislation I have introduced (S. 2820) would make three basic changes in the law. First, before the government could wiretap American citizens in national security cases, it would have to obtain a judicial warrant based on probable cause that a crime had been, or was about to be, committed. The crime involved, moreover, would have to be one affecting this nation's security. Such crimes include those under the Atomic Energy Act, treason, espionage, and sabotage. This change merely reasserts the traditional safeguards provided by the Fourth Amendment. This amendment states that the government can not invade an American citizen's privacy without first obtaining a judicial warrant based on probable cause.

Second, before it can wiretap foreign powers or their agents, the government would have to obtain a judicial warrant. This warrant would be issued if the government satisfied a judge only that the wiretap is necessary to protect the national security. The government need not establish that the commission of a crime is involved. The standards for foreign power taps, therefore, would be less rigorous than the standards applied for American citizens.

This second change is to insure that the power to wiretap foreign powers is not abused in a manner which infringes on the rights of American citizens. A power to conduct warrantless wiretaps for foreign powers and their agents might enable the government to violate the constitutional rights and liberties of American citizens. The recent past provides many occasions when legal restrictions on government wiretapping have been ignored or misinterpreted.

There should be no concern that a requirement of judicial warrants for foreign power wiretaps will undermine the security of this nation. Courts will be most responsive to legitimate requests for foreign power taps. As a result, there will be no restriction on the government's ability to protect the nation against foreign attack or subversion. Moreover, the implementation of

Title III of the Crime Control Act— which requires judicial authorization for domestic criminal wiretaps—demonstrates that judges will jealously guard any sensitive information made available to them.

In short, judicial warrants for foreign power wiretaps will have no adverse consequences for this nation's security. Indeed, former Attorney General Ramsey Clark has testified that the impact of such warrants on national security "would be absolutely zero."

Third, within 30 days after the last authorized interception, the government would have to disclose the existence of the surveillance to those American citizens tapped. This disclosure could be postponed, however, if the government satisfies the court that the individual involved is engaged in a continuing criminal enterprise or that disclosure would endanger national security interests. This option for postponement would prevent disclosures from undermining the government's ability to protect the nation against foreign attack or subversion.

CONCLUSION

For decades, the government has used warrantless wiretaps to serve its view of the national security. These wiretaps have always posed a fundamental danger to the freedoms guaranteed by our Constitution. The Watergate scandals and other recent events have exposed that danger in a dramatic and clear fashion.

We should not fail to heed the warning signs. Constitutional provisions empowering the government to protect the nation's security were never thought to justify the subversion of individual freedoms afforded by other constitutional provisions.

Congress can not, and should not, tolerate governmental violations of the individual's constitutional rights to privacy by wiretaps or any other means. That right to privacy, as well as other constitutional liberties, are the cornerstone of our democratic system. If those rights and liberties are eroded, the very fabric of our constitutional system is imperiled. Congress should, therefore, act *now* to protect our cherished rights and liberties from abusive national security wiretaps.

Emergence of the Dual State

Alan Wolfe

Revelations that the Central Intelligence Agency has been actively involved in spying on the anti-war movement have set off yet another round of breast-beating about this extraordinary agency of state. The pattern is established: every few years, someone discovers that the CIA is not doing what it is supposed to be doing; there is loud declamation; commissions are established; legislators say that now, this time, they will do their job and find out what is really going on; a few agency officials resign; public interest, first intense, begins to wane; things return to "normal," until the next wave of recriminations sweeps in. Meanwhile, the spying goes on and on.

Behind all this activity, and the reason why it takes the form it does, is a contradiction at the heart of American politics and government. Because the

From *The Nation*, March 29, 1975, pp. 363-369. Reprinted with permission.

United States is a class society, in which some obtain most of the wealth and power and others live only to serve them, the state must be able to protect the interests of those wealthy and powerful people, both at home and abroad. At the same time, to win obedience from people who are not stupid and have real expectations about fairness and freedom, the state must give the appearance of being open and democratic. Solving this contradiction has never been easy. Of all the various attempts, the creation of the CIA and related bodies is the most interesting, for the law which established this agency created in the United States what can only be called a dual state. One part of the state was open, democratic, highly visible and generally impotent; the other was covert, lean and ready to operate wherever it had to. As a solution to the central problem of a society that is bound by class yet commited in theory to liberal democracy, the dual state was ingenious—one face for each pole of the contradiction. The only problem has been that it has never fully worked, and what we see in the current revelations about the CIA is an indication of why it is not working now.

The CIA, it should be emphasized, is only one small part of the covert face of the dual state. Intelligence-gathering units operate in the State, Treasury and Justice Departments (as well as in the Atomic Energy Commission) and in each of the armed services. Within the President's staff, the Assistant to the President for National Security Affairs (a post made powerful by McGeorge Bundy), the Foreign Intelligence Advisory Board and the National Security Council are all part of the government that Americans know little about. Finally, within the Department of Defense lies the National Security Agency, with an annual budget of more than $1 billion, 20,000 civilian employees (50,000 to 100,000 military personnel as well) and freedom from public scrutiny (even the "public" Congressional hearings into this agency are held in secret and kept secret). NSA, according to Douglas Watson's recent four-part series in *The Washington Post*, was created not by Congress, but by a secret Presidential directive of 1952, one which has still, despite repeated inquiries, not been made public. No one knows the exact dimensions of what the Prussians used to call this *Staat-im-Staat*, but everyone now guesses that they are bigger than was once thought.

Once it was considered an act of courage and an affirmation of one's political commitment to oppose the actions of the government; now one makes a bold political gesture by trying to find out what those actions are. In a situation of secrecy, the quest for knowledge is a radical act, and so the recent publication of books by former members of the secret state like Victor Marchetti and Philip Agee is most welcome. But behind the mass of facts which have suddenly emerged lie deeper questions. How did this dual state come into being? Through what process was there created a side of government which is as private as the other is public, as closed as the other is open, as specialized as the other is general, one which breaks the laws that the other created, one which denies the public philosophy that the other espouses, one that belittles the values the other holds sacred? A glance into the construction of the dual state becomes a glance into our own future as citizens of a nation that is at once democratic and totalitarian.

The CIA, as all the newspapers have been quick to point out, has a "charter," the Act of 1947 which created it. What is not generally noted is that this Act may have been the single most comprehensive piece of legislation ever passed by the American Congress. The National Security Act of 1947 unified the military services after years of debate, institutionalized the office of the Joint Chiefs of Staff, established the National Security Council and transformed the Central Intelligence Group into an agency. The life of every American was fundamentally altered by the passage of this law, yet it has been the subject of few studies. (The two best, written from widely different political perspectives, are Demetrios Caraley's *The Politics of Military Unification,* and Robert Borosage's article, "The Making of the National Security State," in Rodberg and Shearer, *The Pentagon Watchers.*)

To go back to the events which surrounded this Act is to discover the major dilemmas which the CIA has provided for American democracy and to pose questions about its future. The problem for the decision makers was as follows: if a perfectly workable covert state were created and backed by military might, both its cost and the fact that it violated some key democratic norms could make it unacceptable, once the postwar hysteria subsided, to the people at large. On the other hand, if costs were to be held within tolerable limits and democratic expectations were to be honored, the new state might not be able to satisfy all the imperial dreams of those in power. This problem dominated the thinking of the decision makers.

At the very end of World War II, on June 19, 1945, Secretary of the Navy James Forrestal asked a businessman named Ferdinand Eberstadt to answer three questions: is military unification a good thing? If not, what changes should be made? What should be the scope of the postwar national security organization? Although Eberstadt was a friend of Forrestal, and was expected to issue exactly the suggestions that the Secretary wanted, particularly a recommendation against military unification (which he did), there is nonetheless a hint of chastisement in Eberstadt's letter of transmittal:

Sir: Military efficiency is not the only condition which should influence the form of our postwar military organization. To be acceptable, any such organization must fall within the framework of our traditions and customs. It must be of such size and nature as to command public support. It must be aimed at curbing the weaknesses disclosed in late wars. And finally, it must be conducive to fostering those policies and objectives which contribute to the service and protection of our national security.

The issue had been posed; more than any other participant, Eberstadt insisted that democratic expectations were an important factor to be considered, and that makes his report fascinating reading, even if its most important recommendation, against military unification, was not eventually accepted. The specific "traditions and customs" which became issues in the debate over the law were three: civilian control of the military, the preservation of a democratic façade and high efficiency leading to low taxes.

The concept of civilian control of the military should not be lightly dismissed as some rhetorical nonsense of the ruling class; it may be worthwhile, from the point of view of that class, to sacrifice a bit of military efficiency in return for more faithful adherence to ruling-class needs. Furthermore, civilian control over military affairs softens interservice competition, which can reach severe proportions; having a businessman at the head of the Defense Department suggests to the Army that a Navy man is not, and vice versa. Consequently, there is every reason to believe statements like this one from the Hoover Commission Task Force on National Security Organization, again chaired by Eberstadt:

The completely efficient security system will not be economical. The completely economical security system will not be militarily efficient. . . . Civilian control over military affairs involves some cumbersome and dilatory procedures and may even lead to serious technical mistakes; yet military power freed from civilian control would lead to even more serious mistakes—perhaps irreparable ones.

In furtherance of this principle a number of steps were taken. It was agreed by all that the head of the newly created CIA would be a civilian. When a proposal was worked out to unify the services, it was agreed that a civilian would be, in the words of Sen. Styles Bridges, the new super-deluxe Secretary. Further, Congress, more specifically the two Armed Services Committees, were promised participation in all the important decisions that had to be made. Finally, the National Security Council was placed under the direction of the President, whose role as Commander in Chief was emphasized, and this body, composed of both civilians and the military, was expected to be a policy-making, not just an advice-giving, organization.

Other steps contradicted the same principle. The head of the Defense Department's National Security Agency has always been a military man, though through some kind of bizarre pluralism, the next in command is always a civilian. Further, these designations are not always clear in practice; it was widely known that civilians like Walt Rostow embarrassed the military with their aggressiveness and desire for blood. The point is simply that serious attention had to be paid to reaffirming the notion of civilian control precisely because the principle was in the process of being undermined. Democratic fears about generals could not easily be set aside, even as those in power were trying their hardest to give the brass its head.

A similar problem arose with respect to secrecy. While everyone conceded that covert operations, and a covert apparatus to carry them out, would be part of the postwar structure, some also understood that this might pose for the state a problem of legitimation. Eberstadt's report, as usual, expressed the contradiction: "The [National Security] Council should render annual reports to the President and to Congress. To the extent that national security does not absolutely require secrecy, its reports should be published. Thus the public would be posted on these vital matters by an authoritative and dependable source. In this way, the council could aid in building up public support for clear-cut, consistent and effective foreign and military polices." Too much secrecy was seen as a problem, not because these men were committed in principle to open government, but because a gesture toward openness would elicit the needed public acceptance of the new reality.

But despite this concern, little attention was paid to the problem at that time. Harry Truman said that he never expected the CIA to become an independent, policy-making authority; in his words, it was supposed to be only a gatherer of information. In the Senate hearings on the 1947 law, the CIA came up only three times and only once for substantive discussion. Senator Tydings, a highly conservative Maryland Democrat, who would later fall prey to Joseph McCarthy, expressed fear that the vagueness of Section 202 of the bill, concerning the CIA, would permit no restraints on the agency once it came into existence. Gen. Hoyt Vandenberg, heading the Central Intelligence Group which, characteristically, was acting like an agency even before it was created by law, assured him that this was not so, because a forthcoming bill would specify those exact powers. Had the new bill been prepared? Tydings asked. Yes, was the reply, "but we do not want to submit it until we have reason for it." Evidently there never was a reason, for no serious attempt was made to specify the powers of the CIA until after it had made some of its most serious blunders. Floor debate also was minimal. To be sure, one member of the House said, Cassandra-like:

We must avoid the risk of there ever developing in our government a military Gestapo. As we well know, one of the causes of the last costly war was the fact that the military took over the control of civilian governments. The ordinary citizen lived in constant fear of the military intelligence. He was afraid to express himself. He was afraid of even his own thoughts.

But there was no follow-up to the warning. Besides, for a law of this type, floor debate was for show; any significant legislative contribution would have to come from the two Armed Services Committees, and there the role of the CIA was scarcely discussed. The military chiefs wanted it, and the men on these committees had been selected because they knew how to listen to the military chiefs—quietly and respectfully.

But despite the lack of debate, statements that were made raised all kinds of implications about an organization of professional spies within the state. The whole issue was laid out with precision by Vice Adm. Forrest Sherman on April 2, 1947: "I consider," he said, "the Central Intelligence Agency to be a vital necessity under present world conditions. *Its necessity will increase with our greater international responsibilities* and as

the power of sudden attack is amplified by further developments in long-range weapons and in weapons of mass destruction" (emphasis added here and elsewhere in direct quotation). In an unusual procedure, a private citizen, a lawyer from New York named Allen Dulles, was asked to give his opinion. Since he was leaving for Europe, Dulles filed a deposition with the chairman of the Senate Armed Services Committee. It said that "The Agency should be directed by a relatively small but elite corps of men with a passion for anonymity and a willingness to stick at that particular job." He emphasized that the head of the CIA should be a civilian. Like a member of the high judiciary, Dulles analogized, the head of the agency should have long tenure and should be free "from interference due to political changes"—by which he apparently meant elections. Pointing to the British system as ideal, he called for the CIA to possess "exclusive jurisdiction to carry out secret intelligence operations." In short, testimony in this vein indicated to those who wished to concern themselves that secret intelligence would pose a problem to the maintenance of open democratic structures; the fact that very few chose to recognize the contradiction did not mean that it was nonexistent. The structure in which men like Howard Hunt would exercise their "passion for anonymity" had been created.

Judging by the amount of discussion devoted to it, a third point was considered by the participants to be much more important than either civilian control or democratic structures; that was the question of money. If the existence of a national military establishment were to cost a great deal, there might be a taxpayer revolt; yet if the budgets were kept low, there would be serious damage to the imperial designs of those in power. The first Eberstadt report grasped that issue: "The American people," it said flatly, "will not support a military establishment which they regard as extravagant in its demands upon their services or their pocketbooks." From the Senate hearings on the National Security Act one sees that no other issue so dominated the minds of these conservative gentlemen, most of them from the Middle West. There seemed to be only one way to keep costs down, but it was highly contradictory. As the Hoover Commission report of 1949 explained, "basic criteria" suggested that "the elimination of wasteful duplication is essential to good government, but . . . the preservation, within sound limits, of a healthy competitive spirit and of service pride and tradition are basic to progress and morale." Which was it to be: competition, which would waste the taxpayers' money, or the elimination of distinctive services, which would cost less but would attack vested centers of power? The question thus posed becomes part of a whole new set of considerations which faced the planners of the dual state, the contradiction between common and parochial interest.

As the Eberstadt report emphasized time and again, the major weakness of U.S. military policy during World War II had been lack of coordination, both among the military agencies and between the government and private manufacturers. If that were true, one would expect the report to argue that the military services be unified, but it did exactly the opposite. In an extraordinary passage, one that also reveals the qualified admiration which even liberal members of the ruling class had for both fascism and Stalinism, Eberstadt noted:

The processes of democratic government in this country have sometimes seemed cumbersome and slow, even under the urgent stress of war. *We have often longed for the one-man decision* and have been inclined to minimize the tremendous benefits that arise from the parallel, competitive, and sometimes conflicting efforts which our system permits. *At times we have looked with envy at those systems which we believed dispensed with those time-consuming processes.* It has been enlightening, however, to find on closer examination that they have suffered from similar disadvantages without enjoying the benefits of ours.

This was the manifest reason for opposing military unification, but it was at best a half-truth, since nobody was arguing for one-man rule. The real issue was an intense conflict between Army and Navy. At its root were social considerations much more important than the theories of public administration offered to support each position.

In 1906 Otto Hintze, the German historian and legal theorist, had written that "the Army is an organization which penetrates and shapes the structure of the state. The Navy is only a mailed fist which extends into the outside world. It cannot be employed against the " 'internal enemies.' " Hintze was trying to explain the existence of democratic institutions in England and the lack of them in Germany. His idea was that countries dominated by a Navy will be more likely to adhere to democratic structures, while those dominated by generals will be more repressive. This analysis helps to explain what took place in the United States. By tradition, the Navy Department has been the home of the most patrician segments of the American ruling class; for a time it had seemed that the position of Assistant Secretary of the Navy was an inevitable step in the upbringing of any male Roosevelt child. Elihu Root, a key member of the group which revitalized the U.S. military at the turn of the century, had close Navy ties: Alfred Thayer Mahan, an important apologist for American imperialism, was closely associated with this department. As patricians, those loyal to the Navy had a long-range perspective which emphasized the importance of democratic structures in winning the war for public obedience, even if specific smaller battles might be lost. The Army, on the other hand, was rooted not in New England but in the South and West, more peripheral areas of U.S. society. Its perspective was narrower, geared to immediate needs. Thus when James Forrestal, a perfect representative of the patricians, asked Ferdinand Eberstadt, another, to argue the case against military unification, he was being loyal to a tradition which had historical cogency but which also ran against the temper of the times. The defeat of Forrestal on this issue indicates not only a change in the structure of the state but also in the balance of class forces.

The unification of the armed services revealed that a combination of New Deal Democrats, among them Truman, and conservative Republicans close to the Army hierarchy had joined forces to install a new military establishment— one more parochial, more isolationist (yet, paradoxically, less pacifistic) and more willing to suspend its attachment to democratic forms in the interests of a narrow definition of national security. Faced with the new reality, the patricians had a choice. They could preserve their old focus, becoming, like Chester Bowles, critics of the new arrangements. Or, much more common, they could "prove" that they were as anti-Communist as anyone else. Though Henry Stimson had declared that "gentlemen do not read each other's mail," the men he brought into the government, men like Robert Lovett, Harvey Bundy and John McCloy, and their children (literally in the case of Bundy and Forrestal), showed no hesitancy on that score. It was good for the new order that they had moved with the times, for their very aristocratic and proper mien provided the cover for their vicious and often murderous policies. As Richard Barnet expressed it, "they stood their personal moral codes on their heads when they assumed their public role." This decline in the integrity of the group which had traditionally given the American ruling class its conscience, its Wendell Phillipses and its John Reeds, was the single most important consequence of the struggle over military unification.

The Army position on unification could not have prevailed without Truman, whose role began to be more decisive. Although he at first failed to realize the importance of the National Security Act, when he did he came out in the strongest possible terms for unification. What irked him about the Eberstadt report was one phrase. Eberstadt had written that the National Security Council, during wartime, would turn itself into a "war Cabinet." Much like reform-minded political scientists of this period, who wished to replace the chaos of American political parties with a model borrowed from Britain, Eberstadt and those who agreed with him saw the British system of fighting wars as perfection on earth. But Truman was aghast at the idea: "In some ways," he stated in his memoirs, "a Cabinet government is more efficient, but under the British system there is group responsibility in the Cabinet. Under our system the responsibility rests on one man—the President." The doctrine of Executive supremacy was clearly in the making. Truman wanted, not a war Cabinet but a group of advisers who would work under him, and for this reason, the unification of the various services into one department in his formal Cabinet was preferred to three separate departments each pursuing its own vested interest. Any of Truman's qualms about the covert state were practical, not ideological; it was Truman who in 1952 created the fantastically secret National Security Agency. The final passage of the National Security Act gave the country a law much closer to Truman's ideas than to Forrestal's. It was unification. Trying to save face, Forrestal called it all sorts of things, like merger and incorporation but, when Senator Tydings sarcastically asked him if he was maintaining that a rose by any other name smelled different, the point was conceded.

Truman, however, did not win every point. As Forrestal said on March 18, 1947, "I should be less than candid if I did not admit that this bill is a compromise." Perhaps in return for being a good sport and testifying for the bill, Forrestal was named the new superdeluxe Secretary, head of a Defense Department which he did not want created. Truman, on the other hand, was given the power to ignore the National Security Council, if he so wished; it existed, but it was not a war Cabinet. Further, in 1949 a series of amendments to the law strengthened the office of Secretary of Defense, thereby contribut-

ing simultaneously to Truman's theory but to Forrestal's power. The structure of the state was determined in the way that the American political system determines anything else, by bargaining and compromise among powerful vested interests.

The various parties could compromise because it had become apparent to them that excessive parochial conflict would seriously undermine their common interest in holding power. In 1949, now in his capacity as chairman of the Hoover Commission Task Force on National Security Organizations, Eberstadt indicated that he would accept the new solution. Noting that "one of our greatest needs is to elevate military thinking to a plane above individual service aims and ambitions," his new committee recommended strengthening the office of Secretary of Defense, since "a greater measure of centralized authority is required within the military establishment." If this represented a *volte-face* for the Navy, Army sympathizers also showed themselves willing to compromise. Truman, for one, tempered his opposition to the NSC in practice; before the Korean War he would not even meet with it, but during that "conflict," the NSC was allowed to function in a vaguely policy-making way. The biggest surprise, however, occurred under Eisenhower. Although most people thought that the new President would naturally adopt the Army view on national security matters, since he had faithfully adhered to that position during his testimony on the National Security Act, the new President listened carefully to advisers who spoke otherwise. A committee headed by Nelson Rockefeller, one which may have set the all-time record for the greatest percentage of ruling-class types ever to serve on one committee (Robert Lovett, Vannevar Bush, Milton Eisenhower, Robert Sarnoff, Arthur Fleming, Omar Bradley), joined the Eberstadt group in its recommendations for the Secretary of Defense. Furthermore Eisenhower, unlike Truman, tried to meet with the NSC every week, even calling it into session from Colorado when he became ill. During the Kennedy years it was a popular activity for political scientists like Hans Morgenthau and Henry Kissinger to denounce the Eisenhower staff system as insufficiently hard-headed but, like a rediscovered piece of art deco furniture, it had a certain utility in retrospect. Until the advent of Nixon, it was Democrats, not Republicans, who tried to centralize the national security apparatus into smaller and smaller units.

The compromise worked out over unification solved for a time the contradiction between common and vested interests within the government. But what about the different interests of the men in power and of everyone else in the country? If individual businessmen, for example, pursued their own self-interest, the process of obtaining material for the cold war might be hindered. If labor unions in defense industries went on strike the same thing could occur. If the general public continued in its privatistic ways and did not respond to patriotic appeals, the mobilization necessary for the new structure might not be forthcoming. To deal with these questions, planners turned to every solution in their repertory. Forrestal suggested a vast harmony of interests; the National Security Act, for him, "provided for the integration of foreign policy with national policy, of our civilian economy with military require-

ments. . . ." For a time he was correct, but long after his suicide the war in Vietnam proved to all that what was in the best interests of the military was not in the best interests of Wall Street, let alone everyone else. Another answer was given by Eberstadt: draft the leaders of the private sector directly into the state. His report called for a National Security Resources Board that would exist in peace as well as war. Advisory committees composed of both industry and labor were to be brought directly into the state to make important decisions, for "an important objective of military organization must be the maintenance of close relationships between the military services and the industrial establishments—including the workers —on whom they must rely for the production of most of their weapons." To some extent the creation of the Roy Ash-dominated Office of Management and Budget under Nixon was based on the Eberstadt plan.

There was one other way to win support for the dual state: instead of bringing the military to the people, the people could be brought into the military. The militarization of everyday life would give everyone an interest in supporting the new military establishment, and the problem would be solved. The great appeal of this approach can be seen in the Eberstadt Report:

Today the American people seem to have accpeted the necessity of implementing our ideals for world order with the use of force against aggressor states. In these terms *public support for international cooperation has a high relevance in any planning of military policy.* If this public acceptance is to be fostered and made effective, due consideration must be given in organizational planning to the probable effects of various structural forms upon public understanding and public interest.

Interest of the American people in our Military Establishment is not best obtained simply through appeals to public opinion. It can be based on more substantial grounds if means are provided for *active participation in various phases of military affairs by groups particularly concerned with aspects of military policy.* Thus the degree of public support will be greatly affected by the extent to which the representatives of labor and industry are called upon to cooperate in mobilization and planning, and experts in many other civilian fields are provided with opportunities to contribute their knowledge as it is related to national security problems. *Educational institutions and scientific laboratories can serve as channels of communication between the military and the civilians.* An arrangement with the universities and with industrial and scientific laboratories by which skilled men move back and forth between Washington and their own principal employment is needed. Such arrangements will have the very desirable effect of *breaking down the isolation from the currents of civilian life* that has tended to make the military a group apart.

Aside from anticipating just about every aspect of postwar life in America, this proposed solution worked. For twenty years so many groups—businessmen, labor, scientists and intellectuals— achieved so much self-advantage from the militarization of everyday life that no significant opposition was voiced to the new diarchy.

It is because of all the conflicts which expressed themselves in the period between 1947 and 1949 that Americans in 1975 are confronting the issues that should have been discussed then. In the twenty-five-year history of the dual state, any devices employed to mollify the effects of these contradictions slowly wore away. The militarization of the society, expressed by the fact that even roads had to be built and graduate students supported under the rubric of national security, destroyed the balance between civilian control and military necessity which men like Eberstadt had tried to preserve. The development of the CIA as a domestic police force outside of the Constitution destroyed for many the notion that a genuine democracy existed in this country. The attempt to preserve some equilibrium between military efficiency and low taxes destroyed both principles—not only did the system become inefficient but taxes took off like a Nike missile. Finally, the harmony among vested interests, achieved for a time, broke apart. It was because different factions of the secret state did not like what other factions were doing that the full story finally came out. Americans owe what they know about the Kennedy-Johnson planning for the war in Vietnam, the Watergate episode and the CIA revelations to insiders who went outside. The dual state could be maintained only if all these pressures could be kept in balance; when they could not be, its future had to be questioned.

Some of those responsible for the dual state understand their present dilemma. For example, Tom Charles Huston, the man who proposed Nixon's vast internal security mechanism, urged that the National Security Agency engage in domestic programs. But when doing so, he noted: "Use of this technique is clearly illegal; it amounts to burglary. It is also highly risky and could result in great embarrassment if exposed." Now it has been exposed. Alongside the revelations of CIA domestic spying, Watson's *Washington*

Ed Gamble cartoon reprinted courtesy The Register and Tribune Syndicate, Inc.

"Of course I don't believe it! . . . But to be on the safe side, I'll be spending most of my time out here!"

Post series indicated that the NSA had monitored domestic phone calls. Within the past four months Americans have been told more about the covert part of the state than they had learned in the previous twenty-five years. It is Bella Abzug, not William Colby, who seems on the offensive now, and the profession of spying is probably in lower repute at this moment than ever before. Herbert Philbrick's patriotism has become Gordon Liddy's posturing. One can only hope that publicity—the worst medicine for the body of a secret government—will continue to be administered in ever increasing doses.

Will the CIA survive 1975? Of course

it will. Already men like Nicholas Katzenbach, an important theorist of the dual state under Johnson, has praised the creation of the Rockefeller Commission because the men on it can be trusted to keep the debate totally private. When it is appropriate, Americans will learn what their rulers decide they can be told. Lucien Nedzi (D., Mich.), who failed to ask probing questions about the NSA, will be responsible for investigating the CIA; that is not very different from hiring the man who robbed your store to protect it. Others speak of reforms, so that the structure itself can be maintained. Senator Proxmire, for example, has said that "Immediate and severe action is necessary to preserve confidence in the intelligence establishment, and more importantly, to guarantee the rights of Americans under the Fourth Amendment."

Yet in another sense, the CIA may not survive 1975, at least in the form to which it is accustomed. Our secret state survived this long only because a juggling act was being performed while the audience was watching another spectacle, that of the cold war. With the cold war substantially ended, the juggling act was exposed to direct public view and could no longer be maintained. Signs of the new situation are

everywhere. The patrician fascination with unlimited power may be over; McGeorge Bundy has shifted from taking life to giving charity, and that may be part of a trend. Moreover, détente undermines the base of the covert state; without anti-communism there is simply no need for spies, unless new enemies can be found. And it may take a while to find them. For the time being, the heyday of the National Security State appears to be over. But those who operate it have always shown themselves more ready to retreat than to surrender.

Why Courts Are in Trouble

Interview with Chief Justice Warren E. Burger

Q Mr. Chief Justice, what would you say is the principal problem now facing the federal courts?

A There is not one problem, of course, but many. I can suggest one that qualifies an an overriding problem—the matter of communication with Congress, and to a lesser extent, with the executive branch.

Of course, since the Attorney General and Solicitor General are the chief law officers of the executive branch and at the same time the two ranking legal officers of the Court, we are able to communicate with them rather easily. But communicating with leaders of

Reprinted from *U.S. News and World Report*, March 31, 1975, pp. 28-32.

Congress—which is even more important—is not as readily done.

Q Why is that?

A It is not that Congress resists communication or that I have any hesitancy. It's partly a matter of time. The members of Congress are, as we know, overwhelmed with a multitude of problems, and to reach them we've first got to get their attention. Then we've got to try to focus that attention long enough so they can deal with a particular problem, and that's where the difficulty comes in. And occasionally some people who have not thought the problem through raise a question whether judges should express their views to Congress.

Q Is this because of the separation of powers?

A I suppose that enters into it. The notion of some few people seems to be that we should not even talk to each other—which, of course, is a naïve position not consistent with our constitutional system. Our history rejects this notion.

In the beginning, President Washington and the other leaders wanted to use the Supreme Court as a sounding board to get advisory opinions about treaties and other important public matters. The Supreme Court very wisely declined that invitation and said in effect: "No, we don't give advisory opinions. We deal only in cases and controversies under Article III." But it was common for Presidents from Washington on to ask the Chief Justice about the needs and problems of the federal courts. This was common practice long before Congress created the Judicial Conference to advise the other branches on these matters.

Q Well, how do you explain the present difficulty?

A I've tried to analyze it. It doesn't come from inertia or lack of desire on my part, nor is it from any barrier that members of Congress put up. They are so overwhelmed with demands that finding the time to focus on needs of the courts is extremely difficult, possibly because the judicial budget is so small—one tenth of 1 per cent of the total federal budget. This can have, I think, some very undesirable consequences, particularly if they legislate without adequate background.

When we have an important problem we must see that the Congress hears about it. We don't ask that they always agree with us but that they hear us out before they act.

On some of our most pressing problems I asked the President to call a meeting with the Congressional leadership. He invited the leadership of Congress, and we discussed, first, the need for additional judges and, second, the very disastrous situation we're in on frozen pay scales. These are most urgent problems.

For example, inadequate pay caused us to lose seven judges last year—more judges than resigned for economic reasons in all the previous 34 years. Never before in history have we had that number or percentage of federal judges leave the bench in one year.

Q Will there be more resignations?

A I pointed out to the congressional leadership that there are upwards of 14—perhaps as many as 20—federal judges who have stated that they are considering resigning if the pay is not increased. The pay scales of judges are frozen at 1969 levels. It's simply neither fair nor appropriate that any public leaders be expected to meet 1975 living costs on 1969 salaries.

Today young law-school graduates and law clerks can go with a big law firm and start as high as $24,000, $25,000 a year, if their records are very good. Just think of that small spread between a federal district judge and some neophyte lawyers.

Q On the matter of communicating, are these efforts to express the views of judges to Congress and the President likely to spark criticism?

A No. Much of the negative comment is due to a lack of understanding of our system of government. There's nothing wrong about the judicial, legislative and executive branches discussing the problems of administering the courts—indeed, quite the contrary. Justice [Robert H.] Jackson in his concurring opinion in the steel-seizure case in 1952 was right on target when he said that although the Constitution diffuses power in order to secure liberty, "it also contemplates that practice will integrate the dispersed powers into a workable government. It enjoins upon its branches separateness but interdependence, autonomy but reciprocity."

Now, what he was stating there is a truism of political science that ought to be a regular practice. The three branches can't function in complete isolation. There are countless examples of that. These problems can be solved only by active co-operation among the three branches.

Q Did the special circumstances of the year 1974—and particularly the possibility of an impeachment trial—complicate the problem of communicating with Congress?

A Well, it didn't create the kind of an atmosphere that I hope we have now and will have in the future. Everyone is familiar with the tensions, anxieties that were created by these tragic events of the last year to two years. It was not a propitious time for me to have the kind of meeting we have just had in the White House. I hope we can have more of this kind of communication whenever it is needed.

Q Will this draw the judges into political conflict?

A In our system it is perfectly appropriate for there to be contention between any Administration and the Congress, whether of the same party or of the other party. By the very nature of things, the two political branches of government have something of an adversary relationship. Our constitutional system probably wouldn't work if it did not exist. But there is no basis for an adversary relationship between the judicial branch and either or both of the

other branches when it comes to the "nuts and bolts" problems of the courts.

Now that barriers to communication are out of the way, I believe we can restore the kind of relationship that we must have—as Justice Jackson pointed out.

Q What are the prospects, as you see it?

A I find in discussions with members of Congress in recent months not only willingness, but a recognition on their part that this kind of relationship has been missing and that it hasn't been good for the country. Many members of both Houses have volunteered this view in letters and informally.

Q You emphasize the discussion and communication on matters dealing with the judiciary. What do you think about the communications which go outside the direct concern of the judiciary?

A There is no reason for me to consult either with Congress or the executive branch about matters which do not relate to my responsibilities for the administration of justice. And I stress the word "administration." We have enough to do in strictly judicial matters. Also, I doubt that my views would be very valuable in other areas, but in any event I would consider it inappropriate.

Q As a result of the meeting with congressional leaders at the White House, are you optimistic about getting more judges and more pay for the judiciary?

A Well, if something is not done, we're going to continue to lose some of the most valuable judges—most valuable for this reason: The drain is naturally going to come from those appointed in the past 10 years whose capacities and abilities are such that they have many opportunities to go into private practice—and whose family expenses are at their peak.

Q Do you know which judges are considering resignation?

A I do as to some because they have told me their problems. In addition, I had a meeting with the chief judges of the 11 circuits last week to find out which judges are most likely to be lost by resignation, and a very interesting profile emerged. There are at least 14 of them. The average age is 52. They have an average of 4.6 children. They are in the upper levels in terms of disposing of cases. At age 52 they can still go back into the practice of law. There is value in the prestige of having been a federal judge.

Another factor in the profile is that they are all located in the centers where the heaviest amount of work exists—in one or other of the 25 metropolitan district courts in which, in the aggregate, 69 per cent of all the litigation in federal courts is pending.

By another coincidence, 22 of these 25 large cities are located in one or the other of 20 States which have raised the compensation of State judges up to or substantially higher than the compensation of federal judges. That means they are in communities where we need the ability of these high performers and where the temptation and opportunities to go back into private practice are maximum. Those 20 States found it necessary to increase salaries in order to keep a strong judicial system.

Q What is the pay of a federal judge now?

A Forty thousand dollars for a district judge. And the men who resigned now earn multiples of that. And the ones who are contemplating leaving can command enormously high incomes as lawyers, along with directorships in large corporations.

And I believe that all of them would stay if they had even a 20 per cent increase immediately—that is, $8,000 a year—and provided a commission is promptly created by Congress to deal with the cost-of-living adjustments on a long-range basis.

Q Is this pay problem resulting in lower-quality judges being appointed to the federal bench?

A I wouldn't say that, partly because I would have no basis for judgment. I do know of one situation where it is reported to me, by persons who certainly should know, that 13 lawyers declined the appointment before they found the fourteenth, who took a judgeship. Ten or 20 years ago, a federal judicial appointment was far more attractive to topflight lawyers.

But a judge with four or five children in high school, about to go to college or in college, can't pay tuition on the "psychic income" of the prestige of being on the federal bench. One judge recently told me that the total bill for his children in college had gone from $12,000 to $14,400 this year. Mind you, he has an income of $40,000, on which state and federal taxes must be paid. A person in that situation is under great pressure to accept other opportunities that will provide an income that will avoid these sacrifices.

PAY: "FAR BEHIND PRIVATE INDUSTRY"—

Q How do judges' salaries compare with those of other career Government people and private industry?

A The Comptroller General's report

that came out three weeks ago shows that upper-level career personnel, like judges and Congress, are as much as 50 per cent behind most career federal personnel and far behind their counterparts in private industry.

Q Is it politically realistic to expect to get the 20 per cent immediate pay raise and further adjustments by a commission of judges and Congress during these times of rising unemployment and all the other economic problems?

A I don't know why not. The idea that judges and Congress should be frozen at 1969 pay levels while the private sector has gone up sharply simply doesn't wash. I don't think the people of this country believe that a small segment of key Government people should have to bear this burden, particularly when the immediate 20 per cent increase—the first step that I'm talking about—would cost approximately 5 million dollars a year for judges and about the same for Congress. That's what we're talking about.

One measure of public support for this is shown by the strong editorials in 60 major daily newspapers favoring an increase. I am sure there are other editorials I have not seen.

Q Is it possible the key reason why the judges aren't getting a pay increase is that Congress can't raise its own salary because of the economic and political climate—and therefore won't raise the judges' salaries?

A That is possible, but some members of Congress strongly support an increase for judges. Prior to 1955, salaries of federal district judges were 20 per cent higher than salaries of Congress.

Q Do you have a figure as to what it costs when a vacancy occurs and a new judge is appointed?

A First, there is often a long lag in filling a vacancy. So for a period we are shorthanded, and the work of that court goes down. And then it may be from three to six years before a new judge reaches the peak of his performance. Mind you, every one of the 14 judges I'm talking about who might resign has already reached a high peak. They are among the better performers in the system.

So we have two losses: first, the loss of time in filling the vacancy; then, the loss while a replacement is reaching the peak of judicial performance.

Q Do you think the present situation, with the President of one party and Congress of another, is slowing down the approval of additional judgeships?

A Well, it doesn't expedite it, but it is not our major problem.

HOW THE WORK LOAD HAS GROWN—

Q At this time, when experienced jurists are leaving, what's happening to the work load in the courts?

A In 10 years, we've had an increase of 55 per cent in civil cases and 25 per cent in criminal cases in the district courts. There has been an additional over-all increase of 13 per cent in the first half of the current year.

Q What will new legislation, such as the Speedy Trial Act, do to the court load?

A We don't fully know yet, but it's bound to have a very significant effect.

The Speedy Trial Act is a very complicated piece of legislation passed late in the previous Congress. Its aim over the next five years is to shorten the time allowed to indict an arrested person for a federal crime and to bring that person to trial after the indictment. Ultimately, every defendant must be brought to trial within 100 days from arrest, which is a very large undertaking.

To meet the requirements of this Act we estimate we will need 100 additional employes in the offices of federal court clerks and some in Washington—and we must train them. We'll have to move to a computer system to comply with the Act because the consequence of not meeting complicated calculations of time limits, with some exceptions, will be dismissal of the indictment and release of the defendant.

Q What will happen if you don't get from Congress the authority and funding for additional judges and court staffs?

A It will be that much more difficult to cope with the terms of the Act, while we're also trying to comply with an increasing civil-case load—increasing not only in numbers but in complexity. Cases involving class actions are frequently very protracted and involve new and complex legal issues. Cases involving environmental problems present new issues as yet unexplored in the courts. There is a mass of cases under the Social Security Act that will be flooding into the federal courts.

Those are just a few examples. These cases have a right of access to the courts—just as an accused has a right to a speedy trial—but we must be provided with the tools.

Q Is it likely some defendants will go free because of this flood of litigation?

A There's the real possibility of some indictments being dismissed for want of a speedy trial, but this is not entirely a new problem. There is no disagreement on this, and beginning four years ago we began to look for new ways to eliminate delays—including tactical delays caused by defendants. Not every criminal case can be disposed of in 100 days without risking rights of accused persons. We approached the speedy-trial problems cautiously and experimented in one large district. From that pilot study we evolved our own speedy-trial rule.

The Act swallows up our rule. Judges overwhelmingly would have preferred to experiment with this new rule until we knew that we could make it work and until we received the additional judges necessary to do the job. Now we have no choice. In about three months, the first phase of the Act goes into effect.

Congress did not appropriate one penny even for planning. As you know, a matter this complex—involving 94 federal districts and nearly 500 judges—takes a lot of planning. We're doing that now without having anything in the budget to do it. We're striving to do it with existing manpower.

Q Are you saying that you cannot comply with the requirements of the Act as things stand?

A Some districts—particularly the larger ones—will have grave problems if Congress doesn't appropriate funds for equipment, personnel and additional judges.

Q How many additional judges do you need because of the Speedy Trial Act?

A We aren't able to make a firm estimate yet how many trial judges will be called for. At the moment our informed guess is an additional 20. This is over and above the 52 additional trial judges we asked for in 1972 when Congress required us to study our needs. A Senate Judiciary subcommittee concluded that we should have 29 of the 52 trial judges we requested, but its recommendation has been on the back burner ever since. Mind you, that recommendation was before the Speedy Trial Act was enacted.

Q Why is Congress so slow to provide for more courts and judges?

A The burdens on Congress are so great in all the other areas, and the people who want other things are pounding at their door. It is an old truism that the squeaking wheels get the grease first.

This takes us back to lack of communication. Our committees study the needs, make recommendations to the Judicial Conference, which passes on them, and we send them on to Congress. Only lawyers and concerned citizens can lobby. The American Bar Association, the American Judicature Society and others must pursue these crucial matters with Congress. James Fellers, president of the ABA, and John Clark, of Judicature, have said they will do so.

Q Going back to the Speedy Trial Act, do you think that speedier trials would deter crime?

A Speedy trials—and widespread awareness of the certainty of speedy trials with reasonably predictable finality—would be one of the most forceful deterrents to criminal conduct. When you interviewed Lord Chief Justice Widgery [of England] not long ago, he made the point that one of the strong aspects of their system is that criminal trials are held promptly, and appeals are decided within a few months. There are no long-drawn-out appeals or retrials there.

That their system provides more deterrent than ours can reasonably be inferred from the fact that in all of England there are approximately 100 criminal indictments for homicides annually—for 50 million population. In Washington, D.C., with approximately 750,000 population, there were 295 known criminal homicides in 1974. That comparison is a pretty shocking one.

And that's why we are in complete accord with the Congress—and, in fact, we were four years ahead of Congress in developing our own speedy-trial rule. But we must have the equipment, the staffs and the judges to implement it.

Q Can the appeal process be speeded up?

A We've been working on that in the courts of appeals. One of the major functions of the circuit executive—a new office introduced into the system in the last four years—is to trace what happens to cases from the time of the final judgment in the district court and the filing of a notice of appeal to the time when it comes on for hearing in the court of appeals.

A major bottleneck has been the time-consuming process of transcribing the testimony, and we are making real progress on that at the Federal Judicial Center. The Second Circuit [New York, Connecticut and Vermont] has made great progress on expediting appeals.

Q Do you think that mandatory long-term sentences would be a deterrent to crime? And what about the death penalty as a deterrent?

A Generally speaking, I share the view that I think is common among judges in this country that mandatory terms—such as five years or 10 years, for example—are undesirable. Judges should be allowed some flexibility.

The death sentence is a subject that is again before the Court. I'm not free to go into that.

Q Mr. Chief Justice, do you think that the federal courts have jurisdiction over too many types of cases?

A First, I should emphasize that the Constitution places in the Congress of the United States the power to define the jurisdiction of the federal courts. The point I want to make is: If Congress is going to continue to enlarge the jurisdiction of the courts and the volume of cases, they've got to give us the tools to do the job.

I must add in all fairness that the courts have also made decisions that enlarge our case loads.

Q In the past you have been critical of the quality of trial lawyers. Any change there?

A I hope it's improving. The upper level of trial lawyers in this country is as good as the upper level of the trial lawyers of any country in the world. But we have a relatively thin crust of really competent advocates in this country in relation to the demand, given the number of lawyers we have—300,000 or more.

And I have strongly urged and I intend to continue to urge that, at least as far as the federal courts are concerned, no lawyer be permitted to come into the federal court to try a case simply on a diploma from a law school or a certificate of admission to the State courts—that we require something more: a demonstration that he has had a certain minimal experience in the trial courts of his State.

Q Would this create a barrister system like England's?

A No. But it has been suggested that this would create an "elitist" bar. However, if by "elitist" is meant highly skilled lawyers, my answer is: That's what we should aim for. If I'm going to have a brain tumor operated, or surgery for a detached retina, I want the most talented and skillful surgeon that I can find. By the same token, one who is arrested and charged with a serious crime wants a well-trained lawyer and needs protection against one who is not competent.

Q In addition to more judges, do you also need better judges?

A We always need better judges. In the last few years we have been concentrating on trying to make ourselves better judges. The Federal Judicial Center provides an intensive two-week orientation course soon after a new judge comes on duty.

Q Are there other steps?

A Yes. More and more United States Senators use screening committees to assure that those recommended for judgeships are of high professional competence. And there is general acceptance of the American Bar Association's recommendations.

Q Are the educational programs only for judges?

A We also bring to the Center probation officers, magistrates, clerks of court—all of the personnel of the federal system—not only an initial training, but for advanced training.

Efforts of this type have resulted in an increase in the productivity per judge in the federal system of 30 per cent in a five-year period. Of course, we can't keep on increasing the productivity indefinitely, and I suspect that few areas of government or of any part of our national life can show such an increase. Most federal judges are working harder than at any time in history.

Q When you find a judge who is not up to standards, what can be done?

A Try to help by training and example. We have identified the most effective judges in the system and the most efficient techniques, and we use judges to instruct, and we send them to other courts to demonstrate new techniques. This has been very effective.

Q Other than impeachment, is there any process for removing an incompetent judge?

A No, there is not. The Constitution provides only one method. However, the judicial councils of each circuit, which are made up of the courts-of-appeals judges, have some powers to deal with problems that relate to the effectiveness of the system. But the powers need to be more clearly defined. And the power of these councils has not been used very much.

I should make it plain that problems of incompetence are by no means widespread or general. Given the fact that we have 400 trial judges and 97 appeals judges, and more than 100 experienced senior judges—semiretired—still actively engaged in judicial work, I think it's a tribute to the system and to the people in it that so few problems arise.

Q Didn't the Judicial Conference recently pass on some legislation concerning ailing and infirm judges?

A Leading advocates of judicial improvement in Congress proposed, as far back as 40 years ago, that some mechanism less than impeachment be devised. More recently, other Senators and Congressmen have made proposals. The United States Judicial Conference approved in principle the idea of developing some kind of mechanism that could in certain circumstances suspend a judge's power to hear cases until he was healed of some illness or disability, or censure a judge for behavior that, while improper, is regarded as insufficient to justify impeachment inquiry.

Q Who would censure the judge?

A The proposed act creates a tenure council composed of one judge elected by each of the federal circuits and one judge from each of the special courts—that is, the Court of Claims, Court of Customs and Patent Appeals, and the Customs Court—a total of 14 members. In other words, judges would be judged in a limited area by their peers.

Q What do you think of the proposal that's been made in Congress for review and reconfirmation of federal judges, say, every 10 years?

A That, of course, would require a constitutional amendment. I know of nothing that has occurred in the 40 years I've been a lawyer and a judge that would lead me to believe that the present constitutional tenure of federal judges should be changed. We have a host of other problems that I wish would engage the attention of the Congress—problems that have a much higher priority.

Q What sort of things would help ease the work load of the Supreme Court?

A One would be to totally abolish the three-judge district courts. Another one would be to curtail diversity jurisdiction. All direct appeals to the Supreme Court should be eliminated. The Court can always expedite important cases in which time is crucial.

Q What is "diversity jurisdiction"?

A Diversity jurisdiction is the jurisdiction of the federal court that arises not because of a federal question involved but because the two litigants are residents of different States. Such cases have almost no more reason to be in federal courts than overtime-parking tickets.

Q Mr. Chief Justice, it has been said federal courts today are trying to serve as the cutting edge of social, political and economic reform in this country. How do you react to that?

A I'm not sure the judges are trying to, but sometimes they're forced to. Increasingly, Congress legislates in broad, general terms. Sometimes because the legislation is not as thoroughly considered as it might be, or because it goes through natural processes of compromise, with resulting ambiguity, the courts are compelled to do the best they can using the accepted rules and canons of statutory construction to try to discern the intent of the Congress. This frequently puts courts in the appearance of engaging in what you suggest.

Possibly there are some judges who like that function, but I think most would much prefer to have Congress make the basic social, economic and political decisions. My view is that, under our constitutional system, the elected representatives should make these basic decisions, not tenured judges who cannot be rejected by the people as Senators and Congress members can be.

QUESTIONS FOR DISCUSSION

1. How would you suggest that CIA activities be better monitored?
2. What do you believe are the constitutional grounds for impeachment of the president?
3. Does the decision in *United States* v. *Nixon* open the way for even greater secrecy by allowing presidents to hide behind the shield of national security?
4. Can Congress restrict and define "national security" sufficiently well to serve as a limitation on presidential actions?
5. Could Mr. Nixon have survived the Watergate scandal by citing national security and destroying the tapes shortly after their existence was made known?
6. Would the Watergate cover-up defendants have received a fairer trial in Omaha, Nebraska or Boise, Idaho than in Washington, D.C.?
7. Did press coverage preclude the possibility of a fair trial for Mr. Nixon? In retrospect, did President Ford act properly in issuing the pardon?
8. Why have we allowed the government to use warrantless wiretaps for decades?
9. Does the article on the "dual state" overestimate the power of covert governmental operations in the United States?
10. Chief Justice Burger rejects proposals calling for the removal of federal judges by means other than impeachment. However, legislation introduced by Senator Sam Nunn (D., Ga.) would permit a new organization, the Council on Judicial Tenure, to remove lower federal judges and discipline all federal judges. Does the Constitution place judges beyond the reach of any disciplinary rules?

Editorial cartoon by Paul Conrad; copyright, Los Angeles Times. Reprinted with permission

chapter eight

Watergate in Wider Perspective: Subnational, International, and Economic Implications

"Watergate" continues to raise a variety of fundamental questions. What was it? What did it show? Has it changed American governmental institutions in a significant way? Has its over-all impact been beneficial or harmful?

This book has used the term "Watergate" in a very broad sense. Obviously, it was much more than the burglary of the Democratic party headquarters in the Watergate building. It has come to refer to a whole series of corrupt activities in which various Nixon administration officials were involved—campaign dirty tricks, illegal campaign contributions, the Ellsberg break-in, the partisan use of the FBI and CIA, alleged deals with private interest groups such as the Dairymen's Association, the selling of ambassadorships, fraudulent tax returns, and the cover-up conspiracy. Louis Koenig notes that, "What distinguishes the Nixon Presidency's pattern of malfeasance is its breadth and integration, its attack across the board of governmental processes: all the branches of government, the elections, the press, interest groups, individual freedoms—nothing escapes."[1]

In this broad context, Watergate showed how the growth of the imperial presidency, the existence of weakened political parties, the decline of legislative capacity for action, and the presence of a president who was reluctant to take advice, who was secretive, and who was always ready to sense persecution, could result in widespread corruption of the federal governmental system. On the other hand, it showed that in spite of the president withholding information and his open challenge to both Congress and the courts, a determined press and an increasingly distrustful American public could force the chief executive from office. It also brought to our attention a wide range of government surveillance activities that have been going on since the end of World War II.

Many of the articles in this book have indicated that following the Watergate affair change has occurred throughout the American political system. Clearly, reform is widespread. The American people seemingly have gained a new respect for a free press, for the right of privacy, and for the freedom to criticize governmental officials. Sensitivity to unethical behavior in all walks of life has increased.

[1] Louis W. Koenig, *The Chief Executive*, 3rd ed., (New York: Harcourt, Brace, Jovanovich, 1975), p. 7.

Thus there is reason to believe that the Watergate experience will prove beneficial, or at least more helpful than harmful, to our society. Still, in many areas there has been more talk about reform than action. Righteous indignation does not provide a firm basis for significant reform. Moreover, there is no assurance that "another Watergate" cannot occur. The experience, however, has put us on our guard. At least in the period 1976–1980, voters will be more skeptical of campaign public relations tactics and in many cases public officials will be striving to be more accessible and open.

Besides its major effects on the domestic aspects of the national government, as has been discussed throughout this book, Watergate also has affected the making of foreign policy, the operation of state and local governments, and economic policy.

EFFECTS ON FOREIGN POLICY

As the Watergate scandal continued, it began to affect the ability of an administration, whose president was under congressional investigation, to retain the confidence of foreign governments. Allegations concerning Secretary of State Henry Kissinger's role in wiretapping his aides caused his reputation to suffer. As the Watergate-related allegations continued, Kissinger feared that his "moral authority" would be damaged both at home and abroad.[2] Shortly before the president resigned, Kissinger reportedly told Mr. Nixon that his continuance in office was undermining American diplomatic efforts.

Before becoming president, Nixon said that the country could run itself domestically and that as president he would devote himself primarily to the issue of international peace. He kept that promise, largely ignoring domestic matters. Indeed, as the end drew near, Nixon increasingly used international diplomacy (trips to Moscow and the Middle East) to divert attention from his troubles at home.

As president, Gerald Ford has been urged to concentrate on domestic problems and to forego the attraction of world affairs which has captivated all United States presidents since Franklin D. Roosevelt. In turn, there is evidence that the American people are becoming increasingly isolationist. As the government of South Vietnam collapsed in 1975, members of Congress returning from Easter recess reported that they had encountered practically no support among their constituents for President Ford's plea for further military aid to the Thieu government.

The fall of Vietnam has compounded the problem of post-Watergate distrust of American government. We now know that there were secret agreements between President Nixon and President Thieu. Nixon wrote Thieu giving him "absolute assurance" that if Hanoi violated the Paris peace agreement, "we will respond with full force." Secretary of State

[2] Marvin and Bernard Kalb, *Kissinger* (Boston: Little, Brown, and Co., 1974), p. 443.

Kissinger has said that these agreements were not "obligations," and the president's press secretary has dismissed the issue as one of "semantics."

Yet major questions remain. When a foreign head of state gets an "absolute assurance" from a future American president, should he dismiss it as semantics? When Congress is told there are no secret agreements, should it understand there may be "secret assurances"? European governments note that Congress for six months withheld all major replacement equipment and half or more of the fuel needed by South Vietnamese armed forces before their retreat and defeat. Thus the solidarity of American commitments everywhere in the world—particularly in the face of rising isolationist sentiment—is in doubt. At home can we have compassion for Vietnamese refugees without amnesty for Americans who resisted the war?

Writing in the *New York Times,* Anthony Lewis suggests ". . . that those who do not learn from history are condemned to repeat it. One large reason so many Americans have stopped believing their Government is that successive Presidents have adopted as their own the lies and the secrets of the past on Vietnam. It is time for the lying to stop."

THE POWER OF MULTINATIONAL CORPORATIONS

In the area of international economics, a variety of disclosures have been made regarding corporate bribery of foreign officials. The Northrop Corporation admitted paying bribes of $450,000 to two Saudi Arabian generals for help in selling aircraft; Gulf Oil maintained an illegal campaign fund in South Korea; and United Brands (bananas) made generous bribes in Honduras.

Political scientist Richard J. Barnet (the author with Ronald E. Muller of *Global Reach: The Power of the Multinational Corporations*) suggests that while corporate bribery is not new, there is a growing awareness of the problems of multinational corporations and their standard operating procedures. Multinational corporations can set artificial prices, countries which impose little or no tax burden can be selected for relocation of plants, American workers lose jobs as production is shifted to Hong Kong and Singapore, and American taxpayers bear a heavier burden as the federal government loses potential tax revenues.

Professor Barnet believes that corporate planners have become a public menace because of their power to make crucial decisions, for which they often are accountable to no one. Our tax laws, labor laws, disclosure requirements, and antitrust laws are incapable of dealing with corporate entities which operate with worldwide subsidiaries. Because multinational corporations have become social institutions with power to dominate the political life of many countries, Barnet believes that our laws must be changed to cope with huge enterprises which threaten our public interest.

EFFECTS ON STATE GOVERNMENTS

While the Nixon administration was paralyzed by Watergate and much of the energies of Congress were diverted to Watergate investigations, power began to flow back to state and local governments. In a time of federal inertia, states were showing a willingness for action and leadership. At the national governor's conference in 1974, political scientist Daniel Elazar noted that "some of the strongest leaders in the world today—with the greatest capacity to take action—are the governors of some American states." While states were beginning to initiate major reform before Watergate and the federal government had shown a willingness to decentralize authority, clearly Watergate itself has affected state power.

The Advisory Commission on Intergovernmental Relations reports that states were in the forefront of legislative initiatives in 1974 because they perceived public sentiment on major issues more readily than did the federal government. During 1974 the following actions were taken: 30 states enacted laws governing financing of political campaigns; four states established income tax check-off systems for contributions to campaigns; seven states passed laws regulating the activities of lobbyists; several states, bringing the total to 48, passed open meeting laws for government agencies; and 14 states enacted new requirements for public officials to disclose their financial interests.

The well-being of state governments is also reflected in the fact that in fiscal 1974 only two states operated with a budget deficit. However, this very fact of financial solvency, in part, threatens the federal revenue-sharing program. With a huge federal deficit, it is becoming more difficult to justify the allocation of $6 billion per year to states with budget surpluses. Moreover, there is serious question among members of Congress concerning the way in which revenue-sharing funds have been allocated. Senator Edmund Muskie (D., Maine) has noted that:

> The failure of the allocation formula to insure that those with the greatest need receive the greatest assistance has left ample room for criticism that revenue-sharing means an abdication of our national commitment to alleviate the social ills of poverty, ignorance, and disease.

Senator Muskie is supported by figures from the General Accounting Office which in 1975 showed that 1 percent of revenue sharing funds were spent for children's programs and 0.67 percent were spent for the elderly.

EFFECTS ON ECONOMIC POLICY

The Watergate scandal and American involvement in Southeast Asia, as discussed previously, have made us increasingly aware of government irresponsibility and impotence and have pushed many Americans in the direction of political isolationism. In the area of economics there also has been a deepening anxiety about the ability of government to manage effectively—as the Nixon administration was consumed by attention to Watergate, the economy worsened almost daily. Until January 1975, the Ford administration allowed economic policy to drift and refused to recognize the existence of an economic recession. During this period of drift, industrial production fell 6.5 percent in 1974 and unemployment moved above 9 percent in 1975. Moreover, illegal business contributions reached unprecedented heights in 1972 as Nixon administration officials literally blackmailed business corporations by offering them "protection" from government regulations and oversight.

Our political isolation has been matched by an economic isolation. For example, instead of seeking stable, secure trade arrangements with oil-producing countries, our government has proclaimed a kind of "fortress America" brand of economics and sought "energy independence." In order to achieve energy independence we have encouraged foreign oil producers to keep their prices high so that domestic producers will have an economic incentive to tap expensive sources such as shale oil.

In the general post-Watergate reaction against executive power, the Congressional Budget and Impoundment Act of 1974 represents part of the historic attempt by Congress to control government's purse strings. For the fiscal year 1976, Congress, for the first time, is putting itself through the process of grappling with how much money the federal government should spend during this recessionary period. The new budget act gives Congress the authority to set a budget ceiling rather than processing individual spending and revenue bills without much regard for the total, as in the past. Fiscal conservatives have been shocked with the huge budget deficit, while liberals have pushed to increase the deficit as a means of financing recovery legislation such as public works and public service jobs. Not surprisingly, resolving such competing impulses has been a grueling job for Congress.

RESTORING PUBLIC TRUST

Former Attorney General Elliot Richardson has suggested two basic steps to help restore confidence in the integrity of government after Watergate. They are: (1) ensure greater protection against the invasion of privacy by establishing clear guidelines for the use of electronic surveillance; and (2) lessen government secrecy by assuring greater visibility for the exercise of power. Americans have a strong belief in government's respect for law. Watergate, however, revealed a host of examples of illegality on the part of those sworn to enforce the law. In particular, the Justice Department must adhere to the words of Justice Brandeis—"Decency, security, and liberty alike demand that government officials shall be subjected to the same rules of conduct that are commands to the citizen . . ."

A. James Reichley discusses the roots of Watergate which he believes go back to cold war espionage and dirty tricks. Reichley suggests that the ethical atmosphere of government is largely influenced by unwritten norms of acceptable behavior by politicians. He makes a variety of proposals aimed at avoiding future Watergates.

In his article, Richard Rovere argues that American guarantees to other nations have been strengthened following the end of our involvement in Vietnam. To him, it is unlikely that American disengagement elsewhere will occur. Thus Rovere views American foreign policy at the end of an era in which supporters of the war in Vietnam unfairly labeled their opponents as "isolationists."

The article by Robert Scheer, former editor-in-chief of *Ramparts* magazine, gives particular attention to the rise of multinational corporations and to the inability of the American government to control their activities. Mr. Scheer suggests that the growth of global corporate operations has weakened the power of American labor unions and of the American people in general to influence and control private investment. As Watergate occurred in an atmosphere of government irrationality and impotence, Scheer argues that economic policy has been a part of the same process. Thus Watergate is not an isolated event which can be separated from other government ills.

Political scientist Nelson Polsby, in his essay, attempts to give us an understanding of the causes and effects of Watergate by reviewing the isolation of the Nixon administration and its alienation from Congress, the media, and the American people. Polsby suggests that a president who alienates himself from most of official Washington cannot govern effectively.

Getting at the Roots of Watergate

A. James Reichley

The collection of horrors known as the Watergate affair was to a considerable extent the consequence of errors in judgment and defects of character among the individuals who planned, carried out, or later tried to cover up those strange events. If the congressional committees and federal prosecutors investigating the affair do their work well, the urgent need for determining exactly who was responsible, and to what degree, will be met. But there are deeper roots to the Watergate—trends and tendencies winding through the very heart of the American political system itself. If these roots are not uncovered and cut away, the system could soon be confronted by some new and even greater threats.

Part of the difficulty in coming to grips with the underlying nature of the Watergate is that it seems constantly to change its shape and dimension. When the burglary of the Democratic National Committee was first detected, it seemed an almost clownish act of guerrilla politics planned and executed by fairly low-level operatives within the Nixon campaign. Then, as some of the conspirators began to talk, the stain of guilt began to spread wider and wider not only in the campaign organization but in the executive branch of government itself.

The more serious offense came to be not the initial break-in, but the efforts

Reprinted from the July 1973 issue of *Fortune Magazine* by special permission; © 1973 Time, Inc.

by high officials in the White House, perhaps even the President, to cover it up. Then, gradually, even more startling outrages were revealed: the apparent exchange of government favors for cash contributions to the President's re-election committee, the burglary of the office of Daniel Ellsberg's psychiatrist, FBI Director Patrick Gray's agreement to destroy some incriminating documents, the involvement of the CIA in various aspects of the affair. And finally came President Nixon's own admission that he at one point gave approval—later rescinded—to a plan for a vast domestic intelligence-gathering operation that under some circumstances would have been authorized to use illegal methods.

The issue now is the apparent acceptance at the highest level of U.S. government of police-state tactics and methods. What the country desperately needs to know is what caused this infection and how any recurrence can be prevented.

THE NORMS OF POLITICAL BEHAVIOR

Watergate is not "the same old dirty politics." But one of its aspects, the shenanigans of the Nixon campaign committee, does have roots in traditional American political corruption, which has shown other signs of livening up lately. The last two years alone have seen: the conviction of Federal Judge Otto Kerner for taking a bribe in the form of racetrack stock while he was governor of Illinois; the conviction of Attorney General of Louisiana Jack Gremillion for perjury; the conviction of Gus Mutscher, former Speaker of the Texas House of Representatives, for participation in a stock swindle; the conviction of former U.S. Senator Daniel Brewster of Maryland for taking a bribe; the indictment of close associates of Governor William Cahill of New Jersey for promoting a scheme to evade income-tax laws covering campaign contributions. (Cahill lost his bid for renomination in the Republican primary last month.) None of these deeds approached Watergate in seriousness, but all are evidences of the low level to which ethical standards have fallen in many areas of government.

The ethical atmosphere of government largely reflects unwritten "insider" norms accepted by politicians themselves. These norms are influenced by laws, public expectations, and the availability of large campaign contributions. They are also to some extent the product of habit and tradition. Politicians form a kind of sub-class, and like every such group develop their own standards of behavior, which may be passed on from generation to generation.

In France, for instance, the cynicism that pervades all parties goes back at least to the flagrant corruption permitted by the government of Louis Napoleon under the Second Empire. In Britain, standards derive from a code of gentlemanly political behavior, which gives politicians the sense of belonging to a boisterous but high-minded club. As a rhymester put it during the Profumo scandal in 1963, when the Defense Minister gave a misleading account to the House of Commons of his dalliance

with a call girl named Christine Keeler: "It's the fault of little Christine; she's ruined the party machine. To lie in the nude is no more than lewd, but to lie in the House is obscene!"

OUT OF THE SAME BAG OF TRICKS

Prevailing standards in Washington grant tolerance to a number of ethically dubious and even illegal practices. Few politicians take direct bribes or payoffs, but many have no objections if their fund raisers accept unreported cash contributions. Congressmen who are also lawyers continue to participate in firms representing clients that do business with the federal government. Even reformers on occasion seek support from political machines notorious for tampering with vote results, like those in Chicago, Jersey City, and many one-party rural counties in the South. During national campaigns most candidates give at least tacit sanction to low-level acts of spying and harassment against the opposition. Some of the dirty tricks performed by Nixon operatives in last year's presidential primaries were quite a bit dirtier than is usual—but they came out of essentially the same bag that has often been used by others. "Don't tie all the dirty business against Muskie to the Nixon people," said a top McGovern staff member last fall. "We were doing some of it ourselves."

The invasion of the Watergate offices, however, went well beyond normal campaign standards. Other such political crimes have occurred—the brother of antiwar congressional candidate John Kerry has been indicted for breaking into the headquarters of one of Kerry's opponents prior to last summer's Mas-

Drawing by Mal

Watergate affair were close enough to politics to know that. Several of them belonged to the tribe of campaign technicians who began to enter politics in the early 1960's, prepared, they claimed, to bring new insights and techniques to bear on the political process. They may have felt they were merely adding new refinements to practices already common.

COLD-WAR "TECHNOLOGY"

But other ingredients besides a tradition of political corruption were needed to carry Watergate to its final magnitude. One of these was the complex of attitudes and skills left over from the cold war. Experts in the spy business estimate that the CIA and other intelligence agencies have by now given tens of thousands of Americans training in espionage. Some of these have actually played dirty tricks on leftist or anti-American governments in foreign lands. While most of these who were once so occupied may now be shoe salesmen or ad writers with only an average interest in politics, a few have been permanently seized by the spy mentality. Some of these feel no great compunction against using their skills within the U.S.—particularly when the cause can be defined as roughly the same as the one they formerly served abroad.

Political espionage also had some anticedents within the U.S. The FBI practiced illegal breaking and entering up until 1966—though apparently without direct presidential approval. Surveillance of public figures by the FBI also was nothing new. Robert Kennedy told a journalist after he left the Justice Department that he was certain that J.

sachusetts primary. But the breaking-and-entering aspect of the Watergate case geniunely shocked most Washington politicians. Burgling a building is not at all the same thing as taking unreported cash from the local cement company or even giving false returns from a voting machine. Breaking and entering is the sort of thing that is done by *crooks*. It can lead to people getting hurt—guns going off, property damaged. It is, besides, exactly what the average politician is promising to stamp out when he talks about "law and order."

So it cannot be said that insider norms provided a precedent or a model for Watergate. Indeed, if those who planned or consented to the break-in had been more sensitive to prevailing political standards, they might not have gone so far. But insider political norms do allow for rather casual violation of some laws. The men involved in the

Edgar Hoover used FBI dossiers to coerce support from Congressmen. President Johnson liked to drop hints that the FBI and CIA were providing him with intelligence on his political opponents. These practices—or rumors of practices—were known to the men who planned the events leading to the Watergate.

Sheer excess of campaign funds also helped to encourage illegal activities. The Nixon committee raised almost $60 million—more than twice as much as had ever before been spent on behalf of a presidential candidate. (The McGovern campaign gathered about $28 million—more than was reported for Nixon in 1968, and almost two and a half times as much as had ever before been reported for a Democratic candidate.) "The Republicans were done in by the politics of affluence," says Herbert Alexander, director of the Citizen's Research Foundation in Princeton. "With a lean budget there are no excess funds for stupidities like sabotage or espionage."

"THE WHITE HOUSE SURROUNDED"

Another factor behind Watergate was the gradually evolving view that the President, elected by all the people, has authority to act in the public interest without much regard for what the Constitution or Congress may say. This theory of inherent executive powers began to take shape under Theodore Roosevelt and Woodrow Wilson, gathered momentum during the New Deal, and reached new heights in the Kennedy and Johnson administrations. At least since Franklin Roosevelt's reign, most Republicans have vigor-ously opposed extension of presidential authority. President Eisenhower tried conscientiously to reduce the role of the executive in the national government, and of the national government in the federal system.

Richard Nixon, however, made clear from the start that he believed in a "strong presidency." His military and diplomatic objectives, he felt, required decisive executive action. While he sought to decentralize government and to reduce the impact of government on economic life, Nixon accepted the paradox that decentralization at this stage can probably be accomplished only through firm national leadership from the White House.

During Nixon's first term, his Administration encountered strong opposition from powerful elements in Congress, the press, and the federal bureaucracy. A feeling developed of "the White House surrounded," a former aide recalls. In this atmosphere the President and the White House staff grew increasingly aggressive in their assertions of executive authority. Traditional Republican insistence on limited government was pretty much forgotten. The phrase, "The President wants—," came to be regarded as sufficient warrant for almost any action.

THE PRICE OF SOLITUDE

The exaltation of presidential power was augmented by Nixon's personal style of governing. He dealt with Congress at arm's length, and kept even most leaders of his own party at a distance. Republican politicians who had won elections on their own were for the most part relegated to secondary roles in both the government and the Nixon campaigns.

Political solitude may have given the President time and freedom to develop his plans for governing. But it left him without sound practical counsel when he came to deal with two sensitive issues: unlawful dissent and leakage of government secrets to the press.

During 1970 and 1971, radical groups conducted an offensive of broadening violence: bombings, arson, attacks on police, a mass protest in Washington with the announced purpose of "'shutting down the government for a day," an explosion in the U.S. Capitol. While some of these acts were themselves responses to violent events—the invasion of Cambodia, the shootings at Kent State and Jackson State—they were of a nature that no government and no nation could possibly tolerate. To have believed that they seriously imperiled the existence of the government—as some within the White House inner circle do seem to have believed—was irrational. But the threat they posed to human life and property was clear and real.

In the same period, a series of leaks of highly classified information indicated that some well-placed government employees were giving secret documents to the press. Existence of these breaches in security, the President felt, imperiled the delicate negotiations he was conducting to end the war in Vietnam and to improve relations with the Soviet Union and Communist China.

Some of the Administration's reactions—like tapping the phones of employees of the National Security Council, from which some of the leaks seemed to have come—were probably justified. But in at least two instances, the President's concern for security led

him into serious errors of judgment: when he approved, at least for a short time, the plan that called for illegal breaking and entering; and when he set up a small investigative unit operating out of the White House itself. The plan for breaking and entering, though apparently rescinded after a few days, helped create the climate in which the burglary of Ellsberg's psychiatrist's office and the raid on the Watergate were conceived. The establishment of the White House investigative unit known as the "plumbers" gave political coloration to what should have been kept a police matter. Before long, the plumbers were forging diplomatic cables to stain the record of President Kennedy and hiring thugs to disrupt peace rallies.

Because of these two decisions, Nixon bears a heavy responsibility for the events leading to the Watergate, whether or not he knew of the acts that were later carried out in his name. Most of the forces that produced Watergate, however, will still operate when Nixon is no longer President. The current round of investigations and hearings has temporarily inhibited some of them, but to this date has by no means counteracted their underlying strength.

Nixon, in fact, has probably in some respects *restrained* some of the tendencies that led to the Watergate. As a pragmatic politician, as a lawyer, as a conservative, he has observed limits of legal propriety and tact that some of his subordinates would have been only too happy to exceed. Within the complicated personality that is Richard Nixon, the dogmatic zealot has always had to accommodate and usually yield precedence to the artful politician. What the zealot has yearned for, the politician has often forbidden. Not all political leaders are similarly inhibited. It is entirely possible that the presidency may someday soon be occupied by a more rigid idealist—or by a more ruthless cynic.

DRAINING THE CESSPOOL

The need, then, in addition to exposing the wrongdoers, is to deal with the deeper causes. Since political ethics depend to a great extent on unwritten norms, they are difficult to change. But we should not be so fatalistic as to consider them impervious to conscious efforts at improvement. British political standards were extremely lax in the eighteenth century, during the age of Robert Walpole and the Duke of Newcastle (who kept a careful ledger on the current market prices of leading politicians). Political ethics in Britain did not begin to get better until a reaction against corrupt practices set in following the Napoleonic wars. Watergate could provide a similar impetus for reform in the U.S.

Campaign fund raising, "the cesspool of American politics," as Hubert Humphrey calls it, is particularly in need of reform. The recent revelations will strengthen the case of those advocating that the government should foot the whole bill for campaigns. This would have the desirable effect of preventing candidates from selling governmental favors to particular economic interests. But it would leave business pretty much shorn of means for countering political pressures exerted by big unions and other organized interest groups. It would also handicap less known challengers for political office who generally need to spend more money than those already holding power to get their cases

before the voters. And it would place candidates of modest means at a disadvantage against wealthy opponents who could travel around on lots of "nonpolitical" publicity-making missions at their own expense.

Probably no system of campaign financing can work with perfect fairness for everyone, but the worst abuses would be eliminated by these changes:

—a reasonable upper limit on what can be spent on behalf of any candidate;
—disclosure of all contributions, with enforcement supervised by a bipartisan commission;
—perhaps a limit on contributions from any individual;
—some public financing in general elections, provided equally to candidates of all parties receiving more than an established minimum percentage of the vote in the previous election;
—free access to a specified amount of television time for such candidates.

RESPONDING TO VIOLENCE

To avoid future Watergates we will also have to develop effective *legal* and *constitutional* responses to the genuine security problems that helped lead the Nixon Administration astray: violent protest, and leakage of secrets.

Law-enforcement techniques for handling political protest have been and are being improved. But the more fundamental difficulty lies in developing an over-all governmental strategy for dealing with acts of dissent that go beyond peaceful assembly and petition. If government's approach is too restrictive, rights may be threatened and unnecessary confrontations may be provoked.

But if government or public attitudes are too easygoing, the dissenters may be tempted to escalate their conduct.

Leakage of secrets raises the problem of reconciling legitimate concern for security with freedom of the press. The Nixon Administration, like its recent predecessors, has exaggerated the damage done to the national interest by the publication of government secrets. Still, almost anybody would agree that government has the right and obligation to keep some of its vital operations and communications secret, at least for a limited period. The press seems headed toward the position that reporters and editors should be the sole judges of whether publication of the secrets that come into their hands would actually damage the national interest. There is, unfortunately, no guarantee that the pursuit of truth will always be accompanied by a sense of responsibility. The press might exercise more self-restraint if officials drew a clearer line between information whose divulgence would really endanger national security and information that is withheld because it could be politically embarrassing.

A NEED FOR POLITICIANS

Perhaps more than anything else, Watergate points the need to keep the presidency itself responsible and responsive. With all their imperfections, organized political parties provide the best available means for making the presidency, and indeed the entire governmental system, more responsive to the people. Watergate will have given the wrong signals if it furthers the trend toward a politics built around personalities, rather than national parties. If that trend continues, the inevitable

results will be revival soon again of the doctrine of presidential infallibility, and another White House staff with a sense of anointment by the latest landslide.

To avoid this danger, national politicians should be willing, at least part of the time, to subordinate their hunger for publicity and their quest for personal popularity to common party interests. In the process of building stronger parties, fund raisers and public-relations experts will have a place. But the major responsibility must be carried by public leaders who owe their positions to the votes of the people.

Future Presidents will be wise to move away from the practice, begun by Eisenhower and continued by Kennedy and Nixon, of choosing many of their principal aides and advisers from outside political life. It is important that a President include among his most intimate advisers some practical politicians, who are likely to have a sense of what the people need and want. They are also more likely to be attuned to the subtle arts of dealing with Congress and the press. Except for George Shultz and Henry Kissinger, Nixon's own most effective appointees have been politicians: Elliot Richardson, Melvin Laird, Caspar Weinberger, John Connally, William Ruckelshaus, Donald Rumsfeld.

FULL-TIME PARTIES

At the same time, a stricter line should be drawn between the political and governmental functions of the presidency. Of necessity, the President is both the nation's most important political leader and the head of the executive branch of the federal government. But beneath the President himself, lines of political and governmental authority should not coincide. The poison of Watergate could never have spread so deeply through the government if the White House staff had not been playing so large a role in directing Nixon's re-election campaign.

Separating the President's political from his governmental functions would be facilitated if the parties had more extensive full-time organizations, as the British parties have. The President then could run his political activities through able subordinates within his party organization, rather than through members of his executive team.

Watergate has revealed some grave problems that touch the inner workings of the American political system. These problems should not be passed off lightheartedly, or attributed solely to the misdeeds of a single Administration. But neither should they lead to public disillusion or disenchantment with the system itself. After all, the wonder about the affair to much of the rest of the world is not that it happened, but that it has been exposed and subjected to effective attack.

Now the system provides instruments through which many of the flaws that helped produce Watergate can be corrected or brought under control. Democracy has many shortcomings. But at least it always has at hand the means for bringing about its own reform.

Letter from Washington

Richard H. Rovere

In his State of the World address to a joint session of the Senate and the House, the President outlined what an adviser a few hours earlier had said would be "the Gerald Ford foreign policy." Except for requesting a large increase in non-military aid, it sounded very much like the Lyndon Johnson-Richard Nixon foreign policy. For one thing, more than three-quarters of the sum he requested—almost one billion dollars—was for arms. He also asked congressional approval for using American troops to evacuate American personnel and as many South

Vietnamese citizens as possible who wished haven. He told Congress and the world that he wanted "swift" action—meaning, he explained, within nine days. Everyone knows that this deadline will not be met, and few think that military appropriations or approval for using American troops (the latter being a pro-forma request, at least concerning the evacuation of Americans from South Vietnam, since any President has the authority to provide armed escorts for citizens whose lives may be endangered) will be granted at all. Most people suspect that the President himself was under no illusions about this, and was speaking mainly for the record.

Richard H. Rovere, *The New Yorker*, April 21, 1975.

Indeed, he conceded that it may be "too late" to save Cambodia, for whose government he has asked almost a quarter-billion dollars. The writers of the speech, led in eminence by Henry Kissinger, turned out a spiritless hour of exhortation, with an almost unbroken string of bromides: "We live in a time of testing . . . we build from a solid foundation . . . solemn prayers . . . tonight is a time for straight talk among friends." It was notable that the Southeast Asia passages, constituting about half the speech, drew only one round of applause—mostly from the Republican side of the aisle, and a good deal less than deafening. In a rare and recently unprecedented occurrence, one member of the House hissed when the President spoke of military aid, and he and a colleague walked out. Two veteran supporters of Administration policy—Senators Henry M. Jackson, of Washington, and Robert C. Byrd, of West Virginia—opposed using American troops for the evacuation of Vietnamese citizens. Senator Byrd said he did favor troop action to provide safe passage for Americans.

Ford's speech climaxed a week in which Vietnam has been at the forefront of consciousness here for the first time in several months. Through most of the winter and early spring, it was, of course, apparent that the non-Communist regimes in Cambodia and South Vietnam were doomed. Many newspaper correspondents and politicians had written obituary articles and speeches, and filed them for future use. Few, however, thought that the final collapse was quite as near as it now appears to be. As recently as three weeks ago, the most knowledgeable and disinterested students of military affairs gave Cambodia a month or two, and South

Vietnam a few months more than that. It is, to be sure, still possible that the titular authorities in both countries will be able to hold on to a few coastal enclaves and proclaim their legitimacy after ceding nearly all their territory. It is possible, too, that some currently uninvolved power—perhaps France, which has announced its readiness to do what it can to mediate—will find a place in some coalition regime for officials of the Lon Nol and Nguyen Van Thieu governments, but it seems improbable that they will ever again make policy or command armed forces. Hanoi might find it in its own interest to enlist such prestige as the Lon Nol and Thieu officials still command among the Cambodians and South Vietnamese. In any case, the war is—in a phrase once frequently heard here—"winding down" at a thundering speed.

Had the events of recent months taken place at any time between 1960 and the early months of this year, this city would have been a highly distressed area. The National Security Council would have been in round-the-clock sessions; Congress would have had no Easter recess; military missions would have been dispatched to the war fronts. Nothing of the sort has happened, or has even been seriously proposed. (The only thing resembling a military mission was the one-man canvass of the situation by Army Chief of Staff Frederick Weyand, who reported to the President last week.) While muttering pieties about our "obligations" and "commitments," Henry Kissinger has—quite properly, in the eyes of most people here—been almost single-mindedly concerned with what now seems the nearly inevitable outbreak of war in the Middle East. While disaster in both parts of the world was in the making, the President did not see fit to cut short his vacation in California, where he issued his own pieties from the La Quinta golf course. The word "crisis," so frequently on the lips of everyone in earlier stages of the war, was rarely encountered. Two weeks ago, when one South Vietnamese province after another was falling, the principal topic of conversation here was the brutal wind that swept the entire Northeast. Whenever Vietnam was mentioned, the concern was not the imminence of a Communist victory but the plight of the refugees—the kind of concern that no doubt should have been uppermost in the minds of our leaders for several years. It seems to be a case of all passion spent, of a common realization that our outrage has been misdirected as well as futile. There are only a few people—mainly those more radical veterans of the anti-war movement who some time back concluded that a Communist victory was preferable to a Washington-Saigon one—who rejoice in the prospect of North Vietnamese dominance. Most opponents of the war have felt for years that there was little, if anything, to choose between the kind of terror practiced by North Vietnam and that practiced by South Vietnam; still, they know that it is hardly a blessing for anyone allied with us to be left to the mercy of the Communist chieftains. In the light of the evidence now available, it seems unlikely that the "bloodbath" so authoritatively predicted years ago is about to take place; however, there can be little doubt that Hanoi will deal ruthlessly with anyone it feels may still have some potential for endangering its security. (South Vietnam would surely behave similarly if it won the war. President Thieu has propounded the curious theory that unless the American people

"do something for the people of South Vietnam," they will prove themselves "traitors." If the people of one sovereign nation can commit treason against another by action or inaction, then all Americans who have fought or opposed totalitarian regimes must be regarded as having betrayed several foreign countries.)

Aside from the problems posed by the refugees, it is the fate of the military and civilian leaders of South Vietnam that most occupies the attention of people here. Thanks to the folly of our original intervention, many South Vietnamese—some out of conviction, but others certainly out of venality or gullibility—aligned themselves with us and are, it may be assumed, about to suffer the consequences of their rashness. A realization of this has led Sir Robert Thompson, the British authority on, and practitioner of, guerrilla warfare, to upbraid us for what he regards as the callousness of our approach. He has recently written, "Blessed . . . are the excuse-makers, for they have destroyed the credibility of the United States. It is, so they say, only a corrupt, repressive regime in Saigon. But in that case why are the poor people of Vietnam fleeing yet again from the Communists? Millions are voting with their feet. What has happened to all those lovely newspaper stories that the refugees fled only from American bombing?" To his "Why?" the principal answer would seem to be that these unfortunate people are victims of our government's and their own government's propaganda. A few bourgeois entrepreneurs may be among those trying to escape, and it is not unlikely that Hanoi would give them a hard time, but it is difficult to imagine why a Communist regime would wish to deal harshly with hundreds of thousands of ordinary people, whose only crime was being on the wrong, or losing, side. Hitler and Stalin butchered millions, but Hitler did so out of his crackpot theories of eugenics, while Stalin let the kulaks perish because they would not go along with the collectivization of Russian agriculture. The Hanoi Communists are not, as far as is known, dogmatic Marxist-Leninists. To our credit, we are doing what we can to help out, but what we can is severely limited by our past policies and unbending attitudes; thus, in a sense, the refugees are fleeing from us.

Thompson shares the view of several American Presidents that an abandonment of our "commitment" in South Vietnam will be seen throughout the world as a sign of American cowardliness and fickleness. "Israel," he has written, "realizes that an American President's guarantee is worthless." How he knows this he neglects to explain. To most people here, the opposite appears to be the truth. Our "guarantee" to South Vietnam weakened us immensely—militarily, politically, economically. Had we never made it, we would not have been associated with an abandoned cause, nor would we have lost so much of our confidence in the rightness of the American mission in the world. (It certainly did the French nothing but good to clear out of Indo-China.) However that may be, the Israelis continue to solicit our support —moral as well as industrial. Most of our traditional allies have for years been imploring us to cut our losses in Vietnam precisely so that we could lend a hand to those countries whose national security is vital to our own.

It may be that Thompson is right in a sense he did not intend. Our experience in Vietnam has changed us in many ways. Sympathetic as most Americans are toward Israel, anti-war sentiment— that is, the view that *no* wars are defensible—is perhaps higher than it has ever been in any Western nation, and is not much short of universal among the young. A majority of the people, if one judges by the sentiments of their spokesmen in Congress, is skeptical of all commitments. Even foreign economic aid, once so popular and so seemingly noble, has been revealed as a possible road to war ("protecting our investments") and, in certain receiving countries, as an encouragement of nationalism. (Some historians have always seen protection of our investments as the villain in Vietnam; that is, they feel that our efforts to make South Vietnam a kind of showcase of democracy in Asia led us to respond with arms when the showcase was threatened by the Vietcong.) Fortunately, it would seem, we have developed some capacity for distinguishing between the kind of aid that is likely to compromise our policies and the kind that does not. Few voices now are raised in protest against the Administration's requests for aid to the victims of the war; on the contrary, there are many opponents of our policies who fault the President for requesting too little and for the easy way he has played on the sentiments of a family-oriented society by emphasizing the plight of the orphans above that of other sufferers. (It requires an addiction to some devil theory of history to believe that the Communists would discriminate against homeless children.) But economic aid is another matter, and it may well be that our fear that it would somehow or other draw us into war will prevent us from lending a hand in many just causes—among them Israel's desire to continue to exist as a sovereign state in the Middle East.

With the possible exception of the Civil War, Vietnam has been the biggest trauma in our history. As the nature of our society and our politics changed after that great earlier conflict, so it may change again after this squalid one. Such words as "commitment" and "obligation," rendered ridiculous by the uses to which they have been put, may be restored to their former dignity. It may sometime be possible to formulate a new concept of national interest and base upon it a more rational foreign policy. Supporters of the war in Vietnam often characterized their opponents as "isolationists," and predicted that if we disengaged in Vietnam, we would disengage everywhere. This seems most unlikely. The strongest critics of the Administration's Southeast Asia policies have been dedicated internationalists and have opposed American policy on solid international grounds, the principal one being that the war was rendering it impossible—morally and economically—for this country to make any serious contribution to the global community. Most of those who have opposed foreign aid in recent years have done so not because they regarded it as wrong in itself but because they feared the political and military consequences; the way to avoid these consequences might be international aid, through the United Nations or some concert of powers. Perhaps a new definition of national security could lead to a new role for the armed services. At any rate, we seem to be, as politicians so often put it, at the end of an era.

America after Nixon: The Age of the Multinationals

Robert Scheer

Although Richard Nixon was able to preside over the initiation of a grand new strategy of American foreign policy, he failed miserably to build a new consensus of support. Despite public approval of the lessening of Cold War tension, there is a sense of bewilder-

ment and suspicion about where the new global politics is headed. A host of problems long suppressed under the false Cold War consensus have come bursting to the fore, demanding responses that can no longer be stilled by references to the national security or the needs of the "defense budget." As the economy becomes more and more shaky, the public begins to explore new possibilities in politics. Increasingly

they have come to see that the corporations and their top government allies are
at the center of what ails the society, be
it the destruction of forests, skyrocket-
ing meat prices, or gas shortages.
America has not seemed so democratic
and alive in over twenty-five years.

The striking shift in public opinion
about the large corporations was
documented at a May 1974 meeting of
the American Association for Public
Opinion Research. The findings of these
pollsters "whose firms take periodic
samples of public opinion for some of
the country's largest corporations," was
summarized by *The Washington Post* in
quite dramatic terms:

Big American corporations wield too much
power in society, are insensitive to most social responsibilities, and ought to be broken
up into smaller business units.

These are the views now of a majority of
Americans whose opinions of the business
world have taken a drastic downward turn
in the past decade, a panel of pollsters
agreed today.[1]

The same article quoted Thomas W.
Benham of the Opinion Research Corporation as sayiing that "the anti-
monopoly sentiment is so high that it
already is producing pressure for a new
round of public ownership of transportation and utility companies. It will
spread in 15 or 20 years to other businesses not traditionally subjected to
public regulation." Meanwhile 75 percent of the American public feels that
"too much power is concentrated in a
few large companies" and 53 percent
believe "that many large corporations
should be broken up for the good of the

country."[2] According to the surveys of
the Roper organization, "Big business
leads the list of institutions which are
criticized for having too much power."[3]

As an AFL-CIO report noted, only a
relatively small number of corporate
giants, and not the general public or
even "business," are benefiting from
the current setup:

Although an estimated 25,000 foreign
affiliates are controlled by about 3,500 U.S.
corporations, the bulk of those foreign operations is highly concentrated among the corporate giants. Professor Peggy Musgrave of
Northeastern University reports that, in
1966, "over 80 percent of taxable income
which U.S. corporations received from
foreign sources . . . went to 430 corporations
with asset size in excess of $250 million.[4]

And again citing Professor Musgrave:
"Foreign investment may enhance the
private profitability of U.S. capital, but
it is likely to reduce the real wage to
U.S. labor as well as the Government's
tax share in the profits."[5]

After noting that the world economic
situation had changed dramatically in
the 1960s, as reflected by the development of a new globalism of large scale
multi-national private investment, the
AFL-CIO pointed to what it considered
the main danger—*that the American public was being disenfranchised from*
influencing or controlling those invest-

[1] *Washington Post*, 1 June 1974.

[2] Ibid.

[3] Ibid.

[4] "An American Trade Union View of International Trade and Investment," paper submitted by
AFL-CIO in *Multinational Corporations*, a compen-
dium of papers submitted to the U.S. Senate Subcommittee on International Trade of the Committee on Finance, 21 February 1973, p. 69 (hereafter
cited as *Multinational Corporations*).

[5] Ibid., p. 70.

ments. The multinationals were able to move outside the control of American workers, for the new market situation was no longer based on the export of products manufactured here:

Within the confines of U.S. national frontiers, the spread of large national corporations was met gradually by institutional responses, such as the growth of national trade unions, and by government regulations, standards and controls. In the case of multi-national corporate operations, there is no common international culture or legal structure. There is hardly even an international framework for the rapid development of international social controls and regulations.[6]

In the sixties, with the new globalism of corporate operations, the power of American unions began to slip away. In the process, the marriage between the big-labor bureaucracy and multinational corporations began to disintegrate. As the union report stated: "What may be a rational decision for a U.S.-based multinational company may be harmful to the American economy."[7]

The labor unions are merely the most organized of the disenfranchised. For most Americans, including most American workers who are not in the big unions, what power they had slipped away a long time before, but disillusionment was held in abeyance by the stifling Cold War political climate.

Kissinger has continued to speak as if the disunity caused by the Vietnam War and Watergate were exceptional to those events, and the events themselves accidental and not likely to be repeated: "I realize that we can't put Watergate

behind us. But I hope that we can treat it as a cancer that has been excised . . ."[8] But Watergate's legacy to the American public has been less the revelation of the fact that an American President got caught playing with corporate funds and electronic tapes, and more a growing understanding of how government works. Watergate occurred in an atmosphere of disaffection with government power that had been most sharply increased by Vietnam. But there had been many such examples of government irrationality and public impotence in other areas. Kissinger would have done well to check out the nemesis of the Nixon administration, Walter Hickel, who was forced out of his post as Secretary of the Interior. In 1971, this three-time Nixon campaigner wrote his book, *Who Owns America?* to sound the alarm about public loss of power and, in doing so, spoke for a very widespread mood:

Theodore Roosevelt, the father of enlightened environmental policy in this country, was the first President to see this problem in its entirety. The problem, even in his time, had to do with the obligation of ownership, and the public's residual interest in *any* ownership . . .

It is clearly time to reaffirm that "we" and not "them" are the new voices of America, and that "we" and not "them" really own America.[9]

As Secretary of the Interior he had come smack up against the power of the large corporations on virtually every is-

[6] Ibid., p. 72.
[7] Ibid.

[8] Hugh Sidey, "The Response: 'It Gives Me Faith' " (interview with Henry Kissinger), *Time*, 3 September 1973, p. 15.
[9] Walter J. Hickel, *Who Owns America?* (New York: Paperback Library, 1971), p. 9.

sue, and had been forced back to the populism that had given Estes Kefauver his clarity in an earlier period of confrontation with the companies. Such populism comes to be informed and often radicalized by the recognition that the current institutional setups exclude the public from the key economic issues. These institutions surrender the major areas of decision-making to the "nonpolitical" process of the economic market place—a deceptive way of leaving the government in the position of protecting the property and prerogatives of the corporations, and even ensuring their economic survival, without demanding social obedience or responsibility in their conduct. This double standard of "competitive capitalism" was summarized quite bitterly by Hickel:

The people who criticize government most, are the same people who always come back to government with their hand out for financial help. Meanwhile they say, "The poor should help themselves, but our companies should be helped by the government because it's in the national interest." Bullshit![10]

Whatever the problems of dealing with such companies within the interior of the U.S., the question of regulating their global practices is many times more difficult, beginning with the fact that even the American government is not privy, as the energy crisis showed, to the facts of their operations. Writing before that particular foul-up, the AFL-CIO predicted as much with their description of the new global system:

Multi-national companies attempt to use a systems approach to global production, distribution and sales, which are spread

[10] Ibid., p. 295.

through plants, offices, warehouses, sales agencies and other facilities in as many as 40 or more countries. Such companies can and do juggle the production, distribution and sales of components and finished products across national boundaries and oceans, based on the decisions of the top executives for the companies' private advantage. They can and do transfer currencies across national boundaries, often beyond the reach of the central banks of nations.[11]

These decisions—"beyond the reach"—are life-and-death decisions for people throughout the world, including Americans. When Kissinger talks of a stable world order, it is one in which the norms of this disenfranchisement will be accepted. When he says, "'If we don't tear ourselves to pieces domestically, we can build something that will last beyond this administration,"[12] he implies incorrectly that our domestic arguments are irrelevant to our lives here as well as to the international order.

By dealing with the irritants in the international system (revolutionaries, angry nationalists, etc.) and gaining agreement among the major powers on a "world order" and "stability," it has been Kissinger's hope in the style of a Metternich and the Congress of Vienna to preserve a balance of nation-state power that leaves the outstanding economic questions to be resolved in the international market. But the problem is that the international market is unstable and the multinational corporations are not self-regulating or even compatible with these nation-states. There is a built-in instability to their operations. This was summarized by two British economists:

[11] *Multinational Corporations*, p. 71.
[12] Sidey, "The Response," p. 15.

. . . it is clear that the growth of the multinational corporations, by itself, tends to weaken nation states. Multinational corporations render ineffective many traditional policy instruments, the capacity to tax, to restrict credit, to plan investment, etc., because of their international flexibility. In addition, multinational corporations act as a vehicle for the intrusion of the policies of one country into another with the ultimate effect of lessening the power of both. These tendencies have long been recognized in dependent developing countries, but it is now also evident that the United States as a *nation-state,* is losing some of its "independence" as it attempts to cope with the tangled web woven by its international business.[13]

This last thought contains the basic contradiction of the post-neo-colonial strategy promoted by Nixon and pursued by Kissinger. For, while cutting back on older mechanisms of international control which were found to be inoperative or too costly, it has been forced to rely for basic decision-making on units which have supranational interests that can then come into conflict, not only with American workers, but with the people as a whole, including important sectors of the business community.

The economic isolationism of John Connally spoke for those other business interests within the Nixon administration, and their viewpoints have only temporarily been mollified. In the last chapter of his book (on the Kissinger policies), Henry Brandon points to this as one of the problems with the "balance of mutual weakness":

Connally's outlook was not isolationist, but a mixture of nationalism and protectionism. It troubled not only foreign governments but also American business corporations which are, with their multinational operations and vast holdings overseas, the last American globalists. His views were not typical but they nevertheless reflected the views in the U.S. Treasury and of many in Congress. Mr. Nixon considers himself an expert in foreign policy, and so does Kissinger, but neither has a real understanding of overseas economic affairs. As a consequence, there has been an unfortunate lack of American leadership in this field.[14]

In actuality, leadership has been abandoned to the new American corporate globalists who are free of public restraint. At least this was the case until the energy crisis when the break between their interests and ours became obvious.

America after Nixon will now be continuously plagued by such conflicts of interest, which will cheat the Kissinger-Nixon vision of the domestic consensus needed to build what Kissinger hoped would be "something that will last beyond this administration." America will be plagued because the problems built into the new "structure of peace" will be Nixon's legacy to the nation. There will be no easy going back from that structure. The new administration cannot simply summon the return of the Cold War, no matter how desirable that might seem for ensuring domestic tranquility. It will have one of two choices—either to move to make

---

[13] Stephen Hymer and Robert Rowthorn, "Multinational Corporations and International Oligopoly: The Non-American Challenge," in *The International Corporation,* ed. Charles P. Kindleberger (Cambridge, Mass.: M.I.T. Press, 1970), p. 88.

[14] Henry Brandon, *The Retreat of American Power* (New York: Doubleday & Company, 1973), p. 350.

America's presence in the international economy more responsive to the American and the world's people or to suppress the doubts and opposition of both. To succeed in the second, it would have to do Watergate dirty tricks on the grand level which some would call fascism.

The "new majority" in America is populist in its opposition to centralized power and its determination to restore citizen control over political life. It is a left-of-center majority. With the Cold War basis of his constituency obliterated, Nixon's main public appeal as President came as a result of dovish overtures to China and Russia, and not through the hard line on bombing Vietnam or law and order. Analysis of his 1972 "new majority" which defeated McGovern found that it never existed, if by "new" was meant "conservative." As reported in *The New York Times:*

Louis Harris, the pollster, is sure that the Nixon majority in 1972 was never the "new majority," as described. Mr. Nixon's strongest appeal, the Harris surveys found, was in foreign policy where the emphasis of Mr. Nixon's trip to China and détente with the Russians was change, not conservatism. On economics and the "social issue," including forced school busing, Mr. Nixon did not have majority approval at election time, Mr. Harris asserts.[15]

The inherent conflict of Nixon's administration was between this reasonable posture on the communists and the necessity to maintain an unquestioning climate of opinion in which to support conservative business and social policies. In the event that readers feel I may have overstated the new freedom

to think politically brought about by the end of the Cold War, I would refer them to further findings of the Harris survey concerning those the American people considered enemies. Mark the shift in a mere six-year period. According to the *Times* account:

"In 1967," Mr. Harris observed in an interview, "substantial majorities of our sample—60 to 75 percent—thought the following people were 'dangerous or harmful to the country': people who didn't believe in God, black mulitants, student demonstrators, prostitutes, homosexuals. In the fall of 1973 we couldn't find a majority to say that any one of those groups was dangerous."

"Today," he continued, "the people considered 'dangerous' by a majority of Americans are these: people who hire political spies (52 per cent); generals who conduct secret bombing raids (67 per cent); politicians who engage in secret wiretapping (71 per cent); businessmen who make illegal political contributions (81 per cent); and politicians who try to use the Central Intelligence Agency, the Federal Bureau of Investigation and the Secret Service for political purposes or to try to restrict freedom (88 per cent)." "That," Mr. Harris said, "is what has happened in America."[16]

That is statistical confirmation of the obvious: that the former constituency of the corporate-military alliance is in shambles. And it is in this context that the recent inactivity of the left is most disappointing. For if over 80 percent of the American people now find corporate control over the political process dangerous, and an even greater percentage fear politicians who use the se-

[15] *New York Times,* 21 January 1974, p. 16.

[16] Ibid.

"Didn't You Used To Be In The State Department?"

cret police, then it means that the American people have regained their senses and that serious concern over real enemies has replaced paranoia about the foreign devil.

This return to sanity occurs at a time when there is much to think about—when basic economic and political questions long dormant are now out there in the public domain where ordinary people can get at them. But without a political framework, the information that has come out is just so much startling data and gossip. It can only become the subject of political debate by being put into the context of coherent issues and programs. America very much needs an active, organized left political force but it must be one that moves away from the style that was useful in the sixties. It is no longer the time to shock but rather to build unity. The experience of foreign revolutions should be presented (when it is accurate to do so) as a source of positive hope and not as a hostile and rude awakening. Nor can the stance of anti-intellectualism be any longer justified at a time when clear and accurate analysis of the American power structure is in great public demand.

Most important of all, the left must abandon the idea that the average American benefits from racism and imperialism. For, as even the labor bureaucrats now recognize, the new era of the multinational corporations disenfranchises the American workers as it does their counterparts in Taiwan, by pitting one against the other. If there are any lingering doubts about the disaffection of the labor vote from Nixon, the following results from a Gallup poll reported at the end of 1972 constitute a statistical denial of the hard-hat image:

Among labor union members and their families, another new majority target in 1972, Mr. Nixon's approval has dropped from 61 percent to 20 percent in the last year. George Meany, the labor leader, who was neutral in the President's last campaign, is now calling for Mr. Nixon's impeachment.[17]

Unfortunately George Meany is too entrenched in his old ways to chance a real alternative. Such an alternative would have to begin with a program for dismantling the power of Corporate America as it is manifested in all dimensions—advertising, wage determination, output decisions, political contributions. Unless this is done—and it means, in effect, ending the existence of such corporations as centers of power—the politics of Nixon will continue long after him. Just as the Truman Doctrine was continued by Eisenhower, so too will the Nixon Doctrine be continued by Gerald Ford. For it is not a matter of the personal integrity, individual political outlook of a President, or even the constituency he claims to speak for, but rather of the class interests which he really represents.

In America after Nixon, in the absence of a strong left, power will continue to concentrate in a corporate political structure which is wasteful of our resources, incapable of world-wide planning for economic development, and hence incapable of maintaining peace and prosperity. For the growth and profits of the corporations are not consistent with the long-run needs of a peaceful world. The planning of such units represents an anachronistic restraint on our political imaginations, and their definition of freedom mocks

[17] Ibid.

every effort of ordinary human beings to make sense of their world. In a day when increasing numbers of Americans can see this quite easily, the ultra-left politics of alienation of the recent past becomes reactionary. It is encouraging that former Attorney General Ramsay Clark made the issue of the multinationals central to his recent New York Senate campaign. In a formulation quite compatible with those expressed in this book, he charged: "Where is democracy and how can we solve problems if our energy policy is determined by the oil firms, antitrust enforcement by ITT, foreign policy by the multinationals?"[18]

A major problem of the New Left was its frequent insistence that the college and bohemian community represented the only fruitful base for militant political action. But in the seventies the leadership has more often come from other sectors of the society as in the independent truckers' boycott, consumer revolts, or wildcat strikes. Indeed a recent and in-depth Yankelovich survey concludes:

Working-class young people in the United States are taking on many of the attitudes on sex, politics, patriotism, religion, the family, morals and life-style that marked college student thinking of five years ago. The result . . . is that workers are becoming increasingly dissatisfied and frustrated at a sense of unfulfillment.[19]

This being the case, we must develop politics which presume that most Americans are capable of progressive thought and identification with the goals of social justice. A significant left

force would have to involve the participation of housewives, editors, labor leaders, liberal Senators, as well as the leadership of rank-and-file Americans. Any gap between the left and environmentalists, or youth, or hip, or square, is, in this context, destructive. There is only one basis of unity and that is a denial of the legitimacy of corporate political and economic power. All other differences fall into the category of what Mao has called contradictions among the people. If the thesis of this book is correct as to the role of corporate America then such unity should be a practical possibility, but only if we can overcome the generally corrupting influences, co-option, and divisiveness of the culture within which we must operate.

The thrust of my agrument has been a Marxist one—that class struggle is the dominant feature of the current world reality, as it has no doubt been historically. Unless the masses of poorer and ordinary people in the world fundamentally change their relation to the means of production, the outstanding problems of waste, underdevelopment, alienation, and violence will remain and indeed increase.

The timetable of America's New Left was all wrong. America will now go through decades of sustained struggle for change. This is still the richest and most powerful country in the world. Its ruling elite still has many cards to play and victory against it will not come cheaply. As the system weakens it will thrash about more and more dangerously, the citizenry will often be divided by false consciousness, there will be violent hunts for scapegoats, and there is an ever-present danger that as bourgeois life becomes intolerable, racism, religious frenzy, chauvinism, and

[18] *New York Times*, Section 4, *The Week in Review*, 18 August 1974, p. 7.

[19] *New York Times*, 22 May 1974, p. 45.

cultism will temporarily hold sway over sections of the public. As the years of Watergate have demonstrated, there will be frightening, uncertain times, but also hopeful ones in which Americans will come to be more aware. But to be aware without having strong and positive alternatives is to produce a sense of impotence and cynicism.

The New Left of the sixties was weakened by its victories. There have been other models in the world, and indeed in our own history, of people gaining strength from struggle. The example of Vietnam is never too worn for repetition. No people has suffered more and no people has grown so much. The Vietnamese revolution nurtured rather than drained a people, and perception of the social realities made them stronger rather than weaker. This is the lesson that the walking wounded of past causes should learn from the Vietnamese. It is time to clear the decks of guilt and despair, to politely ask the burnt-out causes to take a rest, but to permit others, hopefully many who have never before moved politically, to get on with the work of changing the face of America and its predatory relation to the world. If we look to our own country's history, we will find that the mass of people have snapped back repeatedly from periods of slumber and reaction, from racism and national chauvinism, to wage a higher level of struggle. One of the side effects of the Cold War was to keep this history from us. The history of populism, socialism, and labor struggles has many lessons and is a source of sustenance. It was a tradition of radicalism which once again rose in the mass antiwar and civil rights politics of the sixties, and, now, in the aftermath of the Cold War, faces its best opportunity.

Watergate: Alienation and Accountability

Nelson W. Polsby

It seems to me appropriate to begin this collection with a sermon about a subject that for a political scientist has to be Topic A. As these words are written, at Christmas 1973, Watergate is still pending business. Impeachment of the President is being taken up by the House.

From *Political Promises: Essays and Commentary on American Politics* by Nelson W. Polsby. Copyright © 1974 by Nelson W. Polsby. Reprinted by permission of Oxford University Press, Inc.

Watergate-related trials are in progress in various courts, and grand jury investigations are continuing. A Special Prosecutor, Leon Jaworski of Texas, is at work, as is a special committee of the U.S. Senate. A great deal more is bound to come out before this issue has run its course, and so the essay printed below must be considered as tentative in character.

What it seeks to do is explain how the

Nixon administration got into the difficulties it has thus far suffered over Watergate, without attempting to explain except indirectly whatever further difficulties may be in store. My interpretation of Watergate relies heavily upon a distinction that political scientists frequently make but which is not commonly used in general discourse about American politics, namely, the distinction between a consensus view that develops in the subculture of Washington elites and the tenor of public opinion generally.

President Nixon's publicity men have frequently argued that the President's extreme unpopularity with the public at large over the Watergate revelations is no worse than that suffered by Harry Truman over the firing of General MacArthur, and therefore could be expected in time to blow over. The key difference, of course, is in the sharply contrasting postures of Washington political elites on the two occassions. When the elites are with the President, he can ride out an unfavorable public opinion rating. When they are against him, general unpopularity comes as still another bale of straw on the camel's back.

Consider the events surrounding the dismissal of Special Prosecutor Archibald Cox by President Nixon in comparison with what happened when Truman fired MacArthur. When Nixon fired Cox, Attorney General Richardson and Deputy Attorney General Ruckelshaus resigned also. The F.B.I. was temporarily instructed to seal off the offices of the departing officials, and to block their access even to personal material stored there. This at a time when ex-Vice-President Agnew, by then a convicted felon, was still riding around town in a government

limousine. For a short while, in the words of a right-wing commentator, official Washington became acutely conscious that they must have seemed to outsiders like "downtown Santiago."

When General MacArthur was fired, his immediate superiors in the Truman administration evidently breathed a sigh of relief. Far from quitting, Secretaries Marshall and Acheson and Undersecretary of Defense Lovett seemed to have fully approved of the move. Republicans, especially in Congress, it is true, took up the hue and cry in MacArthur's behalf. MacArthur returned home to a hero's welcome, and Truman's popularity in the Gallup polls slipped badly. Senator Richard Russell convened an investigation of the Senate Armed Services Committee, however, with the flimsily concealed purpose of letting air out of the MacArthur bubble, which he effectively did.

Can we assign an equally benign purpose, from Mr. Nixon's point of view, to the Senate Watergate committee? Not even all the Republican members of the Committee were at any time favorably impressed with Mr. Nixon's conduct of Watergate-related matters.

In short, the elites were with Truman, and against Nixon. Truman was able to convince members of his own cabinet, substantial numbers of Congressmen, and observers in the press corps that regardless of the risks for his own short-run popularity he had good and sufficient reasons for doing what he did. And so he willingly suffered a nonrecurring loss of political capital in the country at large by dumping MacArthur.

Mr. Nixon's record has in comparison been a tale of misfortune. Cabinet and subcabinet officials and even members of his official White House staff have left, visibly dissatisfied with his response to Watergate. Far from a one-shot liability, Watergate has been for him a running sore, utterly sapping his capacity to deal with most other Presidential business.

Thus, in looking at Watergate, it seems desirable to look beyond the particular precipitating events, beyond even their lessons for the future conduct of public office, and see if we can understand the causes and effects of Watergate in the light of the way the Nixon administration as a whole has situated itself in the American Constitutional order. This is the aim of the essay that follows.

There is little doubt that Watergate is here to stay, in the fundamental sense that observers, analysts, moralists, and historians will be ruminating for years and years to come on the causes and effects of this extraordinary, bizarre injury to the American body politic. It is certainly too soon for a full assessment of the damage that has been done, or for a very convincing argument about how to prevent another such shattering series of events. History never repeats itself with sufficient precision to make very appealing the strategy of locking the particular barn door through which the most recent horse has bolted. Perspective is needed in order for us to see whether in the end it is the faulty architecture of the barn, or an attractive nuisance of the neighborhood, or merely a rusty padlock that needs to be fixed.

At close range, before time has begun to temper judgments and mellow viewpoints, it is possible to indulge in a few speculations about the causes of Watergate. A parallel with the Dreyfus case immediately suggests itself. Musing on the conduct of that celebrated

outrage, Mark Twain said: "To my mind, this is irregular. It is un-English; it is un-American. It is French." Many observers of Watergate find themselves making the same comment. The English, as we all know, have scandals about sex. The American tradition—hallowed by Yazoo, Crédit Mobilier, Teapot Dome, and countless lesser occasions (including the recent unpleasantness surrounding ex-Vice-President Agnew)—is to have scandals about money. It is characteristic of the French civic culture, by contrast, for political belief to curdle into fanaticism, for ideology to justify political irregularity, and consequently ideology is what French political scandals are about.

Yet as the Watergate story has unfolded before our eyes we have seen Americans justify all manner of extraordinary—and irregular—political activity in the name of political commitment. It is un-American . . .

Behind all this there is still another level at which the Gallicization of American politics can be observed, and this is the essentially plebiscitary theory of Presidential accountability that the Nixon administration has apparently embraced. While this theory has strong roots in American history, its major modern exponents have not been Americans at all, but rather continental European adherents to the Rousseauean notion of direct democracy—most notably in recent times General de Gaulle.

This theory holds that public officials are primarily accountable to mass electorates rather than to one another, and that the results of the last election are in principle capable of conferring powers on political leaders that can override the prerogatives, the preferences, and even the legitimacy of competing elites. Thus

I refer to this theory as a mandate theory of accountability.

In this most attractive form, the mandate theory goes by the name of strict majoritarianism; in a slightly different guise, populism. Its beginning as a significant force in American politics dates from the rise of mass political parties and from the Presidency of Andrew Jackson. Of course it is not necessary for there actually to be popular majorities in the electorate in favor of any particular policy for a President to assert that he is operating under a mandate theory of accountability; all that is required for him to make this claim is that he be a duly elected and sworn incumbent of office.

An alternate view holds that in America periodic elections are an essential part of the Constitutional design to secure the accountability of officials, but are the smaller part nonetheless. More significant has been the creation of an interdependent set of governing institutions, each with its own incumbents and prerogatives, constraints and opportunities. From the very beginning, this theory holds, it has been fundamental to our political system to rely upon a plurality of elites as the central device for compelling the accountability of public officials. This structural theory of accountability is, of course, espoused by the authors of *The Federalist*, where it is advocated as the principal means for preventing tyranny. Another adherent of this theory, Thomas Jefferson, as President brought it a logical step forward through his energetic efforts to create out of the "separate battalions" of the Washington community an elite subculture capable of responding to Presidential leadership, but retaining significant autonomy and legitimacy in its component parts.

If I am right in my surmise that our Constitutional order provides for an extensive network of interdependencies among various public officials, it is hazardous even for a President of the United States newly elected by a landslide to proclaim his exclusive devotion to the mandate theory. For others have their mandates as well, and strict pursuit of a patented mandate in our political system means that political leaders, instead of working toward a reconciliation of political aims and an accommodation of policies, may find themselves at loggerheads, unable to conduct their business effectively, suspicious of one another's legitimacy, and ready to invoke ultimate sanctions.

Nothing I have said so far hints of the possibility of wrongdoing among the President's most intimate staff, or by members of the cabinet. That possibility aside, it appears that a significant part of this administration's troubles since the Watergate revelations began is rooted in a loss of confidence among other Washington elites that Mr. Nixon seems to have suffered well before everything came undone as the result of his adoption of the mandate theory of accountability. This explains—if anything can— the satisfaction that nearly everyone in Washington expressed over the dismantling of the high command of the Nixon administration in the summer of 1973. Assistants to the President—even cabinet officers—have fallen from grace before, but never, it appears, to such sustained bipartisan applause from McLean to Chevy Chase, from Georgetown to Hollin Hills. Perhaps it will be worth our while to look again at certain characteristics of the pre-Watergate Nixon Presidency.

It was a strong Presidency, but one uncommonly devoted to enhancing its power by attempting to cripple, discredit, or weaken competing power centers in national politics. In certain respects, this aggressive posture toward competing power centers has been dictated by considerations of policy; in other respects it has been the consequence of President Nixon's administrative style; and in other ways, it appears to be the product of a genuine spirit of alienation between Mr. Nixon's values and those of his closest associates on the one hand, and the values and attitudes that dominate the thinking of leaders of most other Washington elite groups on the other.

For the nation at large, the unfolding Watergate revelations present a profound challenge to the people's sense of trust in their government. Even before Watergate, however, many leaders in our national political life just outside the Presidential orbit may well have had to come to terms with a fundamental unease about the course of the Nixon administration.

This unease did not have anything to do with suspicions of wrongdoing. Rather, what has been at issue is the question of the commitment of the Nixon administration to the underlying legitimacy of government agencies and their rules, the media and their criticisms, cabinet-level officials and their linkages with interest-group constituencies, Congress and its Constitutional prerogatives, or the rest of the Republican party and its political needs.

AN OCCUPATION ARMY

In successive waves over a five-year period, President Nixon has attempted various schemes to govern the executive branch in the manner of a small army of occupation garrisoned amid a vast and hostile population.

The first major Nixon administration reorganization pulled two trusted lieutenants—Secretaries Shultz and Finch—out of day-to-day departmental responsibilities and brought them into the White House. The second move was to change the name of the Budget Bureau and strengthen its powers over government departments. Third, there was a noticeable slowdown in the staffing of the top levels of departments whose programs are given a low priority by the administration. And, finally, there was an effort to move people without any notable background, experience, interest, or qualification into top levels of various government agencies, apparently to provide listening posts for the White House.

Programmatic commitments appear to lie at the heart of the Nixon administration's seeming distrust of many parts of the national government. It is a fairly reliable rule of thumb that government agencies retain forever the political coloration that they have when they are founded, given their central missions, and initially staffed. Undeniably, also, the great expansions of federal agencies have taken place under Democratic Presidents. Thus a Republican President is bound to feel at least a little as though he is surrounded by career-long Democratic bureaucrats, all hot in pursuit of the basically Democratic objectives of their housing, education, welfare, transportation, urban development, and science programs.

A MATTER OF DEGREE

Once written into law and placed in the charge of a government agency, of course, it can be argued that programs are no longer Democratic or Republican programs but simply government programs, and whoever runs the government is obliged to see to them. This rather simple-minded, traditional view was sharply challenged by the Nixon administration decision to dismantle the Office of Economic Opportunity while the law embodying the agency was still in force. It is uncertain how this questionably legal maneuver struck the leaders of other government agencies, but to the OEO staff itself the attack must have seemed flagrant and somehow outside the rules of the game.

Leaders of Congress have expressed themselves in similar terms on the issues of impoundment and executive privilege. It is not that the Nixon administration, in asserting executive privilege and in impounding funds, has done unprecedented things. It is that it has done these things to an unprecedented degree, so much so that a matter of degree is transformed into a difference in kind and has an impact on the normal relations of comity and trust between Congress and the Presidency.

As we all know, the Constitution ordains that Congress and the President were meant to do battle. In the end, their capacity to do business at all rests upon a set of mutual restraints and accommodations, because in the last analysis, either branch can do the other in.

A QUESTION OF POLITICS

It is a matter of the utmost sadness that serious people in Washington and elsewhere could begin, in the summer of 1973, to speak unflinchingly of ulti-

mate sanctions, and specifically of the impeachment or resignation of the President. Before Watergate, it is now clear, the mutual accommodations and understandings that must exist for orderly business to be done between Congress and the President were deeply eroded.

There was the ludicrous and intemperate claim of executive privilege for virtually everybody in the executive branch and on virtually all issues. There was the matter of impoundment—for example, of all public works projects added by Congress to the budget as presented by the President. Likewise, grant and loan programs for water lines and sewers, open spaces, and public facilities were impounded, apparently to coerce the Congress into enacting the administration's special revenue-sharing bill. And there was the attempt to cancel the Rural Environmental Assistance Program.

What is at issue in all of these actions is not whether they represent good public policy or even whether they were legal. Rather, the question is whether they were good politics. The answer must be framed not only in terms of the goals of national constituencies and interest groups and how much the President wants to gratify them, but also in terms of whether or not the President thinks he needs to get along with Congress.

USING UP CREDIT

The Nixon administration attacks on newspapers, on television commentators and the networks, and on the so-called "elitist" Eastern press—somehow these, too, got out of hand. Again, different observers might well draw somewhat different bills of particulars. Some would include as unwise the attempts to get injunctions enforcing prior restraint on publication of what turned out to be innocuous Pentagon Papers. Others remember the petty and futile exclusion of the *Washington Post*'s Dorothy McCardle from coverage of routine White House social functions, and the clumsy investigation of Daniel Schorr of CBS, followed by the patently dishonest rationalizations of the White House press spokesman. Somewhere in between these were the famously abusive speeches of Vice-President Agnew, or opaque references to "ideological plugola" by a White House functionary, accompanied by not-so-opaque administration plans to exert political influence over public broadcasting.

Less noticeable to casual readers was the fact that, well before Watergate, President Nixon was also using up sizable amounts of credit with Republican party leaders. There is always an election-year competition for campaign funds between Presidential candidates and other party standard-bearers further down the ticket. In this contest, the Presidential candidate—especially an incumbent—usually wins. It is then up to him to take the initiative and spread any extra cash around to help the party win some key Senate and House races, once he is fairly certain that his own campaign can be paid for.

This Mr. Nixon apparently neglected to do. Moreover, in his low-profile campaign he made few personal efforts to help fellow Republicans. Now that they are able to see the uses made of some of the money that could have paid for more conventional campaign expenses, it is no wonder that not a few Republican stalwarts are angry.

"PEACE AT THE CENTER"

Some of the disagreeable relations between Mr. Nixon and the rest of official Washington are, as I have indicated, the result of programmatic differences. His dismantling of the President's scientific advice apparatus, for example, can be explained as simply a wish to rid himself of spokesmen for an interest group whose interests he did not want to gratify. Likewise, his dismissal of the American Bar Association as a clearinghouse for future Supreme Court justices came only after the relevant committee of the Association found fault with a couple of his prospective nominees.

Other problems are evidently the inescapable product of Mr. Nixon's work style. His intense desire for "peace at the center," for orderly, private, unharried decision-making, thrust a great burden on his most intimate staff. Not only have they had to protect the President, ruthlessly filter the stimuli to which he is subjected, meanwhile bringing him options and decisions to make, but they have also had to face outward, to deny access to Congressmen, cabinet officers, and others whose responsibilities include shares in the ordering of various aspects of the public business. As time has gone on, it has become evident that there has been too much "peace at the center."

THE WASHINGTON SUBCULTURE

A major by-product of the extreme insularity of this President has been a growing inability to come to terms with the ongoing subculture of official Washington, that noisy little world inhabited by Congressmen, agency heads, jour-

Bob Barnes cartoon reprinted courtesy The Register and Tribune Syndicate, Inc.

"I'm not cynical about politicians. I believe everything the Democrats say about the Republicans, and everything the Republicans say about the Democrats!"

nalists, interest-group leaders, party dignitaries, lawyers, embassy folk, and others, some of whom have been harshly dealt with by the Nixon administration. Of course, these few thousand people are not "the" people, those whom Presidents address on television and who vote by the millions in national elections. But does this mean that official Washington consists of nothing but "nattering nabobs"?

Some of these nabobs are themselves duly elected officials under the Constitution. Others are employed at activities contemplated under statutes of the U.S. government. Still others are doing work that manifestly aids in the proper discharge of governmental functions.

Can a President govern effectively or at all if he systematically alienates himself from most of the rest of official Washington? Can his feelings of alienation, or those of his closest advisers, lead to excessive suspicion, to a frame of mind that encourages the taking of extraordinary precautions, to worries about political opponents that verge on the prurient? If Mr. Nixon's style of work tended to alienate him from official Washington before Watergate, could we reasonably expect that the trauma of Watergate would decrease his alienation from this indispensable community sufficiently to restore to him the capacity to govern?

These sorts of questions have no easy answers, and as time has gone on, and revelation has piled upon revelation, it has been harder and harder to find people in Washington outside the inner moat of the White House itself who could give an optimistic answer.

Indeed, the only cause for optimism in this entire dismal business is the thought that there is something sturdy and enduring about the system of checks and balances that was written into the Constitution, and that at least to some degree, the checks have checked and the balances have balanced in such a way as to bring home to the President, and conceivably to his successors, the fact that legitimacy in our system proceeds not from electoral mandates alone, but also from the mutual account-ability of political leaders. The political process in America occurs not once every four years but continuously. That is one valuable lesson of Watergate.

Persons who value the proper working of American political institutions, and who see in their proper working a marvelous instrument of democratic self-government, are bound to view the unfolding events of Watergate with repugnance. For it is precisely because we Americans are so numerous, so diverse, and so liable to disagree that we must nurture with particular care a government whose leaders are subservient to law, hedged by custom, protected from arbitrary and impulsive acts by inner restraints and by institutionalized rules. That is the public trust that has evidently been so abused and which must be restored.

QUESTIONS FOR DISCUSSION

1. Do you agree that Watergate has been more beneficial than harmful to the American political system?
2. How does the fall of Vietnam affect the credibility of American commitments to such nations as Israel and South Korea?
3. Why have recent presidents devoted more attention to foreign affairs than to domestic affairs?
4. What major governmental reforms remain to be enacted at both the federal and state levels?
5. What is your reaction to the use of bribes by American corporations to secure contracts with foreign governments?
6. Did Watergate really differ significantly from the usual "dirty tricks" in political campaigns?
7. In 1969, from a careful study of Mr. Nixon's early childhood and character development, could one reasonably have predicted a "Watergate-type" crisis?
8. Why do you believe the Watergate burglary occurred?
9. Do you agree with Scheer that the "new majority" in America is populist in its opposition to big business and left-of-center in its political ideology?
10. What does Polsby mean by the phrase "Gallicization of American politics"?